CURATING GRIEF

A CREATIVE GUIDE TO CHOOSING WHAT TO KEEP AFTER A LOVED ONE DIES

CHARLENE LAM

CHROMAFILE PRESS

Author: Charlene Lam

Publisher: Chromafile Press, New York, NY

Original watercolor illustrations by Yeesan Loh

Cover design by KUHN Design Group

Curating Grief® and The Grief Gallery® are registered trademarks of Charlene Lam. All trademarks are the property of their respective owners.

Curating Grief: A Creative Guide to Choosing What to Keep After a Loved One Dies / Charlene Lam —2nd ed.

Library of Congress Control Number: 2024925599

Paperback ISBN 979-8-9919862-1-2

Visit the author's website: www.curatinggrief.com

CONTENTS

PROLOGUE

The soy sauce paralyzed me.

I was standing in my mother's kitchen, more than a year after she died. Staring at a bottle of soy sauce in her maple wood kitchen cabinet.

Every time I looked at the soy sauce, I thought about the meals she had cooked, how much she loved feeding people. Thanksgiving at her house. The Chinese congee that she would make with the leftovers.

How could I let it go?

How was it possible that my mother would never step foot in this kitchen again?

Never cook again?

*Never do **anything** again?*

Those were just some of the impossible questions that ran through my mind after my mother died. That soy sauce bottle was just one of hundreds of objects in her house. If I couldn't toss the soy sauce, how was I supposed to let go of anything else?

INTRODUCTION

Almost a decade after my mom died, I found myself once again transfixed by a bottle of soy sauce. I was no longer bereft and feeling overwhelmed in my mother's kitchen, but instead in a gallery space in Canada, feeling inspired and proud. The Grief Gallery, my creative platform, was presenting an exhibition about grief and loss at Toronto's annual design festival—and the soy sauce had a starring role.

Over the years, the impact of my mother's death and the burden of clearing out her home had evolved. It was still the worst thing that had ever happened to me, still the disaster that derailed my life as I had planned it. But I no longer felt lost.

I had found my compass by leaning into my own creativity— the same creativity we all have, regardless of whether we're artists or not—and discovering a willingness to grieve in *my* way. I had created my own pathway for navigating the practical and emotional aftermath of her death. **Curating, as I'll share with you in this book, was the key.**

That soy sauce represents so much more to me now: Love for her. Love for myself. Where I've been. Where I'm going.

I lost my mother but found myself.

———

Where are you currently with your grief? Are you feeling paralyzed and lost too? Numb? Or overwhelmed with emotion? Feeling conflicted or confused? Are you ready to celebrate their life—or does celebrating anything feel impossible right now?

Or maybe you're experiencing a whole jumble of all of the above. Grief is rarely simple; more a chaotic collage than a straightforward drawing.

And mixed into the patchwork of thoughts, feelings, and emotions are so many important choices, like this one:

How do we choose what to keep after a loved one dies?

That's the same question I agonized over for almost two years after my mother died suddenly and unexpectedly of a stroke in 2013. And maybe it's a problem you're wrestling with now, as you clear out a home after the death of someone you loved or who was significant to you.

Maybe you've got boxes that you've been putting off looking at. Or a storage unit you've been paying the fees on for years. Or maybe what feels heaviest to you now is the emotional stuff, whether you're grappling with guilt, conflicts with others, or feeling overwhelmed by grief.

I want to offer you a gentler, more creative approach to taking on these terrible tasks and challenges.

Welcome to Curating Grief.

EVERYTHING BECAME PRECIOUS

When my amazing mother, Marilyn, died, she left a 3,000-square-foot dream house. A house full of stuff and the belongings from a lifetime.

I soon found out that I had a big problem: Everything in my mother's house became precious after she died.

Her toothbrush.
The box of Band-Aids in her bathroom.
Souvenirs on her shelves.

I couldn't imagine letting any of it go.

It's a common problem. Maybe you've experienced this too? Maybe it was a musical instrument they'll never play again. A computer that holds years of poetry and other writings. Or a leather jacket that still smells like them.

How do we choose what to keep and what to discard when we feel so attached to these people and their objects? How do we choose when they have so much meaning for us?

My uncommon solution was to curate.

When my mother died, I was working as an independent curator in London. I was organizing and presenting exhibitions that featured the work of talented artists and designers, like ceramicists and jewelers. As I stood in my mother's house, overwhelmed by all this responsibility, overwhelmed by all this stuff, out of inspiration—or maybe it was out of desperation!—I put on my curator hat.

I asked myself: *If I were to curate an exhibition about my mother, which 100 objects would I choose?*

CURATING CHANGED EVERYTHING

It was a natural question for me because I was already regularly choosing artwork, jewelry, and accessories for my pop-up exhibitions.

That question—**"If I were to curate an exhibition about my mother, which 100 objects would I choose?"**— changed everything. As a grieving daughter, I couldn't choose. With my curator hat on, I could!

It started off as a creative exercise, as an imaginary exhibition. But more than two years after my mother died, I presented my first physical exhibition featuring my mother's belongings.

Looking back, it was the memorial I really wanted to give her.

———

It's been more than ten years since my mother died . . . Now I use the lens of curating in my grief work in multiple ways to create space for grief, in a world that often fails to give us *any* space for our pain and losses.

I'm passionate about helping grieving people to make sense and make meaning out of the chaos we experience after a major loss, using the lens of curating and the metaphor of exhibitions. I developed the Curating Grief framework to help others process grief in a creative, accessible way. (And no, you don't need to be an artist or creative to curate!)

As a grief coach, I work with grieving individuals to feel lighter and better equipped to move forward with their own fullest lives. As curator of The Grief Gallery, I present international exhibitions featuring the belongings of loved ones lost, with installations at events from New York City to London to Lisbon.

As a speaker, I deliver talks and workshops on the power of art, design, creativity, and storytelling for grieving, sharing my Curating Grief approach with thousands of grievers and wellness professionals. There's even a short film titled *Curating Grief: Loss and Objects*! (Can you tell I'm really passionate about curating?)

My goal is to help grievers like you to navigate the aftermath of loss—and if and when you feel ready, to transform your pain into something beautiful.

In the years since my mom died, I've shared the Curating Grief framework with so many grievers through my individual client work, exhibitions, events, and talks. In each of these opportunities to make space for grief, I ask: "If you were to curate an exhibition about your person, what would you choose to display?"

I invite you to consider the question too. (And no, you don't need to be a curator by profession. Or have any artistic ability. Or even consider yourself creative to curate!)

This book will show you how to use the lens of curating, whether you're sorting through piles of physical stuff or piles of grief after losing a loved one.

A Gentle Note: I'll be sharing examples from my grief journey and from my clients and colleagues, with permission. Whether you see the exact details of your story or not, please know that you are seen.

I will be referring primarily to losing a person to death, but you can apply many of the Curating Grief principles to the death of a pet or another major loss, like losing a person to addiction or estrangement.

I've tried to include examples and case studies from a range of grievers and losses throughout the book. Even if I don't name your specific scenario, please know that your grief *is* valid.

You are welcome here. Your loss matters. Your grief matters.

ABOUT THIS BOOK: WHAT IT IS AND ISN'T

This book is about celebrating our loved ones. But it's not *just* about celebrating. I don't assume that all your memories are positive. It's also about conflict.

Internal and external conflict.
Conflicted feelings.
Conflict with others.
Conflict with ourselves.

This book is also not about crafts as a hobby. It's about curating and what happens when we curate. It's about navigating the field of emotional landmines. It's not as simple as whether an object sparks joy. Sometimes the relationship was complicated. Sometimes the circumstances of the loss are *excruciating*. This book holds a space for all of that.

At the heart of it, this book *is* about:
    Making sense.
    Making meaning.
    Finding beauty.
    Cultivating hope.
    Seeing stories.
    Seeing narratives.
    Choosing.
    Creating.
    Being gentle with ourselves.

WHO CAN CURATE? WHAT DO YOU NEED TO CURATE?

Anyone can engage in the practice of curating. As I'll remind you from time to time in the pages of this book, you don't need to be an artist or even consider yourself creative. And there's more good news: You do not need a formal gallery space. You do not need any of the actual belongings from your person. You do not need a degree, permission, or anyone's blessing.

    All you need is:
    Openness and curiosity.
    Willingness to see in different ways.
    Willingness to make choices.
    Your imagination.

BRING YOUR IMAGINATION

This book offers a series of creative thought exercises, not a master's program in curating. I'm offering you the lens of curating, inviting you to see through the eyes of a museum or art gallery curator. I'm handing you an imaginary curator hat.

When I was little, I loved playing Librarian. I would line up my dolls and stuffed animals as library patrons. All set up at the coffee table with a stack of books and my favorite rubber stamps, I would issue their reading materials, stamping the opening pages with great enthusiasm.

I invite you to bring a similar spirit of make-believe to playing Curator. I approach this work as an art lover, not an art expert. I don't have a degree in art history. Curating came about because I loved museums. My mother loved art and took me to museums often as a kid, so it's my happy place.

Together, we can approach Curating Grief as art lovers and museum enthusiasts, and as human beings who can engage with and be moved by art and the creative process. Experiencing loss, death, and dying can already be grim and serious enough. We're not making light of these experiences here, but I suggest we can make them *lighter*.

Curating Grief is about using our imagination to serve us. Often, after we lose someone or experience a major loss, our imagination works against us. We think, *Who will I lose next?* or *I'll never be happy again!* We use our imagination against ourselves without realizing it. But it doesn't have to be that way, as you will discover here.

After reading the book, you will not be qualified to work at the Guggenheim Museum (unless you are already qualified to do so!); instead, you will have a new set of tools for navigating grief and more ways of seeing life after loss.

HOW TO USE THIS BOOK

Your reading journey starts by checking in with where you are now, with your grief and your loss, giving you and I an opportunity to get oriented and acquainted. The opening chapters offer some Grief Essentials, including myths and misconceptions that may be making your experience of grief more difficult than it needs to be.

For clarity and ease, I've organized the book as a whole in

multiple parts, each addressing specific scenarios where you can use the lens of curating in ways that are both practical and profound:

Curating for Comfort and Connection
Curating for Awareness
Curating for Clearing Out and Making Space
Curating for Healing and Getting Unstuck
Curating for Celebrating and Memorializing

Just like an art exhibition, you can opt to read through the chapters in the suggested order, or you can jump to a section or a chapter that speaks to you.

WHAT TO LOOK FOR ALONG THE WAY: YOUR STEPPINGSTONES THROUGH THE BOOK

Good Questions: Asking good questions is at the heart of a lot of helpful practices: self-coaching, self-inquiry, the Socratic method, the scientific method, and creativity itself—to name just a few! Here you will find a series of Good Questions in most chapters. These are not homework assignments—you certainly won't be graded; instead they are for you to ponder if you feel up to it. You can answer them in your head, on paper, or on a digital device of your choosing. I do encourage taking at least a pause to read the questions!

Creative Thought Exercises: There are Creative Thought Exercises scattered throughout the book, from prompts where you are imagining yourself in a gallery, to visualizing an exhibition about your loved one, to Getting Objective exercises that offer you different, potentially helpful perspectives.

No Ordinary Index: Toward the end of the book, there is **Index: What Hurts?** to help you navigate to a particular issue you may be experiencing.

In various chapters, I invite you to gently consider what hurts—what is specifically triggering emotional pain so that you can turn toward it with compassion, curiosity, and self-kindness. Addressing hurt in this way is so powerful in the healing process that I've included this index as a quick-reference resource. It lists some common situations that grievers experience so you can quickly receive a dose of empathy, clarity, and relief.

Resources: At the end of the book, there is a **Resources** page with a selection of the books and people referenced. For the full and ever-evolving list, visit curatinggrief.com / grief-resources

Book Bonuses: If you find yourself wanting even more at the end of this book (I had a page and word count limit!), you can register your book at curatinggrief.com / book-register to get free bonus content and additional goodies.

From start to finish, I encourage you to go at your own pace and just notice what the Curating Grief pathway opens up for you—what new possibilities for healing your heart and living your life.

NONE OF THIS IS PRESCRIPTIVE

While talking about our losses and being validated can feel therapeutic, I am not a therapist, nor are the contents of this book intended to be a substitute for therapy, or the help of a medical professional or licensed mental health provider. My lawyer said I have to include that disclaimer, but more importantly, I want to stress that none of what I offer in this book is prescriptive—these are all just possibilities. Beautiful possibilities! What's more, the work of Curating Grief is about finding beauty or creating beauty, not *forcing* beauty. Be gentle with yourself, and only do what you feel ready to do. This book will be here; there's no rush.

ARE YOU GOING TO CURATE AND PRESENT AN ACTUAL EXHIBITION ABOUT YOUR LOVED ONE?

If you want to, you sure can! I share creative prompts and inspiration in Part 8: Create. And it doesn't have to be an exhibition—your "curation" can take the form of a book, a film, or other creation.

The key is the *lens* I've been pointing to. The primary purpose of this book is to share with you how to use the *lens* of curating and the metaphor of an exhibition about your loved one to help you navigate grief after a major loss.

If you're reading this book, I'm guessing that you are, like many grievers, feeling overwhelmed by, lost in, or otherwise stuck in some way in your grief. Whether you're dealing with the belongings and the estate, struggling with conflicts with other people in your life, or wanting to feel more connected to your loved one, curating can help.

Curating is, essentially, about seeing and choosing. Together, we're going to help you see and we're going to help you choose. Curating can be a *beautiful* lens for seeing, choosing, and approaching the many challenges we face after we lose someone. That's what really drives my grief work: I want to offer you beauty to balance all the inherent ugliness that comes with being human. Death, dying, illness, loss, and all the circumstances around them can be so ugly.

Here's my hope for all of us: We can still live a beautiful life.

PART ONE
ORIENTATION

Their Cooking Tools

CHAPTER 1
GETTING ORIENTED
WELCOME TO THE GRIEF GALLERY

"I may lose you."

The woman behind me says it loudly, startling me. We're on the Metro North train, departing Grand Central Station and approaching the tunnels that will take us out of Manhattan. She taps her phone and sighs in frustration, her call ending abruptly.

I may lose you, my brain echoes mindlessly, in rhythm with the sounds of the metal train. *I may lose you.*

I've already lost her, another part of me replies grimly.

When my mother was alive, she took this train at least once a week from her suburban house by the lake, traveling the hour south to Manhattan to have lunch with friends, to shop in Chinatown, or when she was working, to deliver talks.

After she died, the train was my connection to the city and a sense of normalcy as I struggled to figure out what to do with her house and, perhaps more perplexingly, what to do with myself.

The automated voice announces the names of the train stops with booming clarity, lending a certain gravitas and grandeur to the curious names of the towns.

The next station is . . .
Katonah
Goldens Bridge
Valhalla

Even a decade later, my husband and I will recite the names to each other, mimicking the announcer's cadence and delivery style. The syllables distinctive like in a chant. The tone authoritative but with a note of enthusiasm. A bit like an emcee introducing a beauty pageant contestant or a drag queen. *Welcome to the stage . . . Miss Massachusetts!*

The next station is . . .
Ka-to-nah
Gol-dens Bridge
Val-ha-lla

All I heard was:
Disaster
Disaster
Di-sa-ster

My mother's sudden death was a disaster. As abrupt and devastating as a violent car crash or train derailment, at least as it impacted my life.

For the first year, I staggered around in a disoriented fog, picking up the pieces of my life and her life, like detritus scattered on the road. I don't remember that first Mother's Day or that first Christmas without her. I didn't feel the deep emotional pain until later. It was as if the shock and adrenaline of the disaster caused me to not realize until later that I was missing a limb—that I had lost a massive part of me.

I have a feeling that you might be able to relate, even if the specifics of your loss may differ.

ORIENTATION

Dear Reader, who or what brings you here? This is the same question I ask at the start of The Grief Gallery's monthly gatherings that I've been hosting over the past two years. We don't attend grief events for no reason, I often say. And if you're reading a grief book, you're here for a reason, too.

What happened?
Who did you lose?
When did they die?

The profound answers to these questions, each a part of a life-altering occurrence, is what brings you here. This is the Event Story, as psychologist Robert A. Neimeyer of the Portland Institute of Loss and Transition calls it. The who, what, when, and where.

The *why* is another thing altogether—it's often elusive, an impossible question. In chapter 2, I'll offer you the space to tell your Event Story, if you wish to do so.

What's your metaphor?

As I shared above, I use the metaphor of being blindsided in a car crash when I think of my mom's sudden death. Do you have a metaphor for your loss or experience of grief?

My client Jen describes it as being lost in dark woods, stumbling toward an unknown future that had seemed so bright before her parents' deaths. Others resonate with a water-related analogy, like feeling adrift and directionless, or feeling like they're drowning and struggling to keep their heads above water as waves of grief crash over them.

I imagine us all, bereft and besieged, struggling to navigate a strange and foreign land after a loss that changes our life. And I invite us all to enter the world of The Grief Gallery, bedraggled, soaked, and disoriented, across the geographical miles, no matter the circumstances of our losses.

Dear Reader: If the metaphor of a car crash or similar is difficult or activating for you, because your loss involves a similar circumstance or you've experienced this traumatic experience yourself, I apologize. Grief and loss can make us particularly sensitive to some imagery or language (like the terms *brain-dead* or *having a heart attack* when used colloquially may take on terrible new meaning for you if your loved one experienced similar medical events or conditions).

It's the imagery that speaks most viscerally to what I personally felt when my mom died. Please insert whatever metaphor or analogy resonates with and feels right for you.

And as always, if you need to take a break or take a walk, and come back to a chapter later, please do so. (You won't hurt my feelings!) It's part of learning how to take care of ourselves as grieving people.

RE-ORIENTING

Finding my way back to my life and myself after my mom died was a process of re-orienting. And it took time—I'm sorry if you didn't want to hear that. Just like it may take weeks, months, and years to re-adjust and rebuild after a disaster, grieving *does* take time. And sometimes help.

Maybe you've tried therapy, grief books, or support groups to try to feel better—to speed up the process, to grieve in "the right way." You might be doubting yourself. You might worry you're stuck because you haven't "moved on" like others have encouraged. You might be wondering, *Is this what the rest of my life will be like?* You might question if you're doing it wrong because you haven't gotten to all the stages of grieving.

Maybe you thought your only option for grief support was

therapy (I love therapy!), and either you lack health insurance, or the only therapist covered isn't the right fit for you.

All of these experiences are so common amongst the grieving people I've spoken to and worked with. I want to reassure you: **You are not grieving wrong.**

You are not the problem. Grief is not the problem.

DIFFERENT KINDS OF SUPPORT

If you're reading this book, you just might be looking for a different *kind* of grief support—a different approach. I've found over more than a decade of processing my own grief and helping others with theirs, that a purely practical or clinical approach is inadequate for most of us. We need the AND:

Practicality *and* poetry
Grit *and* grace
Science *and* art
Intellect *and* intuition

For instance, for some grievers, spirituality is a great source of comfort, while others want to lean more into science and what the research studies say—I personally like a combination!

For some grievers, it's helpful to hear other people's stories so we know we're not alone. For others, it might be emotionally overwhelming. (And what about *your* story? Have you felt truly heard?)

What if you intellectually know what you should do, but something is in the way?

The goal of this book is not to fix you or your grief—or to make you move faster in the grieving process. It's to help you feel witnessed and supported in the way that works for you, and ultimately, to help you access whatever you may need to live the life you want. That may be rediscovering hope, joy, peace, understanding. Or it may be removing a block you're not even aware of yet.

MOVING FORWARD, NOT MOVING ON

"You have to move on"—have you been told this by a friend, family member, or acquaintance? Or even a medical professional? At best, they are well-meaning but misinformed about how grief works. At worst, they are minimizing or dismissing your grief and loss because it's uncomfortable or inconvenient for them.

Most of us live in a grief-illiterate culture that takes a problem-solving, pathologizing approach to grief, treating our natural responses to loss as something to be fixed. This can look like talking about grief as if it were a disease, disorder, or ailment, or implying something is wrong with you because you're "still grieving" or "haven't gotten over it," even though it's been a month, a year, or a decade.

It's one of the major misconceptions about grief: that we need to "move on"—often meaning not talking or thinking about our loved ones who have passed. I'll talk about this and other grief myths in the next chapters.

My practice of Curating Grief is not just a once-a-year occasion like creating an *ofrenda* for the Day of the Dead (*Dia de Los Muertos*) or making an excursion to the cemetery to tidy our ancestors' graves, as my family would do. As meaningful as these occasions are, I find that for many grievers, the reality of our loss is always present, a daily or regular encounter instead of a now-and-then reminder.

I am *not* dwelling or ruminating when I say that Curating Grief is a daily practice for me. On the contrary, instead of keeping me stuck, it's keeping me moving. I am not just surviving after major losses, I am thriving.

We do move on, in some ways. We go on, as author John Onwuchekwa says in his book of the same name. Our lives go on, even though it may feel impossible or inexplicable. I prefer to use the phrase "moving forward"— our grief moves with us, we move grief through us, we move through grief. This movement, toward the experience of the life that we want, is what I gently encourage.

Clients have gone from having guilt and memories tucked away in dusty boxes—physical or metaphorical—to bringing them out into the light. They have made space for their loved one in their life (as much or as little as they'd like!), and more importantly, made space for what's important to them.

"Tragedy doesn't have to be a dead end, if it paves the road to a new beginning."

JOHN ONWUCHEKWA

THE 3CS AND THREE GUIDING QUESTIONS

In the decade since my mom's death, I've developed the core principles and concepts of my creative grieving process—which I later realized was also a self-coaching process!—into a framework called Curating Grief that has shown itself to be uniquely effective.

Why is Curating Grief so helpful?

It comes down to three fundamental questions: When I emptied out my mom's dream house after she died, I used what I call the 3Cs of the Curating Grief framework to get me through the terrible task.

The 3Cs stand for **Collect, Curate, Create**—and they each have a guiding question:

How do I remember the person? (aka Collect)
This is when we unpack and look at everything. Survey all the belongings. All the memories and thoughts. The good, the bad. The nonsensical: A bag of Beanie Babies hidden in the attic, Mom? You were still hoping that might pan out.

With this question, we're not choosing yet. Try to survey everything without judgment. Take this time and space to just acknowledge the person as they were and as they lived.

How do I WANT to remember the person? (aka Curate)
This is when we start choosing. Which memories do you want to cherish? Which objects trigger those memories and stories? For instance, some of the things I kept included: My mom's passports (she loved to travel), cashmere sweaters (I'm glad she learned to treat herself), and cooking utensils (she was an amazing cook).

How do I want the person to be remembered? (aka Create)
What do we want people to know about our loved one? Which stories do we want to share? Which belongings can have pride of place? And where: on a shelf, in a shadowbox, or in a frame?

I'll be referring to the 3Cs and these guiding questions at key points in this book.

MY HOPE FOR YOU – FOR US

Losing my mother forever changed the trajectory of my life—and me. A major loss may shape the rest of your life too, but it doesn't have to define you or your life.

The grief will always be there, in some form. We can learn to co-exist with grief. We can learn to live in the "AND"—*and* is one of my favorite words now, as it's an immensely helpful word for grievers and humans trying to navigate life, death, and all that's in between.

I miss my mom AND I live a beautiful life, partly in tribute to her.

I've expanded my capacity for grief—my own, clients', and the larger world's—AND my capacity for joy.

Loss can devastate our worlds AND we can still lead beautiful, meaningful lives.

That's my hope for my clients and all grievers, including you. (And if that hope feels out of reach for you right now, it's OK. I will hold that hope for you.)

"Healing means, first of all, the creation of an empty but friendly space where those who suffer can tell their story to someone who can listen with real attention."

HENRI NOUWEN

CHAPTER 2
WHO OR WHAT BRINGS YOU HERE?
THE EVENT STORY

In chapter 1, I asked you who or what brings you here—to this grief book and to this possibly impossible-feeling moment in your life. Have you ever told the Event Story, the full story of what happened?

We rarely ever get this opportunity, at least with friends and family. Often people are so uncomfortable with the topic of death and dying that they look away. Our pain is met with shifting eyes, interruptions, platitudes, and diversions. The discomfort can be so loud and visible that our expressions of grief and stories of loss are drowned out and obscured.

Because we've been taught to be mindful of other people's feelings, we tend to hide away our pain and stories so as not to disturb them further.

Often, at the start of working with a client, our first call or two may be just unpacking, telling the story of what happened. Because the loss needs to be named. Because our grief and pain need to be witnessed.

This chapter is your invitation to unpack it all. After all, before we can curate, before we can make choices, we need to unpack. If we were to imagine an art exhibition about your experience of loss, this would be the room toward the start called What Happened?

MY EVENT STORY

"I can't get in touch with your mom." It's January 2013. I'm sitting in a coworking space in East London, with a friend by my side. The email from my aunt is puzzling. My mom, my aunt and I—all fiercely independent women—didn't have a habit of closely tracking each other's activities.

"It's probably fine," my friend assured me.
"I think I need to go home," I replied uneasily.

It was not fine.

My mother, Marilyn—healthy, vibrant, and beloved—had died suddenly and unexpectedly at the age of sixty-six.

We didn't know what happened.
We didn't know *how* this could happen.
All I knew was that I needed to get on a plane.
And that my life would never be the same.

Landing in an Unfamiliar Place

The day before my mom died, I was in Paris for work. The day she died, I was in a snowstorm in London. I sent my mom photos of the unusual phenomenon, but she was already gone. The day after we learned she had died, I was on a transatlantic flight back to New York.

My aunt and uncle—my mom's younger sister and brother—picked me up at JFK. My aunt burst into tears when she saw me, crying "I'm so sorry." My uncle silently gave me a hug.

"I want to go to the house," I said, and we drove directly there. I needed to see in-person what felt like the scene of a crime. How could my energetic mother be gone? Just like that? What could have happened?

I'd brought my digital camera, and as I walked through my mom's house, I documented anything that stood out. My aunt had already done some clean-up: the spoiled fish in the refrigerator that my mom had bought in Chinatown the day she died. Likely other horrors that she never told me about.

I snapped photos of my mom's rumpled bed. Her socks on the floor. Was any of it significant? I didn't know, but it all felt like potential evidence.

Don't touch anything.

Document it.

We could analyze it later.

I had watched a lot of episodes of the TV show *CSI (Crime Scene Investigation)*, and if I'd had the little yellow numbered tents they used as evidence markers, I would have left them everywhere.

It was the first but not the last time that the items in her house would take on new significance for me.

UNPACK, UNLOAD, LET IT ALL OUT

This is your invitation to unpack it all. In a moment, I'm going to ask you to tell me about your person. To unload it all.

Tell me how they died.

Tell me how they lived.

Tell me all the moments and items and memories that come up.

You can make a list. You can recite it with stoic matter-of-factness, like a witness giving testimony. Or you can scream it out into the world. Like a witness to a deep injustice.

The circumstances of loss can vary so much. In my years of grief work, I've concluded that it's all just different flavors of terrible.

My mother died suddenly (from a stroke, we learned), which added layers of shock and disbelief to my experience of grief. Maybe your loved one was sick for a long time, and you're haunted by their physical or mental decline. Maybe you had a mixed experience, where a person was ill, but their actual death was still unexpected.

Just different flavors of terrible.

It's *your* event story. You get to decide what was terrible. If there's anything you're grateful for. If there's nothing you're grateful for. The moments that stand out. A smell, a sight. A phrase that stays with you.

I'm here to witness you and what happened.

————

GOOD QUESTIONS

What happened?

What hurts?

Bonus questions:
What helps? Or what might help?
What heals? Or what might facilitate healing?

————

LEARNING THE LANGUAGE OF GRIEF

Did you feel the urge to edit your answers to those questions, or did it all come pouring out, unchecked? Did you question whether it was OK to mention your ex, to grieve your pet, or to think about that job from long ago?

There are so many misunderstandings about grief and loss—and it's not your fault. In school, I learned about geometry. How to conjugate French verbs. The names of planets. **I didn't learn about grief.**

When I lost my mom, the first thing I did was Google: *What do you do when someone dies?* Maybe you've Googled something similar: *How does grief work? How long does it last?*

Because we're not taught any of it, even though we'll all experience grief and loss. (You know, because we're human beings.)

"Grief is human, and to grieve is to be human."

RACHELLE BENSOUSSAN

In one of my first grief trainings, I was introduced to the concept of Grief Literacy. Most of us live in a culture that's grief illiterate—we don't know how to read it or to comprehend it. We struggle to understand and fumble with the language.

In these initial chapters, I'm going to share some grief basics, because there are so many misconceptions about the grieving process—misconceptions that just add to grievers' pain.

Permission is going to be a recurring theme. You don't need my permission or anyone else's to grieve the way you want and need to, but in case you would like permission, I'm including a couple of Permission Slips that I've strategically placed in segments of the book where you may want a reminder that *you* have the power.

Let's start by defining grief.

Grief is the natural response to losing someone or something you're attached to. Let's say it again: Grief is the *natural* response to losing anything that you are attached to.

Anything that you're attached to, which can be:
a person
a place
a project
a pet
a plan
an old identity
the way things were

the way things could have been
the way things should have been

What's more when we experience the primary loss of a person, we often also have secondary losses: the loss of our identity or routine when they were here, or the loss of a sense of security, for instance. My mom was my security, my anchor.

YOUR GRIEF RESPONSE

The circumstances and context around our losses shape our grief responses. For instance, my mother died suddenly and unexpectedly. Most of the deaths that I've experienced have come out of the blue, whether the death itself or the moment of learning about it.

Thus, my grief response looks like expecting loss to happen at any moment. On some level, I'm always bracing myself to be blindsided at any time by death: my own and other people's. (I *will* assume that you are dead if I do not hear back from you.)

That's how my experience of loss directly shapes my grief and how I sometimes respond to life events, big and small.

Another variation might be health anxiety. Claire Bidwell Smith, grief therapist, author of *Anxiety: The Missing Stage of Grief*, and one of my teachers, lost both her parents by the time she was in her twenties to cancer. Her grief response includes worrying about getting cancer too. For grievers with health anxiety, that can look like getting medical checkups obsessively—or avoiding seeing the doctor altogether.

Anxiety can be just one of the emotional responses we have to major loss. Sadness. Envy. Longing. Relief. Guilt. These are all potential responses to loss. Grief is not just one emotion. The experience of grief includes a whole *range* of emotions!

Maybe you experience envy or jealousy on Mother's Day or Father's Day because you're constantly reminded of your own loss as seemingly everyone else celebrates the importance of a parental relationship.

Or maybe your grief often feels like loneliness or being over-looked, because sibling loss or friendship loss don't get nearly as much attention as other losses. Or feeling misunderstood because people avoid talking about your child who died because they think they'll remind you of a painful event—as if you could forget!

You've likely heard of the famous Five Stages of Grief. As catchy as this concept is, it's widely misunderstood. Grieving is not a linear process. Even more importantly, Swiss-American psychiatrist Elizabeth Kübler-Ross, who introduced the frame-work in her 1969 book *On Death and Dying*, originally intended denial, anger, bargaining, depression, and acceptance to be stages a terminally ill person might experience as they face their own mortality! I like the way death educator and trauma specialist Dr Terri Daniel describes denial, anger, bargaining, depression, and acceptance as five *potential responses* to loss, in no particular order, amongst hundreds of possible responses to loss.

GRIEF IS NOT "JUST" AN EMOTION

Grief is a response to loss that includes emotions, thoughts, behaviors, and physiological changes. It affects our bodies, including our brains. How we think, how we sleep, how we eat —they may all be affected.

Grief after significant loss can be a full body experience. A whole system disruption. A world-shattering event. Give your-self grace.

YOU MAY BE SURPRISED BY YOUR GRIEF RESPONSES

"This isn't like me." One of the most disorienting parts of experi-encing major loss can be when we don't feel like ourselves.

Our grief responses can surprise us: Crying if we're usually stoic, for instance. Or not crying as much as we think we would.

There's a whole range of possible responses. And they can change day by day, moment by moment. You may find yourself tearing up at random things. Or triggered by a song or a smell. You may get overstimulated and overwhelmed—even by simple things like sounds, sights, and touch. You might crave being held, or physical touch might feel like too much stimulus on top of already overwhelming emotions and sensations. You might not recognize yourself for a while.

THERE ARE DIFFERENT GRIEVING STYLES

Just as there are different art styles—Baroque, Modern, Impressionist, Abstract, Cubist—there are different styles of grieving.

And just like artists, your grieving style may change or be seasonal. You may have your abstract expressionism period, when your emotions and thoughts are as seemingly random as a Jackson Pollock painting. You may have your experimental era, when you're trying anything that may help. You may have your Blue Period, like Picasso's monochromatic phase. For me, January tends to be painted in a melancholy slate blue and dipped in grief, like a heavy ganache, because my mom's birthday and death dates are in that month.

In terms of grieving styles, there are, for instance, cognitive processors: people who want to think about things, who want to analyze them, who want to make sense of it all. And there are people who tend toward emotional processing. They want to cry, they want to yell, they want to talk about their feelings and express their emotions. It's not binary. But sometimes there can be a tendency toward one over the other.

If you like being able to put academic names to grieving styles, psychologists Ken Doka and Terry Martin identified these distinct styles as Intuitive (tending toward emotion and feelings) versus Instrumental (tending toward thoughts and actions).

HOW IT LOOKED FOR ME

I am much more of a cognitive processor and instrumental griever: Show me all the grief theory! Let me do all the research. Give me a checklist. One of the first things I did after my mom died was to create a spreadsheet and assemble a binder.

Other people in my family were much more emotional processors after my mother died. They expected me to cry with them and were concerned when I didn't.

Part of my response might have been shock, as my mother's death was so sudden and unexpected. I cried when I first learned that she had died, and then I didn't really cry again for two years. (Not coincidentally, it wasn't until I had sold her house.)

My default when there's a problem is to ask, "What needs to get done?" That tends to be the case for most of my clients. They are the responsible ones. They are the ones who stay calm and create order when everyone else is running around, both in their personal lives and professionally.

This form of instrumental processing is a valid style of grieving *and* processing! It doesn't mean we're cold or uncaring. Intuitive processing—more emotionally oriented—is *also* a valid style of grieving and processing. It doesn't mean the person is hysterical or dramatic. People tend to have default or preferred styles of processing grief, even though we may also have a mix of expressions of our grief.

"Grief is as individual as a fingerprint. We do it our own way, in our own time. And that's OK."

DAVID KESSLER, *FINDING MEANING: THE SIXTH STAGE OF GRIEF*

Ultimately, what did it take for me to navigate the tumultuous earlier days and months after my mom died?

It took time to recognize that my family members and I had different ways of processing.

It took grace to let it be OK that we did have these different styles and not to expect other people to process in the way that I expected them to.

It took effort to not take it too personally when people implied that I wasn't expressing or processing my grief in the way *they* thought was right.

———

GOOD QUESTIONS

What kind of processing feels supportive to you?

Do you want to write, talk, dance, move, draw? Make a list and a spreadsheet? These are all valid forms of processing.

———

YOU'RE NOT DOING IT WRONG

I see so much self-judgment when people are grieving. The flurry of questions and ruminations:

Am I allowed to grieve this? Am I grieving correctly? Shouldn't I be over this already? Is something wrong with me?

So-and-so says I should have gone through the closet already. They said, "It's already been a year since your husband died!" Am I stuck?

We get so many messages about how we should be grieving, and what it should look like:

You need to cry more.
You're crying too much.
You talk about them too much.
You never talk about them.
You need to be strong.
You need to visibly grieve.

A whole range of different expectations!

———

GOOD QUESTIONS

What does *your* grief look like? Are you numb? Weepy? Irritable?

How do you know what's the "right way" for *you* to grieve?

Who's telling you how you *should* grieve: Church? Family? Culture? Friends? Media? You?

———

WHAT HURTS?

"What *doesn't* hurt?" might be your reply. It's OK if it is. It's also OK if you're not feeling much of anything right now. (Remember: Permission to grieve in *your* way, on your own timeline.)

When I ask my clients and workshop attendees "What hurts?" I'm asking them:

What hurts . . . for you?
What hurts . . . currently?
What hurts . . . that needs attention?

You get to decide what is most painful for you. For some of us, it is that our grieving style was questioned, challenged, or invalidated. Or that our grief and loss were ignored entirely.

For others, it might be the conflicts you're having with your siblings or other family members. Or disappointment with friends who haven't come through for you in the way you expected. And yet for others, what feels heaviest right now may be the burden of dealing with the estate or the physical belongings.

And of course, there is the pain of loss itself. Losing a person we loved. Or losing a person who was significant in our lives, who we also had a complicated relationship with. In the following chapters, I'll be diving deeper into these potential painful scenarios and offering the tools from the Curating Grief framework that I use with my clients and for my own grief.

"Adaptive grieving can be understood to involve two forms of narrative processing, centered on the event story of the death itself and on the back story of the relationship with the loved one."

NEIMEYER & SANDS, 2011

CHAPTER 3
MEETING YOURSELF
WHERE YOU ARE

"It's just a potato." July 2019. I'm on a small island between Finland and Sweden. It takes about an hour to circumnavigate the rocky isle by foot. In an airy wooden barn, converted to a retreat and workshop space, we're printing with potatoes, our introduction to learning how to make prints with simple shapes and ink—and unlearning other lessons. Lessons about creativity, what's good and what's enough. Lessons about ourselves.

I've been here before.

I'm lucky enough to be attending this retreat with designer Lotta Jansdotter for the second time. When I first discovered her cheerful Scandinavian patterns in San Francisco, and then interned with her after her move to New York, I could not have imagined that just a decade later, I would be present with her in her beloved homeland of Åland . . . mourning my mom. Some of my mother's ashes are scattered in the chilly waters that surround the island.

The first time I joined Lotta's retreat and encountered the potato as a printing tool, I hated it. I found it uncooperative, unwieldy, and unpredictable.

I wanted to create beauty, and I created messes.

I wanted to create masterpieces, and I created underwhelming *meh's*.

The potatoes slipped, dripped, and eventually crumbled in my inked-stained hands.

What would my mother have said, if she could have seen me struggling with the potato? If she had witnessed me comparing my creative efforts with those of my fellow workshop attendees?

Blaming it (the potato).
Blaming myself.
For not being enough.

I think she would have said: "Silly girl, don't be so hard on yourself. You're doing your best. And so is that poor potato."

And she'd be right. It's just a potato, after all.

Eventually, I learned to love my potato. The weight and shape of it in my hand. Its humble and honest form. It wasn't trying to be anything but its potato self.

Why should I expect a potato to perform like a professional printing block? Why would it? To please me?

Why would it do that? It's a potato.

I learned to stop resisting its potato-ness. Learned to embrace its uneven texture and uncertain printing results. Learned to appreciate its unpretentious nature.

"It's just a potato."

No need to put too much pressure on it. To be too precious about it. It was perfectly enough.

I think of that poor, beleaguered potato, when I think about the expectations we put on ourselves and others when we're devastated by the death of a loved one.

It's just a potato.
We're only human.

Just how are we fallible, flawed human beings supposed to

respond when we are struck by personal disaster? There's a reason we often use the violent language of disasters to try to describe the visceral sensation of losing our loved ones:

Blindsided
Derailed
Destroyed
Shattered

"Cataclysmic" is how Tida described the loss of both her parents within five weeks of each other. "It was a personal catastrophe."

"I felt like my front half had been torn off," said Deirdre after the death of her husband just months after a cancer diagnosis.

Just how are we supposed to be able to cope, to keep carrying on with our normal lives, when we are struck by an event that destroys the world as we knew it?

We aren't.

The human brain can only take so much. I operated in a state of shock for the first two years after my mom died. Often people will report that the period after the death is only a blur. "I saw photos of myself in college, smiling and at parties," confided my client Tracy. "I don't remember any of it."

We're only human, with fascinating, amazing—yet entirely human—brains. A brain that may struggle to make sense of what's happened. That may struggle to grasp the magnitude and depth of the loss in the same way that we can't fully grasp the concept of a billion or the distance between planets—it's just too enormous.

Our human brains may tell us a story about what it means that we weren't there when our loved ones died. Or that we couldn't save them. Or that we can't save all their belongings.

In this book, we're going to look at some of those stories—see them, honor them, and, if it feels right to you, consider rewriting them.

LET'S GO ON A JOURNEY TOGETHER

As your guide, I aim to meet you where you are—in your grief and in your loss. We're going to think about our loved ones and people who have died. About who they were in life and our relationships with them. We're going to look at their belongings and our relationship with all that stuff. (Because their stuff is NOT them, no matter what our brains try to tell us.) And we're going to look at our relationship with ourselves. Because that's what we're left with ultimately: ourselves, our amazing and fallible human brains, our tender hearts, and the lives we are living.

As a fellow griever, I'm going to share my personal experience of losing my mother. I'll crack open my heart as an invitation for you to open yours, and to bear witness to your loss.

As a curator, I'll be putting the belongings of loved ones in the spotlight and sharing the stories of other grievers. We'll use our eyes to see details, connections, and inspiration.

And as a grief coach, I'll be offering you new ways of looking at what's happened and what's been left behind. And a way to reframe the picture and story.

We'll use our brains to gain awareness of our stories—and to choose better ones, if we want—and our hearts to guide us in crafting new narratives.

Ready, fellow potato people? We can do this.

CHECKING IN: WHAT DOES YOUR GRIEF LOOK LIKE RIGHT NOW?

In the same way that we want to pause and take stock after a natural disaster—or at the start of a journey into uncharted territory—let's take a moment to check in with ourselves. How are you doing? How is your loss impacting you currently?

Has your experience changed the way you see the world? Are you interacting with your job, your partner, your children, or your friends differently?

Do you feel pressure to finish grieving quickly or to "do it right"?

If so, grief therapist and author Gina Moffa offers a perspective you might appreciate right now:

"So often after loss, people are tossed into this unknown and foreign emotional landscape, ill-equipped with how to navigate this new world or what next steps to take. It can be a disorienting path, and society is so often looking at their clock and whistling with impatience as we find our way. Society wants us to pack it all up and move on. That's not what grief asks of us."

Permission Slip: Grief has no set timeline. Your grieving doesn't have to be completed after a month or a year—or a lifetime. That doesn't mean it's always going to feel the same, like the searing raw pain earlier on in your experience of loss. You can grieve on your own timeline and at your pace. Same with curating—you don't have to rush to curate, you can do it right away or decades after the loss. See chapter 17 for more about my timeline, as an example.

YOU DON'T HAVE TO KNOW WHAT YOU'RE DOING

Another form of self-judgment I see often is assuming that we should know how to handle grief and loss. The grievers I work with tend to be smart, accomplished professionals and overall brilliant human beings. We may have multiple degrees. We've likely gone to therapy. We have reputations for being the responsible, competent ones. We get things done!

And then we experience major loss.

And we may find ourselves thinking, *Ooh, I have no idea what I'm doing.*

And that is OK. Why should you know? You likely haven't been here before:

You haven't lost a parent. Or both parents.

You haven't had to imagine your life without your partner, child, or sibling.

You haven't seen your planned future crumble in front of you.

Why should you know exactly what you're doing and where you're going when you find yourself in a strange, new land?

My clients and I often laugh about how surreal the experience of grief can be: How are they gone, but this half-eaten jar of pickles is still here? Why am I making decisions that feel incredibly high-stakes financially and emotionally, but there's no road map?

I remember going to the flower district in Manhattan to order floral arrangements for my mom's memorial and feeling so anxious. Yes, I wanted the flowers to be beautiful and meaningful. But here's what I was really anxious about: *I don't want the flower guy to think I'm cheap.* I had no idea how much flowers for a memorial should cost: $200? $2000? *What if he laughs at me. What if he's offended by my small budget and throws me out (it's New York).* In other words . . .

I'd never done this before.

Permission Slip: It's OK if you don't know what you're doing. You've never done this before. You've never been *here* before.

GRIEVING IS A LEARNING PROCESS

The book *The Grieving Brain: The Surprising Science of How We Learn from Love and Loss* by Mary Frances O'Connor explained so much about my own experience of grief after my mom died and the experiences of my clients.

As a cognitive processor, I wanted to understand what was happening. Why do we respond in seemingly inexplicable ways to loss? Why am I so attached to that bottle of soy sauce? Why does my brain keep forgetting my mom is dead?

Although I highly recommend reading the book to get the full impact, my biggest takeaways include the followings gems:

The brain likes to save energy by seeing patterns, remembering by default, and doing things by habit. Of course you expect to wake up next to your life partner of forty years. Of course my mind continued to imagine that my mom was still in her house in New York. That's where our brains expect them to be.

It takes time for our brains to catch up with the new reality. It's like they've been programmed to process our surroundings and lives in a certain way, and when our circumstances change, it takes time for the new programming to take, and the new circuits to connect. It's why you might zone out and drive to your old house after a recent move or pick up your phone to text your person who isn't here to respond.

Neuroplasticity—the ability of our brains to adapt and change—is a wonder. As painful as the process may be (because we are humans and not machines), our brains are designed to update. We can adapt to new places, missing limbs, a different route home—even the reality of our loved ones being dead.

Yay for neuroplasticity! But oh, our poor brains.

Grieving is a learning process for our brains.
Grieving is a learning process for our hearts.
A lifelong learning process.

How will we make it through our first holiday season without our loved one?
We will learn.

How will we live without them?
We will learn.
We *can* learn.

GRIEVING IS AN ACTIVE PROCESS

Have you ever noticed that we often use the words grief and grieving interchangeably, even though one is actually a noun and the other is actually a verb (or more specifically, a gerund, which is a verb form that mainly functions as a noun! Hello to my fellow grammar nerds!)?

I asked Meghan Riordan Jarvis, trauma therapist and author of *Can Anyone Tell Me? Essential Questions About Grief and Loss*, how she describes this difference and love her succinct reply:

"Grief is the energy that is created in the body on account of loss. It's a noun. Grieving is the act of moving that energy through the body. It's a verb. Mourning is the outward expression of grief or grieving that can be witnessed and experienced by others."

We may feel grief. We may experience grief. But **grieving** is something we **do**. (In Chapter 5, we'll dive deeper into mourning.)

As I've discussed earlier, grieving may look very different between individuals, cultures, and even moments in time. Grieving might look like:

Crying. Not crying.
Talking about your loved one.
Staring at the wall in silence.
Walking in nature. Kickboxing in the gym.
Writing a poem.
Reading a novel.
Singing a song.
Dancing in place.

For me, grieving often looked like sorting through my mother's belongings. When I reflect on the first couple of years after my mom died, when tears wouldn't come, it was when I spent time looking through all the stuff in her house that I was moving that energy of grief through my body.

I moved through the world feeling numb, but when I looked at the objects, the emotions would surface—the belongings were my way of accessing my feelings.

- Her toothbrush: disbelief and guilt
- The pictures of us on her bookshelf: love, affection, and regret
- A calendar opened to January 2013: sadness, anger, and disbelief again

In the beginning, I would be surprised by just how triggering each of these seemingly mundane objects could be. But over time, there was no longer the element of surprise. I still couldn't actually bring myself to move or discard many of my mother's belongings, but the way I *felt* started to change.

GRIEVING AS PRODUCTIVE PAIN

How do we deal with grief? How do we feel better? **By grieving.** By taking the *action* of grieving, we are actually changing our *experience* of grief.

I'm not downplaying how painful and uncomfortable it may feel to grieve. If I could skip the snotty crying to my therapist, the anxiety of experiencing more loss, and the blazing anger I felt toward various family members, I would. However, I am reminded of something I read a long time ago, likely as a child flipping through my mom's *Glamour* magazine, about the pain of labor. The article explained that labor pain in childbirth was different from most other types of pain because:

- Labor pain is expected vs. unexpected. There isn't the extra shock that comes with surprise pain.
- Usually pain means that something is wrong. Childbirth pain doesn't mean anything is wrong.

- Labor pain is part of a process and a productive pain. The pain is in service of a desired result.

I now see the pain of grieving similarly. If I know that grieving helps us to move the energy of grief through our bodies and that it's a natural, expected, and productive process, it can make the pain more bearable.

WE NEED TO FEEL SAFE ENOUGH TO GRIEVE

In order to grieve, we need to feel safe—physically, emotionally, psychologically. If you are in the middle of a natural disaster, trying to just survive a tornado, for instance, you are unlikely to have the time and space to grieve!

If you have been told by family members that your tears are upsetting to others, you may learn to repress your emotions. If as a child, you were punished for having Big Feelings, you may adapt by staying small and quiet.

How It Looked for Me: A Delayed Grief Response

Because my mom died so suddenly and unexpectedly, I operated in a state of shock for at least a year. Looking back, it didn't feel like I was actively grieving much. I didn't visibly fall apart— and I didn't feel like I *could* fall apart.

Because I was busy taking care of her house, I was freaking out about her estate. As an only child with divorced parents, I knew most of the decisions would come down to me.

I cannot afford to fall apart right now, was my refrain.

I had things to do. Paperwork to fill out.

A house to empty and sell.

And if I fell apart emotionally, what might happen to the rest of my life?

I was in survival mode. On some level, it did not feel safe to go to the depths of my emotions. Some mornings, I would wake up and remember my mom was dead . . . and it felt like I might lose my mind if I really let it sink in. Actually go mad. Like I might fall into an inescapable anxiety and depression spiral and wind up in a mental hospital.

You might be thinking something similar: *If I start crying, I might not stop. I have to stay strong for my children and my surviving parent. I can't fall apart.*

We have to feel safe enough to grieve. *And* it needs to come out at some point. The reality of the situation and all the emotions that come up all needs to be processed.

That brings me to one of my favorite metaphors: Metabolizing Grief. The metaphor of metabolizing grief helps to illustrate that grieving is a continuous cycle, as well as why it might not happen if you don't feel safe enough.

Just as our bodies metabolize food (to extract nutrients and convert what we eat into energy), the phrase "metabolizing grief" suggests that grief—and all that comes with it—also needs to be processed and digested, broken down into a form that allows for the absorption of what is nourishing and helpful, and the release or disposal of what is not.

Just like animals in fight-or-flight mode, your body may shut down non-essential processes, like digestion and menstruation, if it seems like you're in survival mode. The other items on your list—taking care of others, dealing with the estate, arranging the funeral—may feel urgent, like you're firefighting, leaving little room for your own grieving process.

Therefore, know that if you're feeling numb or concerned by your lack of tears, it doesn't necessarily mean you're not grieving —it might just be how your brain, mind, and body are coping. Trust in your innate wisdom if you can.

———

GOOD QUESTIONS

Do you feel safe enough to grieve? In what spaces do you feel safe?

What would help to create a space that feels safe or comfortable enough, physically, emotionally, and psychologically?

CHAPTER 4
HOW WAS YOUR GRIEF RECEIVED?

A month after my mom died, I commissioned a custom urn for her ashes. The design brief was simple:

> White porcelain.
> A section for a small container of my mom's ashes.
> The ability to function as a vase, because my mom loved flowers.

I knew my wishes would be in safe hands with UK ceramicist Jo Davies, whose work I knew well. Little did I know my grief would be in such good hands as well.

As we shared ideas for the urn in her East London studio, the daylight streaming in from the courtyard, Jo shared that she had lost her mother almost a decade earlier, when she was at university.

I had showcased Jo's beautiful ceramics, with their pleasing porcelain curves and smooth matte glaze, in my pop-up exhibitions for years, but we'd never talked about loss (Why would we? It was hardly considered polite conversation, and I wasn't obsessed with death and grief yet.)

Jo was one of my earliest grief guides, openly sharing her experience and advice with me, and I'll always be grateful for her openness.

A WARM RECEPTION

At the time, I didn't realize how lucky I was to have such a warm and open reception to my grief. So often, I hear clients and other grievers share how isolated and rejected they felt in early grief because of how others reacted to their grief and loss. Friends who changed the subject, family members who turned away.

It wasn't just Jo. I had many grief guides and emotionally supportive figures after my mom died—though they weren't always the people I expected.

"I'm going to call you right now," my friend Marie from my San Francisco days said when I messaged her about my mom. She knew and loved my mom. A workmate turned good friend, Marie calmly and kindly told me I needed to tell my husband, even though he was at work, and I didn't want to bother him. (It's funny where our brains go in these moments.)

My friend Laura offered to stay with me that first night in New York, after I'd flown in from London. Though I'd booked a hotel to have my own space, I so appreciated her offer to just be there. I don't remember her saying much or what we talked about, but her willingness to be present for me in those disorienting early moments was so touching.

Four years before my mom died, my artist friend Jordana, from my textile design degree days, modeled talking about our loved ones, including sharing stories about her mother who had died in her fifties. When her son Silas was stillborn a few months after we met, she again modeled vulnerability and grace, acknowledging the intensely visceral experience of devastating loss.

I may have grown up in a family that avoided talking about illness, death, and grief, but I was so incredibly lucky to be surrounded by emotionally mature and loving individuals who offered me their hands, hearts, and ears after my mom died. Those who had experienced big losses themselves shared their stories—not as advice, nor as a point of comparison—but to let me know I wasn't alone. And those who hadn't experienced these kinds of losses themselves yet remained open to doing their best to provide whatever I needed, out of care for me. They also let me know I wasn't alone.

Each in their own way gave me the precious gift of seeing me, of witnessing this definitive moment in my life.

BEING HELD AND WITNESSED

How about you? Did you feel alone? How was your grief received?

Maybe you were lucky like me. Maybe you had a support network in place, like friends, families, acquaintances, or a therapist, people who were willing and able to receive you and your grief in the way you needed. ("Willing" and "able" being keywords.)

Grief therapist Gina Moffa calls it the *grieffall*—the moment you'll never forget, when your life changed in an instant. "It's a profoundly untethered feeling, like a total free fall into a new reality you never wanted and certainly didn't ask for," she writes in her book *Moving On Doesn't Mean Letting Go*.

When you had your grieffall, was anyone there to catch you? Who was there to cushion your landing? What hurts from the impact of that moment?

Maybe you weren't so lucky.

Maybe, when you shared your grief and loss, you experienced reactions that were painful or isolating.

Maybe you felt rejected.

Maybe you felt shamed.

Maybe it looked like a family member blaming you. Or

telling you that your grief response was wrong: "You should be more upset." Or, "You need to be strong."

Maybe it looked like someone cutting you off. Or giving you platitudes, trying to make you feel better. Or trying to change the subject—to make themselves feel better.

Maybe they couldn't handle your big feelings.

Maybe they couldn't handle your words.

Maybe they couldn't handle reality—your reality.

These kinds of reactions can be so painful, especially when you are in a vulnerable place, in shock, and hurting, looking for that soft landing and gentle reception.

WHAT I LEARNED

Not everyone is a good fit for the grief support you need. I'm grateful I instinctively knew who I could turn to and who would feel safe. There are family members whom I love very much, but I knew their grief responses were not compatible with mine. Their feelings were too big, their expectations of me were too much, and they weren't emotionally equipped to provide what I needed. Their grief responses were valid, but neither of us was in a place to comfort each other effectively.

Not everyone offers your preferred flavor of grief support. I knew early on what kind of support I needed. It needed to be kind, it needed to be calm, it needed to be competent.

The people who were most supportive for me were self-aware, sensitive, and had done a lot of emotional work themselves— whether with a therapist or just in their own processes of healing and mindfulness. (I'm also pretty sure most of them were introverts, like me.)

Jo the ceramicist was kind, calm, and competent. I knew her temperament and trusted her from having worked together during my exhibitions. She had an artist's sensitivity and sensibility. She might not be the most emotionally demonstrative person (she is British, after all). But she had the willingness and ability to be vulnerable with me.

Not everyone has the willingness and ability. Not everyone can be there for you in the way that you want, not even someone who has lost a loved one or experienced a big loss. A friend who has also lost a spouse, for instance, still may not be able to "get" what you're experiencing or be able to respond in the way that you would like them to respond. The pain may still be too fresh for them, or they just don't have the emotional capacity.

Look for the grievers. Beloved television host Mr. Rogers said, "Look for the helpers" in difficult situations and tragedies. My version of this is, "Look for the grievers." Not just any grievers, but those of us who turn *toward* you instead of turning our backs. We are the ones who look you in the eyes instead of looking away. We are the ones who invite you to share your loved one's name and would love to hear a story about them. We are the ones who remember—you, your loss, and your people— because we remember our own.

You might find these supportive grievers in unexpected places. My biggest emotional supports weren't always the people I expected—not the people I was closest to, and not necessarily the family members who were closest to my mother. They were the people who fit the kind, calm, and competent criteria that I needed for support. For you, it may be a classmate or a colleague. An acquaintance at the gym, or a total stranger.

Not all mental health and wellness professionals will get it. This mismatch in styles and lack of understanding extends to people you'd think would know better: therapists, doctors, and other licensed health professionals. I was surprised to learn that many therapists and medical professionals receive little to no grief education during their training! If you're looking for grief support, I personally advise choosing someone who specializes in grief and is trauma-informed, and steering clear of anyone who suggests you can be in "recovery" from grief, as if it were akin to an addiction or mental health problem.

Grief is not a disease nor a disorder. It warrants stating again: Grief is the *natural* response to losing anyone or anything we're attached to!

There is a spectrum of care for grief and loss. Not everyone grieving needs medical treatment, intervention, or a diagnosis. (Because again, grief is not a disease nor a disorder.)

Many grievers never need professional help of any kind! The spectrum of care for grief ranges from medical professionals like psychologists, therapists, and counselors to grief coaches like me to free community support groups, friends, and family.

We would all do so much better individually and on a societal level if we knew that there is a spectrum of care available to us. We don't have to wait until we're in crisis to reach out for support, to be seen and heard. To be held and witnessed.

Note: There is a big difference between missing your grandfather and wanting to talk about him, and not being able to function. If you cannot get out of bed, if you cannot feed yourself, if you're not showering, those are signs to speak to a medical professional.

For more on my take on getting grief support that's right for you, check out the Resources section on my website at curatinggrief.com/grief-resources

———

GOOD QUESTIONS

Take out a piece of paper, or grab your journal or computer, and give yourself a little space to consider the following questions.

What would a soft landing look like for you?

Talking or not talking? Crying or not crying?

Is it in nature, with the sound of birds chirping or the ocean waves?
Or a dark room, with awesome gaming gear?
Are there soft textiles?
Music that's calming or invigorating?

Who might be able to receive you and your grief in the way you want and need?

———

ADDING SUFFERING TO PAIN

Having our experience of grief and pain invalidated can be so painful—it can even get in the way of our normal grieving process.

"Pain and suffering are two different things," says one of my teachers, Megan Devine, psychotherapist and author of *It's OK That You're Not OK*.

"Pain is a healthy, normal response when someone you love is torn from your life. It hurts, but that doesn't make pain wrong," she tells us in a training session. "Suffering comes when we feel dismissed or unsupported in our pain, and when we relentlessly question our choices, our 'normalcy,' our actions and reactions. Suffering is often caused by external forces: other peoples' opinions, events beyond our control, etc. Suffering makes pain harder to bear. It's also where we have the most power to change."

ADDING INJURY TO INJURY

What she describes is what I think of as injury to injury. You know the phrase, "Adding insult to injury"? When I think about what grievers experience after we experience a major loss, what I often see is additional injury to injury.

Having our pain dismissed is just one example of injury to injury. As noted in Megan Devine's quote above, there's the initial wound of being forcefully detached from someone or something that we feel emotionally attached to. There's the essential pain of losing someone who's super important to you, losing a pet who played an immense role in your life, or losing a role that formed your identity for many years.

There's the initial wound and then there are all the other injuries from what we experience after loss:

• Injuries and wounds from living in systems that encourage us to move on from our grief as quickly as possible so we can get back to work.

• Injury from living in a grief-illiterate culture so our grief is not received as warmly or with the understanding that it deserves. People may say or do nonsensical and unhelpful things because they're so uncomfortable with our pain.

• Injury from dealing with a medical system that might not have been able to help our person in the way that we wanted. From dealing with doctors who might have dismissed symptoms, or the harsh realities of necessary treatments like chemotherapy or radiation.

• Injury from the additional stress of a healthcare system that values profit over people, like fighting with insurance companies when your loved one was fighting for their life.

• The injuries that come with living in a culture that expects you to finish your grieving and the tasks that come with the end of life in three days of bereavement leave or if you're lucky, two weeks of unpaid time off, if you're like many in America.

• The injuries that come from encountering healthcare professionals and other practitioners who aren't grief-informed or are working with outdated understandings of grief.

• Injury that comes from bosses who are callous and who expect you to be able to perform in exactly the way that you did before, as if your life as you know it has not been irrevocably changed.

• The injury that comes from your loved one being seen as "less than" because of their race, ethnicity, or identity.

• Injury from judging ourselves so harshly, because we receive so many messages that we're grieving wrong, or not quickly enough. We may doubt ourselves because our very normal grief is pathologized or deemed a problem.

• The injury that comes from your immigrant family member's name being misspelled on their death certificate because it was not a "normal" or standard kind of name.

• The injury that comes from expectations on women and people of color to take on the brunt of caregiving.

• The injury that comes from the pastor or other religious figure insinuating that your loved one is going to hell because they were gay, because they had mental illness, or because of the circumstances of their death.

• The injury that comes from your person being seen as just a statistic, because they died as a result of gun violence, the pandemic, natural disaster, or an overdose.

• The injury of having how they lived be overshadowed by how they died, because homicide, suicide, or other traumatic loss was involved.

• The injury of having your grief minimized or not recognized, because your person was an ex, or "just" a friend. Or maybe even a celebrity or someone you didn't know, but who still meant a lot to you.

• The injury that comes from having a messy and complicated relationship, of grieving someone when elements like abuse, bigotry, estrangement, addiction, neglect, incarceration, mental illness, or other factors were involved.

• The injury that comes from not being seen, heard, and held in the way we needed.

These are all aspects that can add injury at a time when we are feeling most raw and fragile. When we are feeling so vulnerable, all these bumps and seemingly small insults to injury can feel callous. They can leave a mark, leave us feeling bruised and battered.

In chapter 2, we talked about how there are often secondary losses that accompany the primary loss of a person. The additional insults and injuries can also be considered secondary losses, if it results in the loss of friendships, trust, or other things you valued.

I believe it is important to acknowledge this additional injury to injury. I cannot save you from the pain of the initial loss—but my hope is that we can acknowledge and heal from these additional wounds.

CHAPTER 5
MOURNING RITUALS: DID YOU FEEL SEEN?
WAS YOUR LOVED ONE WITNESSED?

We held my mother's memorial at a Chinese restaurant, three months after she died.

She didn't want a funeral. The banquet room had bright red decor with gold accents and big round tables topped with huge Lazy Susans. A slideshow of photos played on the TV screens. Eulogies were delivered. I wanted a red ribbon dance performance, but no dancers were available.

I wore a black and purple dress. I spoke and sang my mother's praises. Most attendees wore black. My mom's friends gave speeches, remembering the old days of their dance company and how relatively tall my mom was for a Chinese woman.

My aunt wore a light lavender pantsuit, and she spoke passionately about her beloved sister.

Everyone went home with paper Chinese containers full of noodles and other dishes. We'd essentially organized a banquet without telling people, and there was way too much food. Looking back, that was very appropriate for our family too. Very Chinese.

HOW DID IT LOOK FOR YOU?

Did you have a funeral, memorial, celebration of life, or other ceremony for your person? And if so, what did you want the gathering to provide?

An opportunity to say goodbye, to sing their praises, to express your love (if you wanted)?

A chance to talk about how much they meant to you, what their life meant to you, or what lessons they taught you?

A time for you to be supported and witnessed by your friends, family, and community?

Mourning rituals, like funerals and memorials, are an occasion for all the above. But maybe you didn't have that occasion. Maybe the pandemic meant you couldn't travel and your family couldn't gather. Maybe relationship dynamics meant people refused to communicate and the time period after the loss was marked by conflict rather than comfort. Maybe the stress of the loss caused your family or friend group to fracture, instead of coming together (an unfortunately quite common experience).

WHAT HURTS? "I DIDN'T LIKE THEIR MEMORIAL"

Since we are, for the purposes of this book, defining curating as choosing with intention, the funeral or memorial could also be considered a curation. After all, there are usually multiple elements chosen with a degree of intention: from who to invite, to what food to serve, to which stories to tell, to what kind of flowers to have. If you're a multicultural family, there may also be a choice of which rituals to perform.

So then, why is the official funeral or memorial often so unsatisfactory?

Timing: The loss is usually recent. People may be in shock or feel drained by grief. Emotions are often high. Attendees may be grappling with their own grief while trying, however clumsily, to be supportive to the family.

Decisions by committee: There are often multiple stakeholders, each with differing opinions and views. The stories they choose may not reflect the person you know.

Cultural mismatches and conflicts: Maybe your person wasn't particularly religious but their family members are. Maybe the pastor who delivered the eulogy barely knew your person or had an agenda of their own. Maybe important parts of your loved one's life were omitted because they were gay or lived a non-traditional lifestyle, or maybe addiction or mental illness was involved.

If you feel dissatisfied with the official funeral or memorial, you're far from alone!

MEMORIALS CAN BE WEIRD

My mom's memorial went smoothly overall. No one fell apart. No fights broke out. I delivered my mother's eulogy without crying, making eye contact with my friends and my husband. I thanked people for coming and smiled reassuringly at them. I had prepared my performance well—and it really did feel like a performance to me.

After all, we were putting on a show.

I've always found this a bizarre aspect of grieving. You mean to tell me that after a loved one dies, we're expected to essentially organize a party? Just when we're reeling from shock and in the throes of acute grief—when our heads are the foggiest, and we're potentially emotionally devastated—we have to sort out an event venue, send out invitations, order food, and then provide programming in the form of speeches? Not to mention all the clean-up afterward.

It seems like a crazy ask to make of grieving people! "It was such a bizarre day," said my client Jen of her father's funeral. "I just focused on making everything as perfect as possible. There were people I hadn't seen for thirty years. I wonder if it was weird for them too."

What was it like for you? Were there arguments about who should be invited? Tension over who showed up and who didn't show up? Upsets over what people said or didn't say? Did you get to tell the stories you wanted about your loved one? Did you recognize the person others described? Did you feel better? Worse?

True to my general experience during that first year after my mom died, I mostly felt calm and sometimes numb.

THE ROLE OF MOURNING RITUALS

As noted, funerals and memorials are mourning rituals. We often use the terms grieving and mourning interchangeably, but there are differences. Grieving is the internal expression or processing of grief and associated emotions, while mourning is an external expression that can be seen by others.

You may notice in this book, and during your own search for grief resources, that there are actually multiple definitions of grief, grieving, and mourning out there, from a range of medical professionals, experts, and authors! (Just like there are thousands of paintings of landscapes, it's like we are all trying to name and make sense of the ever-shifting and evolving terrain of life after loss.) Here's a definition from Dr. Alan Wolfelt:

"After someone you love dies, you grieve inside. You have many different thoughts and feelings, most of them painful. We call this interior experience of loss 'grief.'

Mourning means to express your grief outside of yourself. Mourning is crying, talking to other people about the death, sharing stories, putting together photo albums, journaling, and other actions. Mourning is essential because it's through mourning that you begin to heal."

THE IMPORTANCE OF BEING SEEN

An essential aspect of mourning is being seen. Do you feel seen as a griever? I believe that as grievers we want to be seen when we've experienced a significant loss. Some of the most painful times after losing a person are when we don't feel seen or supported, when we don't have our loss or grief acknowledged.

Companioning one another ...

I'm a big fan of Dr. Wolfelt's approach to how grievers can be supported. In his book *Companioning the Bereaved: A Soulful Guide for Caregivers*, he asserts that if we want to truly support grieving people, we should aim to be companions to people after major loss, to walk and sit alongside those in pain, as opposed to trying to fix or change them.

The fifth tenet of his Companioning model for grief support states, "Companioning is about bearing witness to the struggles of others; it is not about judging or directing these struggles."

He also says in his book, "Bearing witness to the struggles of someone experiencing the darkness of grief—having empathy—is the deepest form of emotional and spiritual interaction you can have with another human being."

One of the ways we talk about being seen after loss is "being witnessed." We need to be seen *and* we need our loved ones to be seen. To know that we are not alone. To feel that our grief matters. To have acknowledged that they matter.

Furthermore, we often desperately want our loved ones to be seen the way we see them.

As not just people who died.
As not just their addiction or disease.
As the individuals we knew and loved.

A hard truth is that not everyone sees our person in the way that we see them. It can often be the case when there's substance abuse, when there is a violent death, if they were incarcerated, or when it's a traumatic loss. Sometimes people can't see them because they can't see past the loss or the circumstances around it.

I have family members who people don't talk about, or have been omitted from the family tree, because it was a traumatic loss, like a suicide. Yet, *I* want them to be seen.

With my mom, I wanted her to be seen as more than just another older Asian lady. I didn't want her to be seen as just another immigrant from a lineage of immigrants with tragic backstories of traumatic loss like the kind recounted in the book *The Joy Luck Club* by Amy Tan. I wanted her to be seen as the amazing Chinese-American woman she was—a woman who had rebuilt her life after divorce, and who was dedicated to helping other people.

And I wanted her to be seen as a mother who was deeply loved by her only daughter. I want *that* to be witnessed too.

Rituals like memorials, funerals, and celebrations of life are ways for our grief and our person to be seen. I believe that curating an exhibition about your loved one can be another form of mourning ritual, a powerful one. The exhibition is an invitation for others to enter your gallery about your person—to witness you as a griever and to see your loved one the way you see them.

The Griever's Request:
I want to be seen.
I want them to be seen.
I want them to be seen the way I see them.

———

DOING RITUAL YOUR WAY

When you think of ritual, what comes to mind for you? Do you think of candles, incense, Druids, or wild dancing? I used to, because I didn't consider myself particularly spiritual or woo, especially before my mom died.

My colleague Mangda Sengvanhpheng is an artist, death doula, and the founder of BACII. As her website notes, her life and death work is guided by her Lao last name, which means "the light of the full moon." (So cool! Mine just means "forest.") Her work with BACII "is influenced by traditional Lao *baci* ceremonies performed at gatherings of birth, life, and death. During the ritual, people wish *baci*, or 'blessings,' onto others in an act of true compassion, unity, and connection."

I asked her about the importance of ritual for her:

"The wild nature of grief oftentimes calls to be tended to beyond the bounds of logic. Rituals create invisible bridges—guiding us through the intangible layers of grief, while offering us what we may need in each moment," she says. "By reconnecting to my severed ancestral rituals, it has chiseled a pathway in soothing an ache that goes beyond words—it reminds me of how grief is a universally shared experience and how this interconnection is a reminder that I am not alone."

Mangda is much more comfortable with the mystical and the use of incense than I am—she's even designed her own line of incense! (I have been known to light a candle or two though. Mostly because I think they're pretty.)

What I'm trying to say here is, I encourage you to be as woo or as religious or as secular as you want. The creative practices I describe are always just ideas, not instructions. Swap in what works for you and your beliefs. For instance, I found solace in scattering my mom's ashes around the world, but your belief system or personal preference may be to keep ashes together. In some grief groups, naming the person who died is a valued part of their ritual, but your community might have name taboos about speaking the name of the dead.

Do ritual your way. For me, the act of presenting an exhibition in a gallery space has plenty of ceremony and ritual. I just have a display plinth instead of an altar!

LOOKING BACK NOW

As awkward as it was, it was helpful to have my mother's memorial gathering for multiple reasons:

- My mom's acquaintances, friends, and colleagues from different social circles got to say goodbye to her.
- It was an efficient way to tell a bunch of people, if they hadn't already heard the news.
- Seeing my mom's friends show up for her did make me happy. It was a visual reminder that she was very loved.
- I got to give a loving eulogy for my mom—a small opportunity to "make amends" for not telling her more often how proud I was of her.
- I'm still so grateful for my friends who showed up for me—from a high school friend, to a best friend from my twenties, to more recent art school classmates. Being able to make eye contact with them when I gave my eulogy helped steady me.
- It gave my cousins and me a project to work on together, which helped strengthen our bond. My quiet, non-emotional cousin put together the photo slideshow. His sister was my rock in many ways—I knew I could rely on her and her partner to calmly deal with anything that came up.

Looking back, I really can see how the memorial and these mourning rituals give us an opportunity to be witnessed and to have our loved one witnessed. (I say opportunity, because not everyone may take us up on the invitation or take advantage of the opportunity!) But it was hard for me to appreciate any of these benefits back then.

THE MEMORIAL I REALLY WANTED

I don't think I felt much better after my mom's memorial. At the time, it was another task, another hurdle, just another item on my long to-do list.

More than two years after the official memorial, I presented my first in-person exhibition about my mother featuring her belongings. Visitors asked about the selected objects, and I told stories about my mom. I always say it was the memorial I really wanted to give her.

In the decade since my mom died, I've curated multiple exhibitions in memory of her—they are my authentic way of celebrating and inviting her to be witnessed anew. They are my continuing mourning rituals.

After all, grief and grieving do not end at the funeral, nor in the first year or two after a loss. We may grieve anew during the holidays or on their birthday. Our grief may surge when we reach the age they were when they died. There are so many reasons we may feel fresh waves of grief throughout our lives— and we deserve to be seen and witnessed through them all.

———

GOOD QUESTIONS

Did you have a funeral, memorial, or other ceremony for your person? If so, what was it like?

What do you wish had been different?

Did you feel seen?

Was your loved one witnessed in the way you wanted?

CHAPTER 6
WHO ELSE IS IN THE ROOM?

I can't believe he said that.
How dare she ask for that.
Why didn't they call?
How could he throw that away?
Why does she still have that?

Our relationships with other people will color our experiences with grief. When grieving people come to me to talk about what hurts and what is most challenging after a major loss, conflicts with other people always come up.

Yes, we talk about the person who died and the death itself. We talk about their relationship with the deceased. Just as often, if not more, we talk about and work on their relationships with people who are still alive. If we imagine a gallery space and an exhibition we've created about our loved one, these would be the other people who may be in the room—or the individuals who either refuse to enter or aren't invited!

Whether it is a family member, spouse, or partner, or whether it's with our children or our friends, often when we experience a significant loss, there is fallout that impacts our relationships with others.

What someone said or didn't say.

What someone did or didn't do.

Clumsy, insensitive, and hurtful words.

Painful interactions and actions. Or inactions.

Baffling and out-of-character or oh-so-painfully predictable behavior.

I find it helpful to separate out the relationships: Your relationship with the person who died, and your relationship with the loss itself. Your relationship with grief, and your relationships with other people. And even more importantly, your relationship with yourself.

Seeing Others

Have your relationships with other people changed since your major loss? If there's been strife, the lens of curating and the metaphor of curating an exhibition about your loved one that we explore throughout this book can be so helpful for untangling these conflicts and seeing them differently.

Curating is going to help you to see the physical objects in a new light. What's more, the meaningful objects and creative exercises in this book can help you to see your loved one in new ways. They can also help you to see other people in your life in different ways, and again, to make choices having to do with them with intention.

But why is it important to consider other people's perspectives and their processes?

"WATCH OUT FOR AFTERSHOCKS"

When I was ten, my parents and I moved from Chinatown in Manhattan to a small town in Northern California for my father's job. We shipped our belongings in boxes ahead of us and drove cross-country, enjoying United States landmarks and tourist attractions like Yellowstone National Park and Devils Tower in Wyoming.

Arriving in California, we were amazed by the land of green lawns, mild winters, single story houses, and beautiful blonde people. I was one of only a handful of Asian students in my elementary school.

The culture shock was immense, but the delights were many: Avocados. Salad bars. Gardens. The beaches of Santa Cruz an easy drive away.

It was also the land of earthquakes. Regular school drills taught us to duck and cover, squeezing ourselves under our wooden desks. Stay inside and don't run outdoors because many injuries come from falling debris, they instructed. Watch out for aftershocks.

If you haven't experienced an earthquake before, typically there is the major shock of the initial quake, followed by the aftershocks or smaller quakes that occur in the subsequent hours and days. They are normal and expected but can be startling, especially when you're already on edge. Buildings damaged in the primary quake may collapse during an aftershock. Structural weaknesses may be revealed, with the additional stress pushing walls and roofs beyond limits.

Earthquakes remind me so much of the fallout and additional damage that can happen in the aftermath of major loss. Earlier, we talked about the secondary losses that can accompany a primary loss. There are also what are called secondary stressors after a major loss. So often, what my clients and I discuss are the ripple effects of the initial loss, and the subsequent damage that follows in the form of family conflicts, tension with friends, and estrangements

"I thought it would bring us together," my client Jen lamented. After the loss of their mother and father, she thought that the siblings would band together to support each other. Instead, she was left largely alone to deal with the house and belongings, after also serving as primary caregiver in their parents' final years. One brother resented not being assigned the executor and questioned every decision she made. Her sister visited once to claim their mother's jewelry (insisting that she deserved it because she had children and Jen did not), and then didn't visit again. Another brother stopped communicating entirely.

Major loss *can* bring some families together. I've seen grievers whose shared grief strengthened their bonds and clarified their values as a family unit and as individuals. I was so impressed by my client Alice's continued resolve to ensure that dealing with the estate did *not* come between her and her beloved sister. Even as she lingered over their mother's collection of vintage linens or their father's assortment of much-mended blue and white ceramics, we kept Alice's eye on what was most important: their sisterly relationship.

And in other instances, existing family rifts are widened, cracks become chasms, and tenuous bonds snap. Instead of rebuilding structures, walls are constructed between siblings and family members.

All of this can cause so much pain and additional suffering. There is the pain of losing a loved one, and then there can be all the extra pain that comes from the aftershocks and additional losses: Injury added to injury. Damage on top of damage. In this chapter, I'm emphasizing the importance of seeing situations and people from different angles because I want to help you minimize the additional damage, if possible.

In chapter 2, we talked about different grief responses and emotional processing styles. I see so often how misunderstandings, a mismatch in expectations, and misconstrued meanings can cause rifts between people. They are like small cracks and chips in the foundations and structures of your relationships that can contribute to eventual collapse after the stress of major loss.

FOR YOUR SAKE

The concepts I'm sharing here are for *your* sake. Not for the sake of maintaining appearances, pleasing others, or not rocking the boat. I have seen how lingering anger, resentment, and blame can weigh people down and wear away at their wellbeing and ability to enjoy their own lives. (I've experienced it myself—after my mom died, all-consuming resentment almost destroyed my health and my marriage.)

If you *want* or need to maintain relationships with particular family and friends, despite your differences, this is for you. If you want to cut ties or limit contact, this is for you. Whatever you choose to do, I encourage you to do it with clear eyes.

INTRODUCING OPP

I like to use the concept of OPP. Do you remember that song "O.P.P." by Naughty by Nature? (Who else loves a good 1990s hip hop jam?) In the song, OPP stands for ahem, *adult relationship dynamics**. But for the purposes of grief and this book, I'm going to say that OPP stands for a range of things:

Other People's Processes
Other People's Pain
Other People's Perspectives and Perceptions
Other People's Priorities and Preferences
Other People's Problems

*Speaking of OPP, when a partner doesn't support you after a major loss in the way you anticipated or needed, the feeling of betrayal can be as searing as the pain of experiencing infidelity or the breaking of other vows. *You said you'd be there for me. I never thought you'd behave like this.* Major loss can cause major strain in marriages and relationships.

I'll refer to OPP throughout this book, because other people's perspectives and grieving processes pop up frequently as secondary stressors for many grievers. In chapter 20, we'll further explore Other People's Perspectives and Perceptions and in chapter 21, Other People's Priorities and our relationships with stuff.

UNTANGLING RELATIONSHIPS

To be clear, this conversation is as much about your relationship to your loved one as the other people in your life. Frequently, I see that a client's story of their loved one is so tangled up in the other stories around the loss: the additional injuries and insults.

When they paint me the proverbial picture of their person, the canvas is dominated by the betrayal of another family member, for instance. Or if we use the visual of their relationship with their loved one as represented by an exhibition, it's like five out of the six gallery spaces are themed around the conflict pertaining to the estate, the squabbles with an aunt, and the lack of support from their partner. Their fondest memories of their person are squeezed in around the conflicts.

How much space in your head and heart is currently occupied by conflicts with others?

Let's untangle your relationships and see them more clearly, so you can create and maintain the relationship you want: with your loved one who's passed, with others still living, and with yourself.

A FULL RANGE OF CHOICES

I want to offer these different ways of seeing your people and their responses, processes, perspectives, and behaviors because I believe it's so important for each of us to see the full range of choices when it comes to the people in our lives. Just as I believe it's vital for us to see the full range of choices when it comes to possessions and the meaningful objects.

If someone is being abusive to you—if someone is just so toxic that you do not want them in your life, and you want to go no-contact—that is definitely a valid choice. I will always support you doing what is right for you.

It's a choice that people make every day. And, that is not your *only* choice.

A SOFT GAZE

In chapter 7, we explore the idea of seeing ourselves with soft eyes. Relationship therapist Esther Perel says that if the goal is to have a connection in our relationships (both romantic and platonic), if the goal is to find peace, then we need to soften. I think of it as softening our gaze.

What do I mean by a soft gaze?

How do we see our loved ones, ourselves, and other people in our lives? With a loving, soft gaze, or a flinty, judging hard glare?

Try it now: Pick an object around you and fix your eyes on it as if you're angry at it. Or imagine a troublesome person in your life and pretend you're looking hard at them. Can you feel your brow furrowing, the tension in your jaw, the way your eyes narrow? I can almost feel the surface of my eyeballs hardening. Or maybe it's yourself that is receiving the stare-down of your inner judge and jury.

Now think of another person who you love and feel tender toward, like a partner, a child, or a pet. Can you feel your gaze softening? Your face relaxing?

The Getting Objective exercise I'll introduce in chapter 10 can be so helpful when we're experiencing conflicts with other people in our lives. Sometimes, when we see the person and their actions in an objective way—paradoxically, looking objectively at what is subjective to them—we can better understand where they're coming from. We can see the person and their responses in a different way. Our soft gaze often allows for an expanded awareness and understanding of everyone involved.

You can *still* choose to take space from them or to cut them out of your life. But you'll be making that choice with clarity.

Remember: seeing and choosing. That's the heart of Curating Grief.

A SOFT HEART

My favorite emoji is the sparkling heart emoji 💖. If you visit my social media, you'll see it everywhere. Google says the sparkling heart emoji expresses love, admiration, and affection. To me, it represents a mantra that's served me well in the years since my mom died:

I can do hard things with a soft heart.

Because you will have to do hard things after the loss of a loved one. Whether you're tasked with planning the funeral or delivering a eulogy. Or dealing with the estate. Or taking care of dependents or a surviving parent. Or "just" picking up the pieces of your own life.

There will be hard things. Emotionally and practically.

It's going to hurt sometimes. Many times.

You will need some armor to get you through the pain. But make it *temporary* armor.

You may have to grit your teeth. Strengthen your resolve. Cry later. But don't harden your heart forever.

Here is my hope for all who are actively grieving: That you emerge with health, sanity, and relationships intact. And that requires keeping your heart soft. Even as you do hard things.

Stay human. Keep your heart soft and vulnerable under that necessary armor.

When I use the sparkling heart emoji, I'm imagining all our grieving hearts: Underneath the sparkles, there are the cracks and repairs from when grief, life, and loss have broken our hearts open. But our hearts can still be whole.

Our hearts—our love, our humanity—can still sparkle, shine, and shimmer.

CHAPTER 7
SEEING OURSELVES
WITH SOFT EYES
WITNESSING OURSELVES

There can be so much judgment when it comes to grief—judgment about the way you grieve, what you think you should be feeling, or where you should be in your grief. That judgment can come directly from ourselves or it can come from outside, whether that's family members, friends, casual acquaintances, or the media.

We can be *so* hard on ourselves. I like to invite grievers and my clients to approach their grief, and our exploration of it, from a place of curiosity and compassion, a place without judgment (or at least setting aside as much judgment as we can). This is an approach that I like to think of as *soft eyes*.

Let's try it out.

I'm going to invite you now to approach your loss with curiosity and compassion as an antidote to the self-incrimination, guilt, and regret that—in grief—so often sound like this:

I couldn't make it in time.
I couldn't keep it.
I should've fought harder.
I fought too much.
I could've done more.

This also applies to the belongings and our relationships with the physical stuff. When we think about the belongings from our loved ones or the objects that we have—or that we do not have— so often there's an element of judgment.

I wish they still had that.
I wish I still had that.
I should've chosen differently.
Why did I do that?

Can we have and hold compassion when we look at the items that we feel attached to after a loved one dies? Often these are things that don't make logical sense. It's the ugly pair of socks. It's the soy sauce in the kitchen. It might be a collection of matchboxes. A stone picked up on vacation. Things that we deem silly.

We judge ourselves for feeling so attached. We question whether we're OK. Or immature. And maybe other people question it too.

Why am I so attached?
Why are we so attached?

We ask ourselves these questions with a note of judgment, with a hint of exasperation or frustration. Impatience with ourselves and our nonsensical hearts.

I'm going to invite you to ask the question, "Why am I so attached?" with a different tone: from a place of curiosity and openness and self-compassion. In the voice of the kindest and most loving person (or fictional character) you know, ask yourself: *Why am I so attached?*

Upon inquiry, we might then see all the reasons, stories, memories, and meanings attached to the object.

Memories with the person.
Stories about them.
Thoughts we have about ourselves.

In chapter 19, "When Everything Becomes Precious," we'll have more opportunity to further explore all that's potentially attached to meaningful objects.

When we approach our grief and attachments with curiosity and compassion, in the same way that we might enter a museum or an art gallery with curiosity, the belongings and meaningful objects can show us so much:

- about our relationship with ourselves.
- our relationship with the person who died.
- our relationship with God or the Universe.
- our relationship with life itself.

Imagine you're attending an art or museum exhibition. You're likely not going to get much out of it if you enter from a place of judgment: judging the value of a piece of art, judging what the artist meant, judging whether it's good or not.

We tend to enter these spaces from a place of curiosity, from a place of wanting to learn, wanting to understand, wanting to see things differently. We want to be inspired. We may want to feel connected to the artist and what they were experiencing. And we find connections to what *we* are experiencing.

And that's why I encourage you to enter into the grief space with openness and curiosity. With a willingness to see. Because these are items that have emotional weight and meaning for you, I also ask that you bring compassion.

Compassion for yourself, as a griever, as a human being.

Also, if possible, compassion for anyone else who might wander into this space, who interacts with these objects, who encounters your grief. (In chapter 6, we go more into who else is in the room.)

Compassion and curiosity will make your experience gentler and more fulfilling. I promise.

And if you can't access compassion right now, that's also OK.

It can be elusive for a while, but my experience tells me that it's always possible. And I'm holding the possibility for compassion for you, like a seed that's ready whenever you're ready to cultivate it.

If you want to be more pro-active in welcoming self-compassion, here are a couple of simple awareness and visualization practices that can help in a big way . . .

BECOMING A (BIRD) WATCHER

I like to use the metaphor of a Garden of Grief for bringing in a sense of curiosity and discovery, especially when we're looking at ourselves and our grief. Sometimes when we notice certain thoughts and feelings we're experiencing, we decide they're "negative." *Oh, I need to chase that feeling away. I need to kill that thought.* In this particular garden, those so-called negative thoughts and feelings are represented by birds—a rich diversity of birds.

So, let's pretend that we are birdwatching.

As we step into the garden, it's essential to know that we are bird*watchers*, not bird hunters. We are not here to shoot the birds. We're not here to chase off that thought. We're not here to evict or eliminate that feeling. We are observers, learning how to be the watcher of ourselves—what is happening in our grief, in our heads, in our bodies, and in our hearts. We are learning how to be the watcher of what we are thinking, what we're feeling, and the sensations we experience in our bodies when we're grieving.

So the first step is really to be that watcher—the gentle, curious observer of that bird.

In the Garden of Grief, we might say, *Huh, I see that bird quite often. I wonder what it's doing right now. Is it squawking a lot? Is it singing? Is it silent? How do I feel when I notice that bird there?*

As we are learning to be the watcher of ourselves, we are learning to be the watcher of our grief. I find this really helpful because it gives us a little bit of distance. It allows us to notice that we are not our grief. We are not the situation. We are not *only* our thoughts. We are not *only* our emotions or the sensations we feel in our bodies. **We are the ones who are watching.**

It gives us the opportunity to practice observing with soft, curious eyes. We are not here to judge ourselves or chase out what doesn't feel good. We are here to see ourselves, to see our grief, to see our situations with compassion, with softness, with love, and with understanding.

THE BEAUTY OF METAPHOR

I love using metaphors, analogies, and similes in my grief work because they elegantly help us to see in different ways. They help us notice how we perceive ourselves, our circumstances, and the people around us. And more, they help us deepen our understanding of the world and our lives.

"Much of what we struggle with in grief is not having answers. There's so much unknown," explains Lisa Keefauver, MSW, grief activist, author, and podcast host of *Grief is a Sneaky Bitch*. "In fact, we often find ourselves questioning everything we thought we knew to be true. This is where metaphor, among other narrative forms, can be such a beautiful vehicle to discover what we do know. Additionally, metaphors give us the protective cover we need to see what we might be frightened to admit, and the language needed to describe what we have no words for."

SEEING OURSELVES THROUGH LOVING EYES

Here's something I've noticed: Grievers judge themselves harshly but have more understanding and compassion for others' actions and inactions.

People who find themselves stuck in this dichotomy will sometimes ask me, "How do *you* access self-compassion? How do you forgive yourself?"

The short answer is: I practice seeing myself with soft, loving eyes. I use the creative visualizations I've shared above regularly, for myself and with clients.

I also practice seeing myself through my mother's loving eyes. I was lucky to have an overall good relationship with a caring mom, so I pretend I'm seeing myself as she saw me: noticing my flaws and mess-ups, but also with true unconditional love.

Not everyone is lucky enough to know that loving gaze from a parent or caregiver, of course. In those cases, I encourage clients to channel the loving gaze of a grandparent or other parental figure, of God or other deity if you believe, or a fictional character from a book or movie. Or you can redirect some of the unconditional love you have for your pets, children, or other loved ones to yourself.

You might suddenly find yourself treating yourself like you would a young child—with great tenderness, an open heart, and encouragement for the future.

———

GOOD QUESTIONS

How good are you at self-compassion?

What does curiosity feel like to you?

What do you need permission for?

How might you try being the watcher of yourself and your grief with love, compassion, curiosity, and soft eyes?

PART TWO
WELCOME TO CURATING GRIEF

Her Favorite Purses

CHAPTER 8
WHY CURATE? AN INTRODUCTION

What is a curator? Many people associate curators with museums, but the Merriam-Webster Dictionary points to wider possibilities. It says the word *curate* "has been used to mean 'carefully choose the right assortment of objects' since the 19th century."

In larger museums, the curator may work with a whole team, including collections managers, exhibition designers, and art handlers. In smaller institutions, the curator may wear all these hats. Because we are individuals and not institutions, for the purpose of Curating Grief, we get to wear *all* the hats!

I was already curating exhibitions when my mom died, but here's how I truly embraced my Curator role in my grief:

A Curator is someone who cares for something. The verb *curate* comes from the Latin *curare* meaning "to care for." Curators can oversee care for the objects in a collection, often working with conservators and registrars, depending on the size of their museum or institution.

Turning again to Merriam-Webster:

We define curator as "one who has the care and superintendence of something . . ." and the verb form of curate as "to act as curator of."

After my mom died, as an only child and the executor of her estate, I became responsible for everything she owned. I continue to care for the items I kept, I serve as custodian of them.

I am now the carer of my mom's belongings—but also of her story and legacy.

A Curator is someone who chooses. In the art world, a curator may choose what goes into a museum's collection. Or what is displayed in an exhibition.

I had to make lots of choices with my mom's estate. Some easy: of course I was keeping the family photos. Some hard: the house itself, for instance. I did my best to choose with intention, and with compassion, for her and myself.

We all make choices every day, even if not all are well-considered choices. And choosing not just things, but thoughts, feelings, experiences.

After a loved one dies, you may have to make choices about objects. Or maybe less tangible things, like memories and stories. These days, you can "curate" anything. A restaurant menu. Your bookshelf. Your Instagram grid.

For this book, let's borrow the lens of curating from the art and museum world. And remember, you don't need to be an artist to curate. Or to even think you're creative to curate. **We are *all* curators.** You do not need to get a degree in art history. Or to gain access to a world-class museum.

————

Here are affirming reasons as to why curating can be such a helpful lens for grieving people:

YES, YOU CAN CURATE!

You are likely already curating. You are choosing what takes up space in your life every day. In your home, in your head, and in your heart. Physical space and emotional space.

Everyone can use the Curating Grief approach. Whether you have physical items or not. Whether your loss is recent or years ago.

Remember: You don't need a gallery space to curate. Your "gallery" can be a shelf. A book. A display case. For more ideas, see chapter 9, "Yes, You Can Curate."

CURATING HELPS YOU CHOOSE – A HELPFUL LENS

Curating is a beautiful lens. After the death of a loved one or a significant loss, we are often faced with difficult choices. What to keep. Who gets what. What to say or do. When we're faced with these situations, we can use curating as a beautiful lens for making these choices.

Curating is Choosing with Intention. That's how I like to define curating. Just as a curator in a museum chooses with intention what goes into a collection or into an exhibition, grieving individuals can choose with intention what they keep after a loved one dies. You can decide with care, consideration, and clarity what you want to spotlight, what stories you want to tell, and what takes up this meaningful space.

AN INVITATION TO SEE

Curating helps us to see in different ways. That's the beauty of art and what I love about coaching, too—it's an invitation to explore seeing from different perspectives.

This ability to shift our views can change our experience of grief, life, and the world for the better.

Curating helps us to see the full range of choices available. It's so easy to slip into black or white thinking when we're grieving. Or to assume things have to be done in a certain way. Let's give you permission to do what's right for you and to see all your options.

AN INVITATION TO GRIEVE

Curating can help us grieve. The belongings and meaningful objects can help us to access emotions and to process our grief in a gentler way. When I was sorting through my mom's belongings, I was also sorting through my thoughts, feelings, and grief.

Curating can give us some necessary emotional distance. As a grieving daughter, I couldn't choose what to keep after my mom died, but with my curator hat on, I could start making choices.

CURATING AS MEANING-MAKING

Curating helps us to make sense and make meaning after a major loss. The death of a significant person in our life can shatter our world as we know it. When we are reconstructing that world view after the death of a loved one, curating an exhibition about them gives us a structure, a creative brief for navigating this new way of existing without them.

The belongings and meaningful objects can teach us so much and help us access greater understanding—about ourselves, about our loved one, about grief.

CURATING FOR CONNECTION

Curating helps us to create a living relationship with our loved one. Our loved ones were people who lived, not just people who died, and talking about them, imagining how they would respond to something we're experiencing now, can be a way to keep their memories alive and continue to feel connected to them.

CURATING FOR AGENCY

Curating is empowering. As grieving people, we are facing so many circumstances outside of our control. Death, illness, loss. It can be empowering to see the choices that we *do* have, to see what we *do* have control over.

As Curator, you decide what's important. After a loved one dies, there can be a lot of decisions by committee. Maybe you're navigating conflicting opinions or difficult family dynamics. Or people just don't value what you find so precious. In your exhibition about your loved one, you get to decide what is valuable.

Reclaim the Narrative. Maybe you're navigating difficult family dynamics or conflicting opinions. Maybe your beloved person is the bad guy in everyone else's story. Maybe people avoid talking about your loved one because of the circumstances around how they died. When suicide, addiction, violent death, incarceration, and other complicating factors are involved, our person's life story may be overshadowed. As Curator, you get to reclaim the narrative, to tell the stories you want about them, to share how *you* see them. See chapter 10 for more about the power of the plinth and reclaiming narrative.

Curating shifts the focus. Our loved ones died. *And* they lived. In the immediate period after a person dies, so much of our focus can be on the death: How they died, why they died, the sheer impossibility of grasping that they're really dead. If you're dealing with the estate, that can be a huge drain on your energy and attention as well. When I invite you to curate an exhibition about your loved one, I'm inviting you to shift focus to how your person lived and the meaning of their life. It doesn't mean papering over the hard parts of their lives and the pain of losing them. But it's an opportunity to spotlight the good parts and the joy of loving them and having been loved by them too.

CURATING AS MOURNING RITUAL – CREATING OPPORTUNITIES TO BE WITNESSED

An exhibition can be an alternative to or complement to a traditional funeral or memorial. As we noted in chapter 5, many grievers find the formal mourning rituals unsatisfactory: emotions are high, you may be in shock. There can be a lot of decision-makers—and your opinion or wishes may have been ignored. Your exhibition can take place months or years after the death. (Or even before death, if your person has a terminal diagnosis.)

An exhibition is an opportunity to evaluate or re-evaluate your person's life and your relationship to them in a meaningful and healing way.

You can curate multiple exhibitions about your person, throughout your life. I've presented over a dozen exhibitions, online and in-person, about my mother in the decade since her death, and I'll likely present others. Your exhibitions and curations can evolve with you and your grief.

CHAPTER 9
YES, YOU CAN CURATE: NO GALLERY OR BELONGINGS NEEDED

In 2017, the artist Maira Kalman recreated her mother's closet at the Metropolitan Museum of Art in New York City. The installation was called "Sara Berman's Closet" and created in collaboration with her son, artist Alex Kalman.

I study the photos from the show: The recreated closet is inset in a museum wall, similar to a hallway closet or a shallow pantry. The horizontal shelves have tidy arrangements of clothing and carefully placed shoes, all white. It has the elegant feel of a high-end boutique. The stacks of shirts—likely all linen or natural textiles—are only a couple of items high, quite the contrast to the teetering towers of colorful T-shirts and sweatshirts my mother had in her closet.

Sara Berman was a Jewish émigré from Belarus to Israel. After divorcing her husband of thirty-eight years, she moved to the US with few possessions to a NYC studio. In her newfound life, she decided to wear only white.

My mother's stockpile of white T-shirts from the Gap weren't an artistic statement, but they were a nod to where she'd been and where she was when she died. In some of her favorite snapshots of herself, she is wearing a white T-shirt. It's the 1990s, and she's standing in her cubicle at Hewlett-Packard Labs in Palo Alto, California, where she worked as an administrator for over twenty-five years.

Much like Sara Berman, my mom found herself in a newfound place of independence after my parents divorced. After a rough period of transition, she reveled in buying a house of her own, picking out furniture that suited her style without having to negotiate with anyone else. She asked me to help her choose paint colors for her room.

Careful planning and lucky timing meant she could afford to count shopping as a hobby, the true American Dream. Nothing too extravagant, but cashmere sweaters on discount at Loehman's, T-shirts from the Gap, and colorful fleece jackets from Kohl's were favorites. I like imagining my mom accumulating white T-shirts as if she had all the time and torsos in the world.

I didn't learn about "Sara Berman's Closet"—the exhibition in 2017 and the book of the same name published in 2018—until recent years. The first exhibition with my mother's items was in 2015. I don't note this to insist, "I didn't copy Maira Kalman, I swear!"—but to notice for myself and to share with you how immersed I was in my grieving when I was sorting through my mom's belongings.

Frankly, I was so deep in my grief and exploring my mom's story that the stories of other artists' mothers weren't of great interest to me at the time. (So if you've ever felt selfish or self-absorbed—or been accused of it—after a major loss, you're not alone! I personally think it makes total sense to be self-absorbed for a while when your world has exploded or imploded.)

I didn't see what I was doing as part of a trend or a movement or a connection to a storied art practice of working with possessions or belongings. I didn't even see my exhibitions of my mother's objects as a creative practice. It was then just a much-needed outlet, an expression of my grief, regret, and love for my mom.

Looking back now though, I can see multiple important reminders for us to take away as grievers:

The belongings can tell us so much. The belongings and

everyday items in a person's house can say so much about their personality and how they lived. They can represent their yearnings, their priorities, their pain and joy. The belongings can serve as a way to have a creative dialogue with the person. Or be a celebration of them. Or an exploration of your relationship.

It bears repeating: You do not need to be an artist or to have a gallery to curate. You do not need to have a formal gallery space to recreate a beloved space. You do not need to be a famous artist —or have access to a world-class museum—in order to curate.

We are all curators—it's my mantra. Anything can become a gallery. I've done installations of The Grief Gallery in spaces as diverse as a community garden and a phone booth, as well as more classic gallery spaces.

The installation "Sara Berman's Closet" actually originated at Mmuseumm, a mini gallery in a freight elevator on the gritty streets of Lower Manhattan, created by artist Alex Kalman— Maira's son and Sara Berman's grandson. When I first came across Mmuseumm, I was so enamored with the idea of turning a freight elevator into a museum space. Anything can be a gallery.

When we curate our loved one's belongings, we are part of a long history and tradition of making sense of loss, making meaning of the world, and connecting to our loved ones through possessions and meaningful objects.

From Mexican *ofrendas* to Buddhist altars, from Frida Kahlo's curated life and wardrobe, to "Sara Berman's Closet," I like to imagine all of us navigating this together.

And isn't that the beautiful thing about art, that it can connect us as human beings and individuals, across the years and our differences in lived experiences?

YOU DO NOT NEED A GALLERY TO CALL YOURSELF A CURATOR

The question, "If I were to curate an exhibition about my mother, which 100 objects would I choose to display?" felt natural to me because I was already curating exhibitions regularly. When my mother died, I was working as an independent curator in London. I was organizing exhibitions featuring the work of artists, ceramicists, and jewelers. For these exhibitions, I would curate—choosing with intention—which pieces of their work went into the gallery space. I chose with intention which pieces told the best stories about them and their work.

When you imagine curating an exhibition about your loved one, you are choosing with intention which objects to include and what stories to tell about them.

You probably don't have a gallery space. You might not be a professional curator with connections to museums. But even though you don't have a gallery, you are still curating. Look around the space you're sitting in now as you read this book. Maybe there's a bookshelf or a wall of framed photos. Maybe there's a fireplace mantle, or a cabinet where the most special pieces are displayed. You are choosing every day what gets put into your space, what gets pride of place.

That's why I say we are all curators. We're all making these choices, whether we know it or not, about what takes up space in our lives, whether it's an office, our closets, or our dresser drawers.

And these choices? They matter. These items take up space in our homes and in our lives and in our hearts. These objects have volume, and they have weight—physical weight, but more importantly, emotional weight. I suggest that it's important that we make these choices consciously, that we choose with intention.

You don't need access to an art gallery to curate an exhibition for your person. Here are some examples of alternatives spaces and formats:

A SHELF

Have a bookshelf or wall shelf? That can be your gallery space. You can arrange meaningful objects and belongings from a loved one. As a permanent display or with a rotation of objects. Galleries and museums change up their displays all the time!

I have a shelf in the bedroom that is my mother's shelf. On it are photos, sculptures, an hourglass, and plants. I rotate items for Mother's Day, Valentine's Day, and Chinese New Year.

A BOOK

My client Marsha made a beautiful book as a tribute to her husband David. She curated stories for each family member, illustrating each one with an object or photograph. A book can be for public consumption, or it can be private—for family or close friends only.

A PHOTO WALL

Or a photo album! Even an Instagram grid. Any place you are curating images, choosing with intention the stories you want to tell, can serve as a gallery space for your exhibition about your person.

AN ALTAR

A variation on the shelf gallery, an altar is important in many cultures. From Mexican *ofrendas* to Buddhist altars, there are often traditional offerings and rituals, like plates of fruit or burning incense. You can create your own altar for your person.

A COLLAGE

Photos, pictures, scraps of handwriting, text—they can all be incorporated into a quasi-exhibition about your person. What might distinguish your exhibition from a purely expressive collage includes the intentionality of your choices and the meaning you're assigning to each element.

A FILM

Independent documentary maker Jamie Max Lee created the short film *Curating Grief: Loss and Objects* after we met at an installation of The Grief Gallery in London. He brought a curation of his father's belongings to Lisbon for the film for us to explore, but I think the film itself is his ultimate curation and creation!

Additional ideas include websites, shadowboxes, and other display cases. In Part 8, we'll go into more detail about the steps for putting together an exhibition, but I hope some ideas have been sparked for you about the form your gallery can take.

———

GOOD QUESTIONS

What space do you currently have available?

What space can you claim, identify, create?

Where do you put special items currently?

Where is your loved one represented in your space now?

What would you like to change about "their" space?

———

YOU DO NOT NEED THEIR BELONGINGS

"What if I don't actually have many or any of my person's belongings?" Does this question apply to you? There is a wide range of experience when it comes to physical possessions, belongings, and meaningful objects, as we explore more in depth in chapter 15, "Circumstances, Capacity, and Collection Criteria."

For me, my problem was that I had too many things. I had too many decisions to make. As the executor and an only child, I had *all* of my mother's possessions. For others, they might not have anything. Where do you land on the spectrum of having and not having?

Maybe you were a child when your loved one died, and the adults made all the decisions. Maybe you weren't given a choice. Maybe you were asked to choose items when you didn't have the capacity or maturity to choose, like my friend Rebecca Feinglos shares in chapter 15 about the difficulty of making decisions about her mother's jewelry as a thirteen-year-old.

Or maybe you were in college, and you didn't have the capacity physically or emotionally to choose or keep anything. Maybe you were in school or living in a dorm room, and you didn't have space to store someone else's possessions. Maybe you couldn't afford to keep a storage unit.

There are so many circumstances and contexts where you might not have many possessions or the meaningful objects that you really want. Sometimes circumstances converge, and preserving items for children may be overlooked.

Taj, Taryll, and TJ, sons of Jackson 5 guitarist Tito Jackson, lost so much when their mom Delores "Dee Dee" Jackson was murdered, several years after their parents' divorce. When I spoke with Taj and TJ on their *Power of Love Show*, they shared how being part of a famous family made the situation even harder for them, on top of losing their mother in such a violent way.

Through a combination of events, their belongings wound up in a storage unit, with the items eventually going up for auction. "Our whole house, basically all our memories were auctioned off," Taj shared.

"It's a really crazy story, because obviously, us being Jacksons, everything was four times as expensive, and they made up stories about what things were. All my mom's stuff . . . her clothing became LaToya's clothing, and so now it's four times as expensive just for a shirt that is my mom's because they said it was LaToya's shirt."

The brothers wound up strategically bidding for their mother's items from the auction site, guided by sentimental choices, with one of the most precious items being a Gizmo doll (the character from the movie *Gremlins*) that had been on their mother's bed.

"This little Gizmo doll cost $300 to get back, which is ridiculous," Taj said. "But at the same time, it represented my mom, and just memories of sitting on her bed with the Gizmo doll there."

They remember their mom best through the Dee Dee Jackson Foundation, honoring their mother's deep love for music—but I'm glad they have some of their meaningful objects back too.

ACKNOWLEDGE HOW PAINFUL THIS CAN BE

I want to acknowledge how painful it can be to not have been given those choices and to not have the belongings that you wanted or that are most meaningful to you. I want to acknowledge how much that can hurt *and* assure you that you can still curate.

If I had my choice, I would have kept my grandmother's incredibly heavy sewing machine. Let's be real: I would have kept a million things! But that wasn't possible.

***And*, even in the face of the impossible, we can still curate.**

Curating Grief doesn't require you to have the actual possessions. You are not the Smithsonian. You are not the Tate Modern in London. No one is checking for authenticity or carbon dating the objects in your collection. You are also not responsible for keeping all of the exact items for the rest of time.

What is important about a meaningful object is the meaning that it has for *you*. I did not have to keep my mother's actual bottle of soy sauce—the bottle that still had her fingerprints—in order to cherish the memories that came with that bottle of soy sauce.

What is important is what the object represents, what it signifies, and the way that it keeps us feeling connected to our loved one. As precious as the belongings can seem, it is ultimately always about the connection, not the artifact, not the object itself.

AND, I'm going to encourage you to collect or acquire some physical objects to represent the belongings, moments, and stories you want to keep as we explore the process of Curating Grief. These external items can be useful for helping us to access our internal feelings!

When we're curating an exhibition about our loved ones, imaginary or otherwise, we are really presenting *stories* about our person. We are presenting how we want to remember them, and how we want them to be remembered. And the objects, the things that are on display, can be thought of as ways to illustrate those stories.

In chapter 35, we will dive deeper into options for curating and creating when we don't have or cannot keep the belongings and meaningful objects. In the meantime, I just want to gently assure you that no matter your circumstances, whether you have physical space or objects or not, you can *still* curate!

CHAPTER 10
THE POWER OF THE PLINTH AND NARRATIVE

Frida Kahlo is on my mind again. Because I am feeling melancholy, I marvel at how much grief and loss the famous Mexican artist experienced in her life. I reflect on how much she did and how young she was when she died at the age of forty-seven—my age now as I write this book.

When you think of Frida Kahlo, what comes to mind? Do you think of her distinctive style, with flowers in her hair and colorful dresses? Do you envision her paintings, like her striking self-portraits? Maybe you remember a visit to her Casa Azul, now home to the Frida Kahlo Museum in Mexico City.

There are so many ways to remember a person. In chapter 8, "Why Curate? An Introduction," we noted that, as curator, you decide what's important and what's in the spotlight: which objects, stories, and meanings.

THE POWER OF THE PLINTH

Throughout this book, I refer to the plinth. A plinth is the base that supports a statue, object, or artwork. The pedestal might be made out of wood, stone, or acrylic. It might be painted or not. Sometimes there is a protective case of acrylic or glass over it.

Placing an object on a plinth spotlights it, singling it out for extra attention and inviting a viewer to look closer.

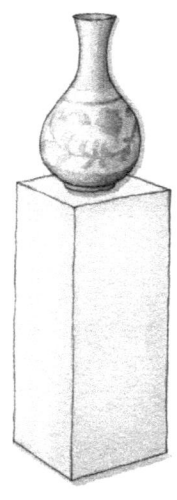

In several chapters, in our Getting Objective exercises, I'll invite you to imagine a white rectangular box (aka the plinth) with a sculpture or object on top, like you often see in a gallery space.

Putting an object on a display pedestal also elevates it, literally and figuratively. People see the object differently. It's been deemed important—by someone. The people we have lost and their objects and stories are also important—to us. They deserve at least a moment on the proverbial plinth.

Here's what I want to highlight about Curating Grief though: **YOU get to choose what goes on the plinth**. Not your family. Not the media. Not the priest or pastor. In *your* exhibition about your person, you choose what deserves attention, and what you want to spotlight.

Have you ever paused to consider:

Who decides which stories are told?
Who decides which people and moments are worthy of memorials?
Who deserves a statue, a portrait, or a museum retrospective?

Often these decisions are made by committee, by institutions and people in power. As much as I love museums, it's been a time of reckoning for many cultural institutions, with important questions being asked about how items are acquired and who determines what is significant.

By assuming the role of curator, we get to decide what is worthy of showing. We get to select the stories. And we get to shape the narrative, reflecting the aspects of our persons, relationships, cultures, and heritage that *we* want to highlight.

NARRATIVE

There are hundreds of ways to approach telling the story of a person, of a life, of a place, of a moment. Exhibitions have narratives, or perhaps more accurately, exhibitions *are* narratives. A narrative is defined as a spoken or written account of connected events—it's a story, or a series of connected stories.

We can think of an exhibition as a structure for your stories about your person.

There is an order and flow to the stories, in the same way that you can imagine visitors taking a path through the rooms of an art gallery. (That's part of what an exhibition designer does, deciding on the recommended path through the space!)

As curator, you get to choose the narrative.

RECLAIMING THE NARRATIVE

This can be one of the hardest truths after a loved one dies: Other people are not always going to see your loved one in the way that you do.

Maybe a parent who was cold and neglectful to you became an amazing grandparent to your children. Maybe you were the family scapegoat or the target of abuse, but others had a drastically different experience. Maybe they were dazzled by the charisma of your narcissistic or mentally ill partner. Maybe they've blocked out and rewritten what actually happened when you were growing up.

Maybe your person died in a natural disaster, a mass shooting, or other event covered by the media. Maybe your person was a public figure or celebrity. Their narrative has been co-opted, twisted, obfuscated, or forgotten by others.

Maybe substance abuse, mental illness, criminal activity, or other potentially difficult circumstances and taboo topics were involved—and their narrative of your person is dominated by these factors.

Perhaps your beloved sibling is seen as a troublemaker or

black sheep by other family members. Maybe they avoid talking about them entirely. Maybe they only speak of them negatively. Maybe they only see them as an angel, ignoring all the dimensions of how they lived.

As curator, you get to reclaim the narrative.

The exhibition "Jean-Michel Basquiat: King Pleasure," which was on show in New York City in 2022 and in Los Angeles in 2023, is a great example of reclaiming narrative. For many, the life of the Brooklyn-born artist of Haitian and Puerto Rican descent is told in three major points: His immense talent and meteoric art career in New York City, his mentor-like relationship with established artist Andy Warhol, and his death in 1988 from a heroin overdose at the age of twenty-seven.

But this exhibition was particularly powerful and poignant because its narrative was crafted by his family. "Organized and curated by The Estate of Jean-Michel Basquiat, this exhibition featured over 200 never-before-seen and rarely shown paintings, drawings, multimedia presentations, ephemera, and artifacts," the exhibition website explains. "This intimate perspective is shared through the lens of his family—intertwining his artistic endeavors with his personal life, influences, and the times in which he lived."

In a *Los Angeles Times* interview, his sisters, Lisane Basquiat and Jeanine Heriveaux, now in their fifties, are pictured sitting in a re-creation of the family's living room, part of an immersive experience in the exhibition designed by Ghanaian-British architect David Adjaye.

"They spent about five years digging through their brother's artworks and personal effects—paintings and drawings, but also clothing, notebooks, dinner china, travel souvenirs—to produce the exhibition. The goal: to show from their point of view who their brother really was," the article says.

The interview notes that "in order for Basquiat's family to 'own the narrative,' the estate paid for everything out of pocket

—insurance, shipping, venue rental, exhibition design, construction, video production, staffing and other costs—and didn't apply for grant funding."

I find it so touching that the sisters co-curated and executive-produced this incredible exhibition about their brother. To others, Basquiat was a legend, an icon, an inspiration, or even a cautionary tale. To them, he was, most importantly, their brother.

JUST PART OF THEIR STORY

I often reference shows about artists when I'm working with clients who are struggling with how to celebrate and remember their loved one without painting them as an angel instead of a flawed human being. Many artists have grappled with addiction, substance abuse disorders, or mental illness in their lives. It is part of their story, but not the *entirety* of their story.

Exhibitions will vary in terms of how much they reference these factors. For instance, the vast majority of shows about Vincent van Gogh will touch on his mental illness. It is part of his life story, but unless mental health is a focus of the exhibition, there may only be one wall label, display, or room that discusses it. It may be similar for your person—in your imagined exhibition about them, maybe there is a room or a couple of references to their illness or vices, but it likely doesn't take over every room of your gallery space. You can acknowledge their reality without sanitizing who they were to the point of being unrecognizable.

A formative experience for me was when an art docent visited my class in elementary school. I was forever changed when that lady turned off the lights and showed us a slideshow of Van Gogh's brilliant paintings while Don McLean's song "Vincent" played. The hauntingly beautiful song starts with "Starry, starry night . . . ," and at a certain point the lyrics "and when no hope was left in sight / on that starry, starry night / you took your life / as lovers often do" ring out with devastating clarity and gentleness.

Eleven-year-old Me was never the same. I can't imagine this

curriculum being allowed now in American schools (unfortunate, I think), but I suspect that this inspired art docent might have planted the seed for me turning Goth in high school. She's certainly the reason there was a poster of the painting "Starry, Starry Night" on my college dorm room wall. But I digress.

The point is: Telling this tragic part of his story humanized the Dutch artist for me, and it also didn't overshadow what he created!

As curator, you get to take back the narrative and to allocate as much or as little space as you'd like to the various facets of how your person was in life.

————

GOOD QUESTIONS

How do other people describe your loved one?

Is it different from how you describe them?

What stories do they tell about your loved one?

Would you choose different ones?

What do they see as the key events in the life of your loved one?

What would you choose?

————

THE NARRATIVE ABOUT MY MOTHER

I know that my amazing mother would be the villain in another person's story and narrative. As much as I want to insist that my family member sees how amazing she was and publicly acknowledges how much she generously did for people, I have decided to let it be. He has his own perspective and narrative about my mother. That is my hard truth.

It may be similar with your loved one. Therefore, I'll say it again: Other people are not necessarily going to see your person in the same light and in the same way.

And that's why being curator of an exhibition about your person can be so powerful.

For more about the different narratives I *could* tell about my mother, check out chapter 32, "Regret, Perspective, and Interpretations."

EXAMPLES OF NARRATIVES

Let me give you an example of a narrative in an exhibition. Say I want to curate an exhibition about Frida Kahlo. Obviously, she is one of the most famous artists in the world. And I still have a whole range of narrative-shaping options for an exhibition about her!

Questions I might ask myself as curator include:

What facts am I including?
What stories am I telling?
What key life events am I spotlighting?
What themes or concepts am I focusing on?
What facets of her personal or professional life am I showing?
What feeling, insight, or concept do I want visitors to come away with?

As the subject of a section of the exhibition or even the whole exhibition, I can identify and pull out different themes about both her life and her work. For instance, themes might include identity, power, strength, or self-portraiture. We can tell the story of Frida Kahlo's life in various ways by changing up the overall narrative and themes:

• The exhibition can be a comprehensive telling of every aspect and every facet of her life. The Frida Kahlo Museum in Mexico City does this, telling the story of her life from birth to death.

• We could present just the facts, in chronological order: She was born on July 6, 1907, in Coyoacán, Mexico. She married artist Diego Rivera in August 1929. She died on July 13, 1954, at the age of forty-seven. The Frida Kahlo Museum's website includes a timeline that actually starts with the births of her father, mother, and her future husband.

• The exhibition could feature her renowned self-portraits and explore how she took control of her own image amidst many circumstances outside of her control—from catastrophic injury and illness, to multiple miscarriages, to her famous husband's infidelity.

• The exhibition could focus just on her relationship with Diego Rivera, who was twenty years her senior and an internationally recognized painter, showing their work side by side and exploring how our closest relationships can shape our lives, personally and professionally.

• The exhibition could focus just on her clothing and accessories, like the exhibition "Frida Kahlo: Making Her Self Up," presented at the Victoria & Albert Museum in 2018 in London, after its debut in Mexico. Described as "a fresh perspective on Kahlo's compelling life story through her most intimate personal belongings," the exhibition was the result of an extraordinary find. "In 1954, following her death, Frida Kahlo's possessions were locked away in La Casa Azul (The Blue House) in Mexico City, her lifelong home. Half a century later, her collection of clothing, jewelry, cosmetics, and other personal items was discovered," the exhibition website explains.

CONTEXT MATTERS

Even when we decide to focus on a certain category or theme, like Frida's clothing, our exhibition can vary greatly, depending on the context, lens, and intended audience. For instance:

• The Fashion Institute of Technology in New York City, where I studied surface and textile design, would likely focus on details of construction and perhaps the cultural significance of Frida's traditional Tehuana dress, and how it was received when she and Diego briefly lived in New York in 1931, during his one-man exhibition at the Museum of Modern Art (MoMA).

• In an interview with the *New York Times*, Circe Henestrosa and Claire Wilcox, co-curators of the "Frida Kahlo: Making Her Self Up" exhibition, spoke about how Frida's choice of dress reflected a desire to distract from her physical disabilities: "The last thing you'd be thinking of when you saw her were her disabilities." An exhibition about Frida's clothing through the lens of a disabled curator would be fascinating.

• An anti-capitalist lens could be applied to an exhibition exploring how the ardently communist Frida might feel about her stylish image being used to sell all kinds of merchandise— from posters in museum gift shops, to beach bags at yoga retreats, to T-shirts in fast fashion stores.

• A Mexican curator might explore how their culture is represented—or misrepresented —by Frida's immense popularity.

In 2013, Japanese photographer Ishiuchi Miyako photographed Frida's clothing and accessories, including her prosthetic leg. The description of the show by Michael Hoppen Gallery is fascinating, including glimpses into Diego Rivera's grieving process:

"*Frida* by Ishiuchi Miyako (2013) is a photographic record of

Mexican artist Frida Kahlo's wardrobe and belongings. Following Kahlo's death in 1954 her husband Diego Rivera began placing her personal effects into the bathroom of their Mexico City house, "The Blue House", which later became the Museo Frida Kahlo. Rivera gave instructions that this room should remain sealed until fifteen years after his death and it in fact remained unopened until 2004 when the museum decided to organise and catalogue the contents. Ishiuchi Miyako was invited to photograph these artefacts, over 300 unseen relics of Kahlo's life."

There are also references to the photographer's personal and professional context for her engagement with Frida's clothing:

"In her earlier series, Mother's (2000-2005) and ひろしま / Hiroshima (2007), she photographed previously worn garments, evoking the lives and memories of the people who wore them as well as the social climate of post-war Japan."

I was lucky enough to stumble upon the photo exhibition at Michael Hoppen Gallery in London 2015, and looking back, it must have inspired me to start commissioning beautiful photographs of my mom's belongings! I'd already commissioned illustrations of my mom's possessions, but I'm sure seeing a famous artist's personal effects captured beautifully prompted a desire to have my mom's glasses, scarves, and other accessories showcased beautifully, too. She may not have been famous, but she was monumental to me.

So many layers: I was a Chinese-American grieving daughter in London, viewing photographs by a Japanese artist who was also a grieving daughter, of the belongings of a Mexican painter who had experienced so much grief and loss herself!

I could go on and on! Can you see how there are so many ways we can tell Frida Kahlo's story? So many potential themes, angles, perspectives, and lenses!

Exhibitions have narratives. Soy sauce can tell the story of a lifetime of celebrations and gatherings. Or it can illustrate a narrative about the loss of heritage and longing for cultural connection. As curator, *you* get to choose the narrative.

PART THREE
CURATING FOR COMFORT AND CONNECTION

CHAPTER 11
CONTINUING BONDS: STAYING CONNECTED

"I don't want to move forward without them."

Marking the passage of time without our loved ones can be so hard. The new year. Birthdays. Anniversaries. Weddings. For grieving people, even the happiest of occasions can be bittersweet and sometimes just bitter.

Sentiments I hear include:

"I don't want to go into the new year without my dad."

"2018 was the last year we were a whole family."

"This year will mark twenty years since she's been gone."

There can be a lot of pain associated with the idea of leaving behind the loved ones we have lost.

But what if we don't have to leave them behind?

CONTINUING BONDS: A SHIFT

"You have to move on." Have you been told this by others? Have you said it to yourself? What do we even mean by "moving on"?

Am I supposed to forget my mom existed? Are you supposed to forget that you shared your life with your spouse for decades? Are we to suddenly wipe them from our memories, delete them from our calendars, routines, and lives? Forget their birthdays. Ignore our anniversaries?

The phrase "moving on" speaks to many of the misunderstandings about grief. There's also been so much change in how we understand how people grieve.

A little grief history lesson: There was a period of time where the emphasis in grief theory was on the idea of moving on. After a period of grieving, you go on with your own life, was the general approach. You cut ties with the person who died because they're dead. And then you live your own life, and you redirect your energy and your attention. The implication was that you were supposed to do the work of grieving and then move on.

But there was a big shift about thirty years ago with the introduction of grief theories like Continuing Bonds, which is one of my favorite models of grief. Published in 1996 by grief researchers Dennis Klass, Phyllis Silverman, and Steven Nickman, the book *Continuing Bonds: New Understandings of Grief (Death Education, Aging, and Health Care)* offered a premise that might seem obvious now:

If we lose a loved one, we might *want* to stay connected. We might want to continue feeling like we have a bond with them. Of course, the bond isn't going to look the same. They're no longer physically here. But there are other ways to continue to feel connected to the person that we loved.

Continuing Bonds challenged the idea that you're supposed to be done and move on. Some of us like to use the term "moving forward" rather than moving on. Because we're moving forward with our own lives. *And* we can stay connected if we want.

I feel like I'm moving forward in so many ways. *And* I carry my mom with me. Not in a heavy way, but in a way that feels beautiful and meaningful. She gets to come along on the journey with me.

Here's how I describe my experience of moving forward, with a nod to the poem "The Dash" by Linda Ellis:

After my mom died, I started to compulsively do a form of math.

1947 – 2013

The year she was born. The year she died. A dash between. The difference was sixty-six.

My mom had just turned sixty-six when she died suddenly and unexpectedly of a stroke.

Sixty-six years. It doesn't seem like a lot considering how health conscious and active she was. It doesn't seem like enough considering all the plans she still had.

My grandmother had died at the age of sixty-seven from cervical cancer. And my mother had always lamented that was so young. And then for my mom to die even younger —that seemed so wrong.

The math seemed off. Calculate it again.

It seemed like that math problem was everywhere: year of birth, year of death. What's the difference in years?

In museums and galleries, the label next to a piece usually features the artist's year of birth and year of death prominently, right by their name.

And I calculated and I figured: How long did that person get? How did that painter who lived in poverty in the 1800s live to eighty-something when my healthy, vibrant mother only got sixty-six years?

Some people had open-ended dashes—a living artist! And

I puzzled: How is that sculptor born in 1930 is still alive? Calculate it again.

But over time and many calculations, I realized: What was important wasn't the year of birth and the year of death. It was that dash between.

Not even the length of it, but the quality of it. The breadth and depth of it. Not when a person was born and when they died, but what was done between: what works created, what lives touched, what meaning left behind.

The dash between is what really matters.
The dash between is ALL that matters.

My mom didn't know she would only have sixty-six years. Most of us don't know what our end dates will be, how long our own dash will be.

But what matters is our dashes are still open-ended. Our dates are not set. We don't know how many years we'll get.

My mom's dash has ended. But mine is still *open-ended.* And when I look closer, my dash—my ongoing life—is now more textured, more colorful, more faceted, brighter, more bitter *and* more beautiful. Because of my mom.

And I bring my mom forward with me, forward into each new year. She continues: Like in a relay race, her memory is carried on. Like a baton or a torch.
And I'll keep carrying her forward, as long as my dash goes on.

So keep going on. Keep carrying them forward.

And may all our own dashes be better and brighter for it.

———

GOOD QUESTIONS

Who are you going to be carrying forward with you?

How is your dash, your life, moving forward, different and better for having had them in your life?

Is it more delicious? More glittery? Softer? Bolder?

———

CREATIVE EXERCISE

At The Grief Gallery's events, both online and in-person, I invite attendees to bring an item to share—to *choose* an item. During our online gatherings on Zoom, we imagine that we are connecting from across the world and meeting up in an imaginary gallery space together.

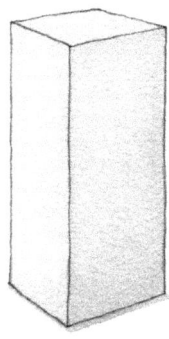

I say, "Imagine that in front of each of you is a white display pedestal (aka a plinth). What would you like to share with us? What would you put on that plinth for us all to see and witness?"

Sometimes people have the actual item, and they hold it up to their device's camera, and we all lean in to see it more clearly. They share a story and tell us the significance of the meaningful object. Other times, the person sharing just has a story, and that's beautiful too, as they sketch for us a picture of their person and a facet of their relationship.

. . .

And now I turn the questions to you:

- Imagine that in front of you is a white display pedestal (aka a plinth). What would you like to share? What object would you put on that plinth to be seen and witnessed?

- What is the significance of this object for you?

- Is there a story or specific memory attached to it?

WHAT HAPPENS WHEN YOU CHOOSE?

When you're choosing which object to share, in effect you're quickly running through the three Cs and three key guiding questions, which I encourage you to contemplate on the heels of the questions above:

COLLECT - Question 1: How do you remember your person? Stories and moments. Different memories. Different facets of them.

CURATE - Question 2: How do you *want* to remember your person? You start choosing, filtering, and spotlighting our favorite memories and what feels good.

CREATE - Question 3: How do you want your person to be remembered? What do you want others to know about them?

Earlier in this chapter, we talked about the concept of Continuing Bonds. In a conversation I had with grief therapist Nathalie Himmelrich on her *How to Deal with Grief & Trauma* podcast, she shared this insight about the connection between Curating Grief and Continuing Bonds theory:

"It's like a process of creation and deciding of how the continuous bond is being lived."

She notes that the third question—"How do I want my person to be remembered?"—is like a continuation of Continuing Bonds. Typically, when we talk about Continuing Bonds, we tend to focus on the bond between the griever and the person who died. But as Nathalie notes, we can expand that definition: "How do I want this continuous bond to be lived by other people?"

This expanded view of Continuing Bonds is actually a vital part of the model, as I learned in a conversation with co-originator of the theory Dr. Dennis Klass for The Grief Academy. There is the bond between the individual griever and the person who died, he said. But there are also the bonds between the person and the larger community. And what's more, bonds between community members. I like to imagine a constellation of bonds, with the person who died being a connecting star.

Isn't it powerful and beautiful, that we have the option of continuing our bonds?

Grief and love are sisters, woven together from the beginning. Their kinship reminds us that there is no love that does not contain loss and no loss that is not a reminder of the love we carry for what we once held close."

FRANCIS WELLER, *THE WILD EDGE OF SORROW: RITUALS OF RENEWAL AND THE SACRED WORK OF GRIEF*

CHAPTER 12
PAINTING A PICTURE OF YOUR PERSON

I like to imagine my mom traveling.

When my mother died, she was planning a trip to Asia. And a separate trip to Alaska. She'd figured out that she had $14,000 in expendable income every year to spend on travel, trips, and holidays. She had it all figured out—other than dying.

Her adventurous, post-retirement trips started with an expedition to Tibet, a place she'd always wanted to visit. She came back with photos of herself in front of temples and with a yak. And a story about how she'd spotted the actor Colin Farrell and asked him what he was doing in Tibet. She was curious, straightforward, and fearless like that.

When I travel now, I like using her LeSportsac backpack and wearing her purse, the one with all the zippers. I cherish her passports and vintage luggage tags, often featuring them in The Grief Gallery's exhibitions.

When I moved to Portugal, I wished so desperately that she could visit me. I want to show her my new home and the river views. Treat her to a meal of fresh fish. Take selfies with her in front of tourist spots.

But maybe she's traveling still. That's how I like to imagine her: Traveling the world, exploring new places. Finally making the trip to Machu Picchu. Going up to the peaks of mountains, without worrying about her asthma or the hiking.

I imagine her traveling everywhere—just without the airport security and hassles the rest of us have to endure.

How do you imagine your person now?

THE POWER OF BELIEF

I didn't grow up in a religion. My family wasn't very religious either, even the ones who went to church. I don't have a Buddhist philosophy, Christian faith, or Muslim principles to reference. But in doing my work with grief, I've grown to appreciate how important the role of belief can be after a significant loss.

I've seen firsthand how a client who believes her mother is in heaven finds deep comfort in believing her mom is watching out for her, along with her other ancestors. It can be such a source of solace to many.

Other clients believe that we are connected to everyone and everything, through energy, through vibes, through a connection to the universe. Others have more traditional religious beliefs—or a variation of what they were taught.

I still don't have a particular religious or spiritual belief about where we go, if there is a heaven, and what it might look like. But I do enjoy believing. I like believing that when I see the number 39, it's a sign from my mom. I do enjoy imagining—using my imagination in a way that helps me to feel loved and connected to my mother.

I like to believe that she's watching out for me. I imagine she checks in on me and she sends me good luck on my travels. When I get an upgrade, when my luggage doesn't get permanently lost, I thank her, sometimes aloud. For me, that is all just in my head. That is all just in my heart. It's all just the stories that I tell about her to other people and to myself. It helps me to construct what I think is a very beautiful, supportive relationship with her.

. . .

When you think of your loved one, where do your thoughts go?

How do you picture them? It might not all be rosy. How they died might come up. How they looked in the hospital or when they were in decline. What comes up might be guilt. Or regret about not being there when they died. All of these may come up.

And what else is there?

Can you also access happier moments? The moments you would want to frame, to have on display in your home or in a museum?

PAINTING A PICTURE

When I described at the start of this chapter how I imagine my mother traveling the world, looking out for me from whichever exotic location she's in currently, I'm painting a picture of her now and of our relationship together. It's a creative process, and a constant one—it's like every time I envision it, I'm painting the picture anew or at least touching up a cherished image, like a much-valued piece of art in a gallery.

Here's my take on why this matters:

Much of the relationship we have with people, living or dead, is an internal construct, a creation we're continually making in our heads and in our hearts. What makes a relationship, after all? Is it seeing the person every day? Speaking with them? Spending time with them? Is it dependent on being able to do all of these things?

Take my friend Maren, for example. We worked together twenty years ago and became instant friends. I see her every couple of years. We check in by email or text message every month or so. And I'd say we have a great relationship!

Do you have a friend like that? You don't actually talk that often, but when you do, you pick up where you left off. You know you'll be happy to hear from them whenever they get in touch. You have a good relationship.

Why do I have a great relationship with Maren? In part,

because when I think of her, I think of the fun times we had together:

Cracking each other up on the job.

Meeting up in Paris and Barcelona during her work trips.

Geeking out about stationery and the best strategies for packing luggage.

The funny thing is, it doesn't even matter what she's thinking of me or if she's thinking of me! I am having the experience *now* of a great relationship with her just by the memories and thoughts I'm focusing on. When I sip tea from the blue and white ceramic mug I bought in Paris when I visited her and crashed in her hotel room, I think fondly of her and feel the warmth of connection.

MY RELATIONSHIP WITH MY MOTHER NOW

It reflects how I think about my relationship with my mother now. More than ten years after she died, I can honestly say we have a great relationship.

When I think of her, I feel love. I feel joy. Even if it's bitter-sweet. I miss her a lot and feel sad sometimes, of course. But it doesn't eclipse the good feelings and memories. I also have so much more understanding for her now: As an adult. As a whole person. As a mother, a wife, and a woman. As a person with her own career, emotions, life experiences, and goals. I have so much more understanding and compassion for her now.

When I think of her, I often smile, because I'm remembering the good times:

Christmas at her house by the lake.

Meals out together in Chinatown.

Going to MoMA and getting Mister Frostee ice cream cones afterward.

Of course there are regrets and less rosy memories, but over time, I no longer focus as much on those. In the gallery in my mind, the framed images of the good times take up more wall space than the images of the bad times.

YOU MIGHT NOT LIKE THIS

You might object: *How can you say that? She's no longer alive!* Maybe you're thinking, *No, I don't want to have an imaginary relationship with my person. They should be here!*

I get it. Is it the relationship I want to have with my mom? That we *should* have?

Obviously, if I had the choice, I would have my mom be alive. Even with my occasional frustration and impatience with her. Even with her likely concern for my life choices. Even with my internal eye-rolling and judgment of her picking up more random things at garage sales.

Part of me definitely says: She should be here. She should be traveling the world for real and enjoying her house by the lake. She should be spending her social security checks, going to the library, and taking classes at the gym. She should be doing her social work and helping people in the Asian immigrant community she cared so much about.

She should be here, a part of me cries. But she isn't. She's gone. I'm working within the constraints of the reality of our relationship as it is now.

YOUR RELATIONSHIP DOESN'T HAVE TO END

Here's the key point: Your relationship with your person who died doesn't have to end, if you don't want it to end. In the previous chapter, we talked about Continuing Bonds theory and the possibility of staying connected to our loved ones.

"In my work with grievers, I am careful to stress that a relationship exists between two people whether they are alive or dead," says trauma therapist Meghan Riordan Jarvis in her book *Can Anyone Tell Me? Essential Questions About Grief and Loss* in a chapter titled "Why Do I Think That Butterfly Is My Mom?"

Of course, our relationship is going to look different because they are no longer physically here on this earth. They're not present in the same way.

Of course it hurts and it's a jarring change: You can't just go over to their house. You can't go on holiday with them. You can't hug them and be hugged back. You can't pick up the phone to call them. You won't get a text back.

And the part that *is* in your control is how you think about them, how you feel about them. The stories you tell, the pictures you paint of them, and the aspects of your relationship that you cultivate. The ways you *practice* being intentional about how you remember them. That is in your control.

If you *want* your relationship to continue, what kind of relationship do you want to have?

OUR BRAIN'S PATHWAYS

When you curate your memories, stories and how you think about your relationship, even with its flaws, you are strengthening your neural pathways.

Our brains are making connections all the time. I think of my mom and a memory comes up—the more I practice that mental association, the more it strengthens that neural pathway. For instance, if every time I think of my mom, my mind goes to forgetting her last birthday and the assigned meaning that I was a terrible daughter, that neural pathway is reinforced. Maybe I don't revisit more pleasant memories, like standing together in her garden and admiring her beloved rose bushes. That memory starts to fade.

We can look at it this way, in the form of pathways through a patch of grass: Imagine you're going back and forth between the thought of your person and the painful memory, wearing a groove into the grass. That thought pattern can become ingrained and automatic. By focusing on the painful story, you may not be walking the path to the happier memories that you would rather highlight, and that pathway starts to fade. That's the potential cost of not being intentional about the stories and meanings we choose.

I CAN MAKE NEW MEMORIES WITH MY MOM

I've scattered her ashes in the waters of Peru, Paris, and the Pacific, and now I smile every time I visit those places, thinking of her. By being deliberate with the memories we choose to replay and share, we get to create and continue our relationships with our lost loved one, every day.

It doesn't all have to be happy memories—that wouldn't be true to our relationship with our person either. Sure, a gallery can have only cheerful paintings. But more often, an art gallery has paintings that encompass a whole range of human experiences and emotions, including excruciating pain and loss, as well as deep love and joy. I suggest that as grievers, our minds and hearts can also expand to encompass multiple facets of how we remember our loved ones.

Collect: How do you remember them?

Curate: How do you *want* to remember them?

This is how you set the intention for the kind of relationship you want to have with your person moving forward. This is how you curate and create it, every day.

————

GOOD QUESTIONS

What relationship do you want with your person moving forward?

How do you want to feel when you think of them?

What do you want to believe?

What do you want to think about?

What aspects of them do you want to spotlight?

What stories do you want to tell?

CHAPTER 13
CURATING GRIEF IS A FORM OF INTERIOR DESIGN

Curating is a way of making space for grief. And it's a way of making space for our loved ones—in tangible and intangible ways. When we imagine curating an exhibition about our loved one . . . when we choose with intention what takes up room in our homes . . . and when we choose how to use these meaningful objects and belongings to stay connected with our loved one, we are . . .

making space for grief
making space for grieving
making space for our loved ones **in our lives**.

It may be physically, in the form of an altar, a shelf, or a picture wall. More importantly, we're making space for them in our hearts and in our heads.

Stick with me here . . .

In my work with clients and grieving people, I have found it fascinating how often what is in their physical space is representative of what is going on with them in their interior space. For instance:

If there's a storage unit or boxes that the person has resisted opening or looking at, they are also likely resisting looking at an internal aspect of their grief or loss.

If belongings are all still in the same place, untouched, the person may be feeling stuck or afraid to change things.

If a person has meaningful objects of their loved one integrated into how they live, they are more likely to have integrated the grief and loss, as well as the person's memory, into their life.

This is a phenomenon that interior designers and professional organizers will quickly recognize. A classic example would be how a cluttered home might correspond with a cluttered mind. If you have a mental health condition, you may be aware of how your home's hygiene or physical tidiness may correlate to your general wellness. (When my living space starts getting chaotic, it's certainly a warning sign for me that I might be neglecting my mental health and potentially approaching an anxiety or depression spiral.)

Caroline of HelloCollo Organizing, a Philadelphia-based professional organizer who specializes in life transitions and grief, agrees that our physical surroundings can give us clues into what may be happening inside us. "The reasons why we choose to store our items in a particular way (or neglect them, or avoid decisions around them, or put care into some versus others) shines a light on something to learn about ourselves," she says.

I asked what she's observed in her work with individuals:

"With some of my clients, the inability to let go of certain collectables or items from an earlier time in their life has surfaced their unhappiness with their present-day self. These items represent the preference of past-self versus present-self," she reveals.

"Other clients who live in a typically cluttered lifestyle often face the realities of their inner chaos or unrealistic expectations.

There will never be enough time in their world to accomplish all they 'need' to or wish to."

Inner life and outer manifestation — sometimes they match up, and sometimes they don't!

INTERNAL CONSTRUCT AND EXTERNAL EXPRESSION

I've also seen this phenomenon in my work with grieving people when it comes to their relationships after a loved one dies. How the meaningful objects and possessions are integrated—or *not* integrated—into a client's living space can be indicative of what's going on for them internally in terms of their relationship with grief, their relationship with the loss, and their relationship with the person who died.

For example, my client Jen had an aha when we talked about what's on our shelves at home. She said, "You know what, the shelves around me don't actually have anything of mine. My shelves are full of dead people's things!"

She had inherited other people's possessions, items that had been meaningful to them—not necessarily to her. Her own belongings had been put in storage when she moved back to her childhood home to take care of her parents.

Jen's spaces were not hers. This was representative of where she was in her life. Other people's priorities, other people's opinions, and other people's drama were taking up most of her energy and focus. Her own life and priorities had been put on hold when she took on the challenging role of caregiver.

She couldn't even recall what the boxes of her own stuff contained. No wonder she felt disconnected from herself and unsure of who she was now! It really took opening those boxes, seeing what was from her past life and the past vision of her life, for Jen to start choosing how she wanted to move forward.

We also explored in what ways she wanted to bring her parents forward with her as she prepared to move out of the family home to embark on the next phase of her own life. You may be in a similar place, of figuring out how to find your way back to yourself. Ask yourself:

How do I want to live the rest of my life?

Do I *want* to bring my person with me as I move forward?

If I do, how might I bring them with me, in tangible and intangible ways?

Curating and choosing with intention are so vital for making space for your loved one, in your current life and in your life moving forward, whether you're moving house or making a more metaphorical change.

A SPLENDID MEMORY PALACE

Have you heard of the term *memory palace*? It's a technique for remembering lots of information by imagining a large space with many rooms, where different memories and pieces of knowledge can be deposited for future retrieval as needed. In the TV show *Sherlock*, Sherlock Holmes has a similar concept of a "mind palace"—like a mental map of all his knowledge. In the original books by Sir Arthur Conan Doyle, the famous detective makes reference to a brain-attic, which, interestingly, has more limited space—and thus requires more deliberate curation of its contents — than the seemingly infinite space of a memory palace!

One way to look at what we're doing with Curating Grief is creating a memory palace or brain-attic about your loved one. If we use the exhibition metaphor, the curating question is a prompt for constructing a gallery in your mind— and I would say also in your heart!

Here's what I believe: When you have a gallery space in your mind for your loved one, the choices you make about the exhibition and items you put in there are going to affect how you grieve, how you remember them, and how you move through life. (Your gallery space for your person is also going to look very different from the gallery space that someone else has!)

For instance, a sibling's associations and memories of the person may be related to gardening, and that will be what's featured in their imaginary gallery. When they go out into the world, they might feel more emotional in a gardening store because it reminds them of their loved one. Another sibling might feel connected when they're making coffee because that's what is in their gallery space and how they remember their person. You get to decide what is in your gallery space.

Why is it helpful to consider these creative exercises of creating a gallery space and curating an exhibition about your person after a major loss?

Because most people never go through the process of sorting through what is in their minds and hearts about their loved one. Most times, it's just a jumbled pile of memories, stories, and meanings! You have a happy memory about gardening, and then you have a terrible memory about being in the hospital with your person. They're all mixed together, not sorted, reviewed, and organized, nor filtered in any way. The process of curating is a way to sort through and make sense of the potential chaos in your head and in your heart.

Your imaginary Grief Gallery is an internal construct—a powerful one. Whether you choose to create a display in your home or to curate an exhibition for others to witness, that's an external expression. Regardless of which you choose, you can curate.

FEAR OF UNPACKING

What if your problem is that you are afraid to look at the piles of stagnant stuff and piles of unattended grief? Do you have a storage unit you've been resisting looking at for years? Or is it the metaphorical boxes you're more afraid of unpacking? Maybe you've carried a story of guilt for thirty years, hauling its weight with you through your life. (There's a reason the term *emotional baggage* persists.)

The question that I offer, with gentle curiosity, is: **What are you afraid of?**

What are you afraid of feeling? What are you afraid of experiencing? Is it your own emotions?

Are you afraid that you're going to feel overwhelmed by the sheer amount of stuff? Are you afraid that you're going to feel overwhelmed by emotion? Are you worried that you're not going to be able to handle your grief? Are you afraid that you're going to break down? Are you afraid of someone else's reaction?

Are you afraid that you're going to get pressure from family members or from your spouse to choose a certain way? Are you afraid that others are going to pressure you to throw away things that are important to you?

When we know what you're afraid of, we can start to make a strategy for how to handle the situation. We can ask if those fears are warranted. How true are they? Maybe it's something that you want to work on with a coach or a therapist. If your fears are unfounded, you might be able to empower yourself by saying, for instance, *Oh, maybe as a child I wasn't given the choice, but now I'm an adult. Now I can choose.*

Maybe when those items went into a storage unit, you were so raw in your grief. And you didn't feel like you had the strength, or the focus, or the resilience. But maybe now you do. Maybe now you are ready. And maybe you didn't have the support then. Maybe you were in an unsupportive partnership or marriage. But maybe now you do. It always comes back to our available resources, like space, time, support, and capacity.

How can we—you and I together—increase your capacity, your resources, and your support options? That's a big goal of my work with grievers. How can we give you the capacity to face what you are fearing, and how can we dismantle some of those fears? What concepts and skills can we give you to pack in your toolbox when you're embarking on a task that may be emotionally or physically arduous? Remember, we can do hard things, with a soft heart.

THE VITAL ROLE OF DESIGN

Thus far, we've primarily been talking about curating and creating as a form of expression for our grief, our love, our pain, and all that may be coming up for us through loss. When it comes to presenting an exhibition, design also plays a vital part. *Who is it for? How is the space distributed?* These are just some of the many considerations for the curator and exhibition design team!

We can design not just for a desired aesthetic but also for function: *Does this work? Is it helpful?*

As I shared previously, when my mom died, I was working with independent designers, helping them to show and sell their work through exhibitions, consulting, and business coaching. I always found it fascinating that the designers were *so* creative in their work, but so *rigid* in the way they approached their businesses. They often hadn't questioned the design of their businesses: Do you want employees or to be a solopreneur? Do you want to make just a couple of pieces a year for collectors, or to license your creations for mass production—or both? Those are the kinds of questions we might ask when we're talking about business design, and there are so many ways to get creative with it!

When we think about grief, I think of it similarly: We can get creative with it. Yes, it can be scary to realize there's no one way to grieve or a surefire blueprint for rebuilding your life after disaster . . . and my hope is that there may also be a feeling of freedom in that expanse of possibilities.

When you lose your life partner or spouse, when you lose your child, when you lose a person who was a massive part of you, the vision of what your life was going to look like may shatter or turn to ash. So we have to rebuild, we have to reconstruct our lives. But we can also get creative about how we rebuild and reorient ourselves.

I like what grief coach Krista St-Germain, who specializes in helping widowed moms, says about our options for reconstructing our lives after disaster strikes, whether it's a storm or the death of a person.

In an episode of her podcast called "Tornadoes and Post-Traumatic Growth," she compares the devastation of a major loss to a tornado knocking your house down and suggests that we can not only rebuild, but rebuild better. "It's just an opportunity that we can take if we want to," she says. "To take what we've learned and build a new building that is even more aligned with what we want."

Some grievers want to return to the life they had before a major loss, but that's not always possible—or even desirable. There's no shame in wanting something different. *And* you're not doomed if you are forever changed, like many of us are after the death of a significant person.

There's the art part of Curating Grief, giving ourselves space to express ourselves without editing. And there's the design aspect to it. *How do I want the rest of my life to look now? How do I want to experience the world now?* I find that really fascinating and encouraging, the idea that we can have creative input that shapes our grieving processes, and we can design—with beautiful intention—what our lives might look like now and in the future.

WE CAN CURATE FOR CONNECTION

What happens when we make space for grief and to think about our loved ones in a more intentional way?

The more I do this grief work, the more I believe it's inextricably linked: When we make space for grief, when we take time to grieve—remember, it's an active process—we are inevitably making connections. Grieving is connecting. It's connecting with ourselves and our own emotions. It's connecting with our loved ones and how we're remembering and potentially missing them, as well as cultivating our ongoing connections with them.

As you move forward now as the perfect interior designer for your precious inner world, prepare to make ample space for the important things that are calling you . . .

Make space for grief.

Make space for grieving.

Make space for love, make space for sadness.

Make space for all of it.

Make space for connection.

We'll go into what *kind* of space in chapter 18, "Making Sacred Space for Grief."

PART FOUR
PREPARING TO CURATE

Things They Wore

CHAPTER 14
PERMISSION TO KEEP, PERMISSION TO LET GO

You don't need permission to do what's right for you. But if you want permission? Granted! No matter what others say you *should* do. You can choose what's right for you.

Have you noticed that a lot of people have different opinions about how to grieve? Some grieving people are told: Don't cry. Others may get feedback that they're not crying enough!

It's similar when it comes to the belongings. I've had clients say, "I'm not ready to sort through my loved one's things, but my family is telling me I should."

Or, "My brother is pressuring me to keep my grandma's piano to honor her memory, but I don't have room in my house."

Or maybe it's your own voice that's most challenging for you, as you ponder:

What should I keep?
What if I want to keep everything?
What if I don't want to keep anything?
Do I really need to let things go?

IT'S OK TO KEEP THINGS

I'm not saying you need to get rid of everything. I am not a minimalist. I really like my stuff! I'm not a professional organizer. I do *not* find it easy to let go of things.

I want to be clear about this because sometimes there's a misconception that the Curating Grief approach is focused on getting rid of things—it's not!

It's OK to keep things.
It's OK to spend time with the objects.
It's OK to take it slowly.

Maybe other people have been telling you: *You shouldn't keep that. You need to move on. You should be over this already. If you're keeping all the things, it means you're not progressing with your grief.*

My reaction: *Grrr . . .*

If those are the messages that you've been hearing, then of course you might be feeling resistance. You might be feeling fiercely, *No, I want to keep the things. People keep telling me that I need to get rid of things, but I want to keep things.*

You have permission to keep things.

In case you haven't noticed yet, throughout this book, permission is a recurring theme. You don't *need* permission, but if you want it, I will happily give it to you.

The goal of this book is not to tell you to get rid of things *or* to keep everything. The goal of Curating Grief is to give you *options* and a creative way of looking at how to choose what to keep and what to let go of—because sometimes we don't have a choice. Sometimes there are circumstances and constraints that mean that we have to choose, even though we don't feel ready to let go. In chapter 15, we look at more of these potential situations.

If you like to hold, be near, look at, sleep with, caress, or even smell a special belonging of the person who died, you're not crazy. You're simply trying to hold on to a tangible, physical connection to the person.

DR. ALAN WOLFELT, *THE WILDERNESS OF GRIEF: FINDING YOUR WAY*

IT'S OK TO LET THINGS GO

What if you have the opposite problem? What if the message you're actually getting from people is:

Hmm, your grandmother would want you to keep that.

It was your mother's!

Your aunt really would have wanted you to keep that. This was really meaningful to us. That's the family crystal—it's been handed down for generations.

Your father put so much work into that piece. It meant so much to him.

And again, maybe the reproach is in your voice, because the message you've internalized is *If I let that piano go, I will be letting my grandmother down. I will not be honoring her memory.*

Some grievers worry they'll forget or let someone down:

If I let go, will I be betraying my husband?

If I release that, does that mean I didn't love my partner?

If I change my child's room, do I risk forgetting her?

What would it mean to let go of an object?

First, if you really want to discard items, but people are guilt tripping you, I am happy to offer permission:

You have permission to let things go.

You have a permission slip to let things go, despite what other people think you should do with them.

Now, if it's an internal *should*? That's really good to be aware of too. In chapter 32, "Regret, Perspective, and Interpretations," we go deeper into these *shoulds* and "what if" questions.

IT'S OK TO CHOOSE WHAT YOU WANT

We may feel inexplicably attached to the most mundane things after a loved one dies—or to what others may consider morbid or nonsensical. I've had visitors to The Grief Gallery's events name the hospital bed, bottles of medicine, and an ashtray as examples of items they would want to include in their imaginary exhibition about their loved one. As curator, you get to choose.

Barri Leiner Grant, Chief Grief Officer of The Memory Circle, offers us a poignant example of an item she kept from the day her mother died:

> "I lost my mom Ellen in 1993. She was fifty. She went to Sandy Hook, the beach in New Jersey that she loved, for the day. She was a realtor and took the day off. It was really hot, she said, too hot to sell a house to anyone. So she set up with a great book and we have a receipt for three pounds of Santa Rosa plums that she adored.
>
> I'm not sure whose idea it was, whether it was my sister Danna or me, but someone had the wherewithal to save the sand that was in her beach bag from that day.
>
> It's not of any monetary value at all, but we put it in a Ziploc, and to this day, I treasure the decrepit baggie and the sand from her last day on Earth, her last hours. Having it seems like a piece of that day, a piece of her favorite place—and holding on to some part of what remains.

She loved the beach. She grew up in New Jersey near the beach and so did we. So it holds meaning for many reasons because it was probably her favorite place on earth. I often think, thirty years later, that if she chose a way to go, she may have written that ending.

I keep the sand next to some old pieces of her jewelry, and it actually holds much more value to me than anything else I have.

I recently took some of the sand and had some charms made for my sister and me so we can wear them. It's a little bit of sand, inside a clear vessel. It holds meaning to me because it feels like the remains of that day.

It's bittersweet, but it's also beautiful because I imagine her feet in the sand. I imagine her tossing her book in the bag. Her sunglasses. Just the way that sand gets in all the crevices. And that was what was left. Having a piece of it just feels like a piece of her somehow."

Barri shares that she finds solace in knowing that there was no suffering, that her mother didn't even know she had a brain aneurysm. I've seen the little charm with the sand in it that she wears on a necklace—it is beautiful in so many ways. A daughter remembering her beloved mother. Sisters supporting each other. A griever creating beauty. A human being grieving in the way that's right for her.

CHAPTER 15
CIRCUMSTANCES, CAPACITY, AND COLLECTION CRITERIA

How you approach your loved one's belongings and the meaningful objects is influenced by a long list of potential factors. A good starting place is to consider the following four elements:

Circumstances
Constraints
Capacity
Context

Everyone has different circumstances. I took almost two years to figure out what to do with my mother's house and its contents. Not everyone has that luxury. My colleague Kelli had two weeks to clear out her mother's apartment. Time was a limited resource for Kelli during an already challenging time.

Sometimes we have limited resources when we need them the most. Time and money are two big ones. The important thing to remember is that you get to choose—to curate—what is right for you based on your needs and resources.

And there are the relationship dynamics and external factors that impact how and what you choose and your capacity to do so. Let's take a look and see what you may be working with.

LIMITED RESOURCES — TIME, MONEY, ACCESS, SPACE, AND ENERGY

Time: Maybe your job only gives you three days of bereavement leave—or none at all. Maybe you have other responsibilities as a parent or other caregiver. Time is a constraint for you.

Money: I burned through savings to try to keep my mother's house. Ultimately, I couldn't afford to keep paying the mortgage. Others can't afford to keep a storage unit to buy themselves more time. Money is a constraint.

Access: Maybe someone else is the next of kin or handling the estate. Maybe a stepfather, sibling, or other family member is withholding access to the belongings. This can be so painful. (*And* you can still curate.)

Space: My mother had a three-bedroom house in the suburbs. I lived in a one-bedroom apartment in London. There was no way I could bring everything home. Others may still be in college or university. Available space may be an issue for you.

Energy: You may have a chronic illness. Your other responsibilities to your family, clients, or job may demand your energy and focus. Grief itself can be an incredible drain on our energy. Our capacity will be impacted. After I sold my mom's house, even seemingly straightforward tasks like getting a new driver's license were too much to handle. (In chapter 16, we go more into emotional, mental, and cognitive capacity.)

RELATIONSHIP DYNAMICS AND CULTURAL NORMS THAT SHAPE OUR EXPERIENCE WITH THE STUFF

Your Relationship to The Person: Maybe your relationship was strained, or you were estranged. Or maybe it's your relationship with other family members that complicates your experience.

Support from Other People: Maybe you have practical and emotional support from family members, friends, or neighbors. And for others, family dynamics can make it *more* difficult. Maybe there's distance, which can be geographical like living far from family, or can be in the form of estrangements and other types of separation, by choice or circumstance. You may not have a lot of friends or people you feel you can call on for help. You may feel misunderstood, ostracized, or otherwise isolated, which just adds to how lonely grief can feel.

Your Roles and Abilities, Assigned and Implied: My problem was I had too much stuff to sort through, and too many decisions to make. For other people, what hurts is that they didn't get to make any choices. Maybe they didn't get to keep *anything* from their loved one.

As I learned from meeting other grievers, particularly in the supportive Motherless Daughters community led by Hope Edelman, author of *Motherless Daughters* and *The AfterGrief*, this can often happen if you were young when your loved one died. Maybe a parent made all the decisions about what to keep, and nothing was kept for you, or not the things you would have chosen.

Maybe a stepmother cleared out your mother's belongings, like my client Tracy's experience. (And reminder, many stepparents are amazing and really do honor the memory of the deceased or missing parent!)

Maybe you were young and given a choice, but when you're so young, how do you know what to choose? That was the case with Rebecca Feinglos, the founder of Grieve Leave. As a thirteen-year-old. she was given agency over what to keep, but she was not really equipped to make those kinds of choices. (I lost my mother when I was thirty-five, and I *still* didn't really feel equipped to make those choices!) Rebecca shares her vulnerable story:

> "My mom died when I was thirteen. I remember in the days afterward, my dad (and, I think, my godmother) were going through her closet. It had been untouched. My mother was in a nursing home late in her life. She was quite unwell—brain cancer will do that. My dad hadn't touched her things, but when she died, he wanted to clear them out. I think that was important to him.
>
> I remember being summoned to the bedroom. All of my mom's jewelry was laid out on the bed—her clothes, her shoes—but the jewelry is what stood out. He told me to pick what I wanted, not in a mean way, but because he needed closure and to move forward. As a thirteen-year-old, I thought, *Holy sh*t, what are my tastes now?* I didn't like any of the jewelry because I was thirteen and didn't care about the Tiffany's necklace. But I remember playing it out in my mind: What might I want in the future? How could I possibly know?
>
> It was too emotional for my dad to advise me much. He did keep the nicer pieces aside in a safe, saying he'd hang on to those for me. But I just randomly picked things because I had no clue, choosing some things I liked and guessing what Future Me might like.
>
> Looking back, I wish my dad had gotten a storage unit and put everything there for me to decide on later. That would have been emotionally hard for him, and I get why he didn't do it. But for me, I wish I could have gone through her belongings as an adult. I'm not the same as I was at thirteen.

I kept some wonderful things, and I'm wearing one of those Tiffany's necklaces now. I know you can't keep everything, but I wasn't equipped to make those decisions at the time.

That was tough. I wish my dad had just let me be a kid and made those choices later as an adult. After all, my brother didn't have to make those decisions when she died—that was my burden as the daughter."

I feel so much empathy for thirteen-year-old Rebecca. And empathy for her father as well, who loved her deeply and was also doing his best in his own time of early grief and very difficult circumstances.

Did you experience a similar situation as a child? I encourage you to have compassion for your past self as well, whether you were able to choose or not. And compassion for your current, adult self if you find yourself feeling regret or other painful emotions associated with the belongings.

EXTERNAL FACTORS

World Events: During the height of the COVID-19 pandemic, many people couldn't organize or travel to attend funerals or memorials. Similarly, others couldn't travel to clean out the house or sort through the belongings.

Your personal context matters. It's important to acknowledge and to notice what the context and those constraints and circumstances are. And no matter what, **you can still curate**.

IT'S OK TO GRIEVE THE CIRCUMSTANCES

It's OK to grieve the circumstances around the belongings and the objects. Maybe no one helped you. Maybe your problem was that you had too many things. Maybe you were stuck with all the responsibility. It's OK to grieve that.

Your relationship with your siblings may never be the same. It's OK to grieve that people didn't show up in the way that you thought they would. It's OK to grieve that people seemed to prioritize monetary value over connection and family.

Maybe you had the opposite problem: Maybe you weren't given any choices. It's OK to grieve that you weren't given a choice. Maybe a surviving parent couldn't bear to look at the belongings and threw everything away. Maybe a family member withheld items from you, even though you requested them, even though you expressed that they would be important.

Let it out: *It's not fair! We weren't raised that way. They should have been there for me. I feel so let down. I'm so angry. I'm full of resentment.*

It bears repeating: It's OK to grieve all the circumstances and the context around the belongings or the objects.

THE BELONGINGS CAN REVEAL OUR LONGINGS

This is another way that the belongings and meaningful objects can give us awareness. They can reveal to us what we're longing for. They can reveal to us all the hurt around the circumstances of losing someone.

We can grieve family dynamics. We can grieve people's short-comings. We can grieve what happened. We can grieve what *should* have happened and what *could* have happened.

———

GOOD QUESTIONS

What constraints and considerations do you have?

Do you have limited resources: Time? Money? Space? Access? Energy?

What factors affect your capacity?

What other responsibilities do you have?

What drains your emotional and practical resources?

What helps you to replenish your resources? What is re-energizing? What is restorative?

———

A MATTER OF READINESS

Sometimes, as we've been exploring, there are circumstances and constraints that mean that you have to choose, even though you don't feel ready to let go. For example, maybe your partner is getting frustrated by all the boxes of your loved one's stuff that are in the garage or in your living space. Maybe you don't have the money to keep covering the costs of two homes—yours and theirs. There may be several overlapping factors.

At a certain point, you may decide that it's time. *OK, I'm ready to look at this. I'm ready to make some choices now.* This is when you'll especially find that curating is an accessible, creative, and supportive way of making these choices.

COLLECTION CRITERIA — MUSEUMS HAVE COLLECTION CRITERIA, YOU CAN TOO

I wanted to keep everything after my mom died—if I had all the money in the world, I would have kept my mom's house like a museum and just visited it to touch her things and talk to her. But I couldn't do that.

A big part of a curator's role at a museum may be deciding what goes into its permanent collection. Think of artwork at a modern art museum. Or vintage ship models at a nautical museum.

Just like you, museums also have limited resources, like space, money, and time. They have to *choose with intention* what makes it into their collection. They have a set of collection criteria—and I suggest that we all would benefit from having collection criteria too! The collections team—the curator and other people who are stakeholders—look to the collection criteria to decide if an item gets added.

What might be part of the collection criteria?

Mission: It begins with whether an item fits the mission or purpose of the museum or organization. For instance, it likely wouldn't make sense for the nautical museum to accept a vintage car, no matter how nice the condition. Or a good case would have to be made for why the car fits the organization's mission.

Space available: Even a car museum wouldn't automatically accept the donation of a nice vintage car. There might not be adequate space to store it or display it.

Object role: Maybe the car museum already has another vehicle from that era. Maybe the museum's priority for acquisitions currently is strengthening their automotive design collection, so they're looking for sketches and schematics—they have enough vehicles for now.

Money: It costs money to maintain and display objects. There are electricity costs for keeping items in temperature-controlled storage. Objects need to be cleaned, repaired, and cataloged.

Museums and art galleries have to decide how to allocate limited resources. We as grievers have to do the same. Determining your own collection criteria can help immensely.

Some criteria I had for my mother's things when I was selling her house included:

fits in my suitcase
fits in my small London flat
won't break in my suitcase
isn't already better represented by something else I've already chosen
genuinely makes me smile when I look at it . . . or
tells a powerful story about who she was and how she lived

Ask yourself: What criteria might you use?

———

Fun Fact: The process of adding an item to a museum or art gallery's collection is called *accessioning*. The term is also used when adding items to libraries and other archives. Items are given an *accession number,* a unique identifier that indicates when it was added to the collection and other key information. The accession number is at the bottom of this example of a wall label that might accompany an object that's been added to The Grief Gallery's collection!

> **Pendant with Sand from Her Last Day**
> Metal and glass vessel with sand on chain
> Contributed by Barri Leiner Grant, 2023
> In memory of her mother Ellen
>
> 2023.NY.BLG.1

CHAPTER 16

CATEGORY: TOO PAINFUL TO DEAL WITH RIGHT NOW

I kept a storage unit for almost ten years after selling my mom's house. Though Marie Kondo, author of *The Life-Changing Magic of Tidying Up*, may not approve, I'm not sorry.

Keep. Donate. Trash. Those are the categories home organizers advise you use when you're sorting and decluttering. But after a loved one dies, there's a category missing: Too Painful to Deal with Right Now. If I hadn't allowed myself this category, emptying out her house would have been even more excruciating, more impossible-seeming than it was.

After my mom died, I spent the following months shuffling around her house, trying to deal with a lifetime of belongings. I picked up objects. Set them down again. Decisions had to be made, but grief can fog your brain and paralyze your decision-making skills.

That pile of never-worn T-shirts? Easier to decide: Donate or Discard. But other items: Divorce papers, photo albums, medical records . . . They were just too painful to handle at the time.

I granted myself grace. The grace of time.

I had the privilege of being able to throw money at the problem, largely thanks to my mom's savings and her premature death. I'm grateful for the privilege. I'm grateful for the time.

So, I offer this category to you as well, if it's helpful: Too painful to deal with right now. In the previous chapter, we spoke about the concept of capacity. Grief is exhausting! Remember that grief is a full-body and full-system experience. Grieving can take so much energy—no wonder we may not feel like ourselves or up to our usual capacity emotionally or cognitively.

Litsa Williams, a skilled grief therapist and co-founder of What's Your Grief, emphasizes the importance of allowing space and gentleness in decision-making during grief. She explains:

"There's value in saying, 'I'm not ready yet. My grief will keep evolving, and I'll keep evolving. Next time, it might feel very different and a lot easier to let some things go.'"

PAINFUL SURPRISES AND EMOTIONAL LANDMINES

You might also find painful surprises after a loved one dies. Long-held secrets may come out into the open. A houseful of belongings is full of potential emotional landmines, but some are bigger bombs than others: Unexpected adoption papers. Evidence of infidelity. Diaries and journals with private thoughts that are potentially ugly or offensive—never meant to be seen by others. Secrets kept. Birth certificates. Death certificates. It's not uncommon for people to learn unexpected things about their loved ones when they're cleaning out their homes.

As CNN anchor Anderson Cooper so vividly shares on his podcast *All There Is*, when he started excavating his mother Gloria Vanderbilt's belongings after her death, he found items from some of the most painful points in her long and storied life. Mementos from his father who died of a heart attack at the age of 50. The clothing she was wearing when his brother Cooper died by suicide in his twenties.

The physical stuff can be the stuff of nightmares. Give yourself grace.

MEETING YOU WHERE YOU ARE: A STILL LIFE

Art Inspiration: A still life is a depiction of a collection of everyday objects: imagine a bowl of fruit, a stack of books, a vase of flowers. As a genre of Western art, still life can serve as either a celebration of material pleasures or a reminder of the fleeting nature of life. A form of memento mori ("remember you must die" in Latin).

After a loved one dies, we might experience the phenomenon of Still Life in our living spaces. Like a still life painting or arrangement, the objects stay frozen in place, untouched.

In my mother's house, her bedroom and her dining table, both of which served as command centers for her home, remained largely as she left them. The scattered papers that she was looking at in the days before she died—they stayed there for months. Like an art installation, a tableau. I couldn't bring myself to move them.

Other grieving people have said, "My husband's shoes—I couldn't touch them. They had to stay where he left them, in our closet and by the front door." Author Kristine Carlson, *New York Times* bestselling author, best known for her work with her late husband, Dr. Richard Carlson of the *Don't Sweat the Small Stuff* series, still keeps Richard's leather jacket on the back of his work chair—now her work chair.

For others, it's their person's desk with all the scraps of paper on it. Post-its and other notes, often in their handwriting—all can become like still life.

If you've experienced this, you're not crazy. Or alone.

ARE YOU READY TO CURATE?

It's OK if you don't feel ready to move the belongings or to start curating. There may be many reasons to feel that way.

For instance, when you've lost a spouse who's been such a big part of your life and living space, it can be really hard to change that comfortingly familiar environment. Or when you've been a caregiver to a parent, when they die, there can be a dramatic impact on your routine and sense of identity.

Maybe you're still trying to make sense of what happened—perhaps of a situation that will never make sense—and making meaning doesn't feel possible yet. It can take a while for us to adapt internally, so it makes sense that it may also take time for us to adjust externally, including with physical objects.

It's all OK. Grief time is not like normal time.

In the next chapter, I'll share more about my timeline for dealing with my mother's belongings.

PRESSURE TO MAKE DECISIONS

Do you feel pressure to let things go? "That pressure, when time is limited, ends up being one of the things that causes so much strain for families," says Litsa Williams. "In early grief, our cognitive processing isn't working the same way it would before. Emotions are so high, it's so overwhelming, and then having to tackle going through belongings in those early weeks and months is so difficult."

Litsa and I had similar experiences dealing with our mother's homes. I first heard the phrase "piles of grief" from her, and it made so much sense to me that we may avoid looking at the piles of physical stuff, because of the piles of grief we will also encounter. By the time we finished preparing our respective houses for sale, we just didn't have enough energy left in us to sort through all the belongings too.

We had a great conversation about it:

"One of the reasons I'm all for my own grief confessions is because when you work in the grief space, like as a grief thera-pist, there's often this idea that when you're going through your own grief, you must really have it all together because you know about grief," she said.

"But no, what I know just allows me to give myself **a little more permission for it to be messy**. To just be able to say, 'Of course, this isn't easy. Of course, I'm struggling with this. It's not supposed to be easy.' You can know all the things and still struggle with figuring out how to approach it."

I love how openly Litsa speaks about this reality of being a griever. Information and implementation are totally different! Reading about strategies is one thing, and then applying it to how our brains work and our particular attachments in relation to the stuff and our loved ones is another.

HOW DID IT LOOK FOR YOU?

For you, your exhaustion might be from caregiving or supporting your loved one through physical or mental decline—or doing all that *in addition to* dealing with the estate!

If we compare our major loss to going through a natural disaster, it's like we survived the storm and its immediate aftermath, but now we're depleted. We've just barely gotten through it, and now we're being asked to tidy up, declutter, and make more decisions!?

MENTAL HEALTH MATH: CALCULATING THE COST OF KEEPING AND LETTING GO

Financial experts would have likely told me, "Sell the house. Get rid of the belongings. Don't get a storage unit." But I did a mental calculation: If I forced myself to clear out my mother's house while struggling with the fact that she's gone, the cost to my mental health would be so high that I might end up in an inpatient program. And those cost $100,000 or more. By that calculation—the cost of her mortgage and then the storage unit, because there was still so much that was too painful to handle at the time—it made sense to keep them. It was a *bargain* to pay her mortgage so I wouldn't lose my mind.

"Taking care of our mental health and calculating that in—it's hard to do," Litsa affirmed. "It feels abstract. Sometimes it's hard to know what the impact will be, but for me, it was very similar.

I just knew I wasn't in a place mentally where I could deal with it. There was a lot of emotion tied to my mom's house. The process of fixing it up to sell was emotionally draining, and I was so spent by the time it was ready to sell. Initially, I thought I'd go through the storage space right away, but I was emotionally depleted. If I had tried to tackle those belongings then, it would have taken everything out of me. I had to be OK with leaving it until I felt ready to deal with it."

I'm grateful to Litsa and other grief colleagues who have shared so openly about their own timelines for dealing with the physical stuff. If you need or want reassurance that you're normal for "not feeling ready" to tackle the house and its contents, please know that's the case for so many grievers, even grief experts!

THE PHYSICAL AND EMOTIONAL COST

I definitely felt depleted after selling my mom's house. We were moving homes in London at the same time, and my marriage was strained. The physical and emotional stress showed up in a lot of ways. I developed a gum infection and had to have an emergency root canal—it was the best part of my week because I could finally stop, do nothing, and just be cared for.

A month later, a scan showed I had a grapefruit-sized fibroid (a benign tumor) that would need surgical removal. I had major abdominal surgery six months after selling my mom's house and developed a serious eye infection about a year afterward. (I generally have very poor memory for when most events happened, but I find myself anchoring events to traumatic dates around my mom's death and her house!)

Two years after I sold her house, once again in mid-September, I realized I was wearing clothing that didn't fit, I couldn't wear my contacts because my eyes could no longer tolerate them, and my glasses were falling apart. Dealing with the estate and my mom's house had taken a huge toll on my physical and mental health, and many areas of my life were impacted, from my relationships to my self-care.

Grief is mentally and emotionally exhausting. The additional grief and death admin duties (aka "sadmin") drain us further.

OUR CAPACITY CHANGES

My experience of grief has changed over time. My relationship with my mother's belongings has evolved. My capacity has grown.

Earlier on in grief, so much is draining and challenging, even small tasks. I almost had a breakdown when I had to renew my passport shortly after I sold my mom's house. I was so tired and emotionally battered from that process, I cried multiple times before and after going to the passport office. (Needless to say, my photo was not great.)

I renewed my passport this summer, ten years later, via the embassy here in Lisbon. I was amazed at how relatively chill I was about the process, even though I was navigating a different language and even though they momentarily misplaced my new passport. (Portuguese bureaucracy is . . . special.)

If you find yourself feeling overwhelmed by seemingly small bureaucratic tasks or crying over a pair of old socks, there's nothing wrong with you. You're not crazy—grief can just make us feel crazy. It's OK to say, this is just too painful to deal with right now.

For more wisdom from Litsa, and more about our respective storage units, go to chapter 26, "Storage Unit Confessions."

———

GOOD QUESTIONS

I put the "too painful" things into a storage unit, but not everyone can afford this temporary solution. If you find yourself saying, "It's too painful to deal with ____," try completing the following sentences to find potential solutions.

It's too painful to deal with ____ **right now**. Can you buy yourself more time, with money, or asking for a favor?

It's too painful to deal with ____ **on my own**. Can you ask for or hire additional support? This can be friends, movers, or other professionals, like a therapist, coach, or home organizer. A new industry of after-loss services has popped up in recent years as well. Check out the Resources section at curatinggrief.com/grief-resources

It's too painful to deal with ____ **in a perfect, ideal way**. Do it imperfectly!

Worried about choosing the wrong thing? Check out chapter 32, "Regret, Perspective, and Interpretations."

Concerned about when it might actually be a bad idea to hold on to items? See chapter 30, "Holding On: When Is It Unhealthy?"

CHAPTER 17
YOUR TIMELINE FOR GRIEF AND CURATING

Proof of Life

In the beginning, everyone wants proof of death.
How did she die? When did he die?
How could this happen?
Is she really gone?
There are forms to fill out
Paperwork to complete
Obituaries to write
Questions to attempt to answer
Later, sometimes much later
After the forms have been filed
The piles of paper have diminished
Our focus turns to proof of life
We remember not how the person died
But how they lived
Not the beginning and end dates of a life
But the dash between
This is where we celebrate PROOF OF LIFE

London, October 2015

This poem was my curator's note for the first exhibition of The Grief Gallery, which was called *Proof of Life*. Up until that point, my life had largely revolved around the end date of my mom's life. I focused primarily on surviving and navigating the impact and fallout from her sudden death.

The first couple of years were mired in what I call the Proof of Death stage—taking care of all the paperwork, emptying her dream house, just barely coping. After all the forms were filled out, her estate settled, and her ashes scattered, I felt like I had the luxury and the pleasure of celebrating my mom's life.

If you're deep in the process of dealing with probate, the estate, sorting through the belongings and other death admin, I want you to know at some point this *will* be done.

TIMELINE FOR CURATING

If you don't feel ready right now to curate or to present a mini exhibition about your person, it's OK. Or maybe there are other family members who don't feel ready. You don't have to do it right now.

I'll offer you an example with my timeline: My mother died suddenly in January 2013. A couple of months later, we hosted a celebration-of-life gathering for friends and family as her memorial.

I did not present my first in-person exhibition with her belongings until October 2015—more than two and a half years after she died.

How It Looked for Me: In the Beginning

The lens of curating was helpful for me to sort through the belongings in my mom's home and make decisions about what was important, but that initial curation was for *me*. It was just in my mind at first. And then I started staging an imaginary exhibition in her home, using her shelves and table surfaces.

Looking back, I wouldn't have been ready emotionally and energy-wise for an audience then. As I'll share in chapter 18, I like to imagine now that I was in my own art studio during that period, working through my grief with a creative lens, and developing experimental work in a safe space.

It's no coincidence that I had to get past the milestone of dealing with her estate, clearing out her home, and selling the house before I could do a public showing about my mom. I sold her house in September of 2014, and my first exhibition in London was about a year later.

How It Might Look for You

Your timing may be different. Maybe your person had been ill for a long time, so you were already preparing yourself, mentally, emotionally, and practically. Maybe you'd already had discussions with your loved one about how they wanted to be remembered. Maybe your grieving process is calling for you to create and present something now.

I'm always in favor of doing what is most supportive for you in your grief.

Take Your Time

Take your time if you want to and if you can. The more formal, traditional funerals and memorials can serve a good purpose. If you feel up to having a mini gallery, exhibition, or altar during the funeral or memorial, you can certainly do that! If you feel like you have the energy and the focus to do it, that's wonderful, follow your intuition. In chapter 34, I share a couple of examples of exhibitions and Grief Galleries from other grievers.

But if grief fog is making decisions difficult or you're already feeling drained, or if your family members' grieving processes are conflicting with yours, you don't need to put pressure on yourself.

You can curate an exhibition, or some other show or representation of your loved one at any time—and more than once.

As you sort through the belongings, you can gather materials for your someday exhibition, setting aside the most likely candidates. You can sketch or jot down ideas. You can gather inspiration on a mood board. Imagine it as your own mini art studio.

You Can Have More Than One Exhibition

I've presented over a dozen exhibitions about my mom since she died, both online and in-person. Don't feel the need to come up with *one* definitive exhibition about your loved one. Just as museums and galleries may present different exhibitions and switch up their displays regularly, you can as well.

Each time I curate an exhibition about my mom, I learn more about her, about myself, and about grief. Having these continuing mourning rituals, beyond the initial funeral or memorial, is one of the best parts of Curating Grief. We can use the lens of curating and the metaphor of exhibitions to create ongoing opportunities for us to celebrate our person and for us to be witnessed in our continuing process of grieving.

YOUR RELATIONSHIP TO GRIEF CAN CHANGE

What's your relationship with grief? Is grief a scary figure to you, something to be feared or avoided? Is grief more of a companion? Or a roommate that you tolerate? Some of my clients fear grief. They're afraid that once they open the floodgates of grief, they won't be able to close them. *What if I start crying and I can't stop?*

Maybe they liken grief to an ocean that can't be contained. *I feel like I'm drowning.*

Over time, my relationship with grief changed.

Grief as a Task

172

In the beginning, grief was a task. Yet another task on my long to-do list. I knew that I would have to process it, go through it like a class or *endure it* like a boot camp.

When my mother died, I had already had enough therapy to know I'd have to face my grief at some point. Key words: At some point. Not now. Later.

My instinct was to make a checklist. Pull out a spreadsheet. Add grieving to the list.

For a while there, I operated under the assumption: "I can't afford to fall apart."

I can't afford to fall apart.
There are things I have to do.
There are things I have to take care of.
But grief is on the list. Grieving is on the list. I will get to it.

Whether or not I was aware of it, that was my view of grieving. I couldn't afford to fall apart, so I couldn't afford to grieve. (Notice the wording here: "Couldn't afford." What did I think grieving might cost me?)

Grief as a Companion

Then I learned in my training that the goal of dealing with grief is not to eliminate it, or to fix it, or to get rid of it, but to learn to coexist with it.

I resigned myself to having grief as a companion. *Fine, I'll learn to coexist with grief.* To begrudgingly have it alongside for the rest of my life, like a roommate who won't move out, or a permanent passenger along for the ride.

Or maybe it would be like a lifelong companion that surfaces now and then. Maybe it's cyclical like my period. Maybe it's seasonal. Like doing taxes. Every year, grief would show up. Every January, which is when my mom died, and also the month of her birthday. Every May, for Mother's Day and my birthday.

During those times of year, I learned to expect that grief

would show up on my doorstep, like a guest that I don't particularly like but will put up with. I was willing to tolerate grief.

Grief as a Helpful Companion

Then I played around with: Can grief be a *helpful* companion? Can grief be a gift? Are there upsides to it?

I learned about the concept of Post-Traumatic Growth, where we might emerge from a traumatic life event with positive changes. I've heard it referred to as the potential of "growing through what we go through."

Though I'm naturally inclined to search for silver linings and look on the bright side of situations, I am aware that too often grief advice focuses on the silver linings and rainbows when the grieving person may not be ready for them. (It's called brightsiding: *Look on the bright side. At least they left you money. At least you got to say goodbye. At least you didn't have to watch them die.*)

I didn't want to slap a toxic positivity sticker with unicorns and rainbows on my grief. But I liked the idea of emerging from the devastation of losing my mother as a stronger, better version of myself. Maybe by carrying around my grief, I could get the side benefit of stronger muscles and greater resilience, the same way weights at the gym can give me better biceps.

Recently my relationship with grief has shifted again. What if grief is not just an inconvenient but sometimes helpful companion? What if it's a *welcome* companion?

I've started seeing grief as a creative collaborator.

What if instead of grief showing up now and then at my door like an unwelcome guest, I actually invite it in sometimes?

Because I know that grief will be a lifelong companion.

I know that as long as I'm alive, I will miss my mom.

That on certain days and times of the year, my grief is going to be really strong and really present.

What if it could be a creative collaborator? What if I could learn to dance with it? Team up with it? What then?

In the decade since my mom died, grief has helped me to create so much. Grief has helped me to create The Grief Gallery and to connect with grievers like you. It has helped me to create the different ways that I work with people using the lens of curating. It has inspired me to commission illustrations and artwork to honor my mother's memory

Sometimes it's painful. Just like the creative process, it's not always easy.

But it feels good to me to think of grief as a creative collaborator, in the art studio with me. I also find it encouraging to notice how our relationship with grief can change.

———

GOOD QUESTIONS

What's your relationship with grief currently?

Have you seen it change?

What would you like your relationship with grief to look like?

Even if you're not an artist, or consider yourself creative, what might it feel like to collaborate with your grief?

CHAPTER 18
MAKING SACRED SPACE FOR GRIEF

When I learned about Mecca and the way believers make regular pilgrimages, I immediately thought of Paris. Paris was our family's Mecca, and its museums our holy sites. My mother was a travel agent when I was little, and my father was a professor. During his summers off, our little family of three would explore Europe. Paris was our favorite, and my childhood memories include postcard snapshots in the city:

Me, adorable at age 4-5, with head tilted to the side and smiling in front of the Eiffel Tower.

Aged 7-8, skinny, with a bowl cut, bangs, and huge glasses . . . leaning against my father at the Centre Pompidou.

Aged about 10, in a sculpture garden, scowling at my dad who's grinning in the background because he got in my photo.

(It's funny now to notice that the shot of me scowling at my dad is the one my mom chose to put in the photo album—she must have been amused by the scene. I also realize now how relatively few photos exist of her from those years; she was always behind the camera, capturing these moments.)

We had our regular circuit of art museums: The Centre

Pompidou noted above, also known as Beaubourg, with its striking modern "inside out" architecture of colorful pipes on the exterior of the glass and metal building, completed in 1977—the year of my birth.

The Musee D'Orsay, housed in a gorgeous Beaux-Arts train station that became a firm favorite when it opened in 1986. The Musee Rodin with its beautiful rose gardens and converted house full of romantic marble figures.

We visited the Louvre, of course, both before and after the installation of the controversial (at the time) Louvre Pyramid by the Chinese-American architect I. M. Pei in 1989.

I wasn't raised with religion. But we did our circuit of the cultural institutions in Paris as faithfully as any devotee and approached the masterpieces with as much reverence as any holy site.

At the Louvre, we would give the *Mona Lisa* a quick nod, and then always visited the same sculpture: *Cupid and Psyche* by the Italian sculptor Canova. In exquisite detail, the white marble depicts a winged Cupid awakening his love Psyche from her poisoned slumber. Cupid is bent gently over her face, she has her arms gracefully raised over her head, reaching for him. They are about to kiss. I didn't read romance novels much as a kid, but this statue was as romantic and swoon-worthy as any scene I could imagine.

I reflect now too that my parents must have admired and even had this level of romance at some point, despite what happened to their marriage later. On our visits to Paris, we visited this statue of Cupid and Psyche with the regularity of paying a visit to a relative or an old family friend. When I went to Paris with my high school boyfriend, I took him to see this statue. (He had no real interest in museums though and wanted to eat at McDonald's. We broke up shortly after the trip.)

After college, when I learned that my otherwise well-traveled boyfriend had never been to Paris, I was as shocked as a heavily devout person hearing a friend had never been to church. What sacrilege; he had even grown up in Europe!

"I have to take you," I said, as fervently as a true believer intent on saving a soul.

I brought him to the Louvre and we paid our respects to *Cupid and Psyche*. He was impressed by the Musee D'Orsay. His favorite was the Centre Pompidou. (I married him a couple of years later.)

For me, museums and galleries are my sacred spaces— revered and holy, where I feel both truest to myself and connected to something greater than me.

"Your sacred space is where you find yourself again and again"

JOSEPH CAMPBELL

WHAT IS YOUR SACRED SPACE?

Is it a religious space for worship, like a church, temple, or mosque? Is it in nature, like the woods or the ocean? Is it on the dance floor or yoga mat?

Maybe you grew up with religion. Maybe you're still a part of that faith or have chosen another belief system, or none. Major loss itself can also cause a crisis in faith, leaving us spiritually "homeless" for a time. Either way, you can curate in parallel or as an alternative to what your faith offers or your preferred form of spirituality. I encourage you to integrate the practice of curating into your *current* life.

If you're like me and agnostic, or an atheist, or just without many existing rituals, the practice of curating an exhibition, imaginary or otherwise, can introduce ritual, ceremony, and a contemplative practice to support your grieving process.

In your own designated sacred space for grief you can tune into the divine, connect to the inner wisdom, align with the

Universe, or just play with channeling grief's emotions in a different way. Add as much or as little "woo" to the process as you'd like!

For some, grief itself is sacred. Fellow grief coach Shelby Forsythia, author of *Your Grief, Your Way*, stocks a T-shirt emblazoned with the words Grief is Holy on her website. It's her bestseller. I asked Shelby what prompted her to create merch with those words, and I adore her reply:

"In our society we worship at so many altars—youth, fame, wealth, power, and very narrow forms of love (romantic, unconditional, motherly).

But we don't give grief that sort of space and reverence. Grief is often cast aside or relegated to a private, hidden part of our lives. It is not shared openly. It is not given the freedom to exist in the same ways as our other altars.

When I say 'Grief is holy," I don't mean that with any religious connotation. I mean that grief is sacred in that it connects us more deeply to ourselves, others, and the world. It reminds us of where we have been and shows us —in some ways—where we are going. It forces us to be OK with having no answers while simultaneously marinating us in questions. It's an experience unlike anything else worth making space and time for, worth prioritizing."

THE QUALITIES OF SACRED SPACE

Here are some of the reasons why I love art galleries and exhibitions as sacred spaces for grieving:

A Container: The gallery space, whether it's physical or virtual, is a container: for artwork, for absorbing and digesting, for storytelling, for connecting.

A Designated Space and Time: People grieving need time and space to mourn and process their emotions. If we're not accustomed to creating this for ourselves, an exhibition inherently has a time and place, an opening date and a closing date. A designated place to meet, an invitation to see and be with our thoughts and inner world.

A Quiet Place: An exhibition is an invitation to be in a quiet, contemplative space. Conversations with and among visitors are still one of my favorite parts of my exhibitions. But visitors are also welcome to just keep to themselves, to sit on a bench and just be. I've silently wept in many museums and been grateful to be left alone.

Across Cultures: Museums and art galleries span across most world cultures, with cultural spaces, institutions and historical societies in cities and rural areas alike. I like the secular nature of creating a mini museum, because I'm agnostic and I didn't grow up with a practice of creating altars. For your version of a Grief Gallery, you can bring in as much or as little of your faith and culture as you'd like!

The Power of Art: Art has the ability to connect personal experience with universal experiences. Everyone will experience death and loss at some point in their lives. It is personal. It is universal. Let's embrace art and design, and their ability to connect people (with themselves and others).

MY MOM'S HOUSE BECAME MY SPACE FOR GRIEF

Ultimately, my mother's empty dream house became my sacred space, my own personal retreat. Looking back now, I see it also became my art studio to express, experiment, and explore my grief and emotions.

I had a creative brief, which is the set of goals and considerations for a project:

Imagine an exhibition about my mother
and choose 100 objects for it.

I used the walls of the guest room as inspiration boards, taping up photos, images, and snippets of poetry. I commandeered my mom's tables and surfaces as workspace for sorting, cataloging, and evaluating her belongings. Her shelves became staging areas for my displays. I labeled a plastic container with a "100 Objects" sign, as a shortlist for what I could carry back with me to London. It was essentially a self-initiated art residency.

A SPACE WITHOUT JUDGMENT AND EDITING

As I sorted through my mom's belongings, I was working through my grief. I was sorting through my feelings while accessing my stories and my emotions through the objects. It was a creative space for me to express myself without judgment. To speak without editing, to say what I wanted without words, and to just be. In
, I noted that we need to feel safe enough to grieve. For me, being away from judging eyes was part of what I needed to feel safe and comfortable enough to be with grief.

And now I invite you to do the same—I invite you into an imaginary art space, part studio and part gallery. A safe space to be with grief. Our cultures, social groups, and everyday lives rarely give us the space to just be with our grief. (Three days of bereavement leave from work is laughably inadequate!) We almost never get the chance to just be curious about our grief, to look at our losses from different angles, to just see what comes up.

In the same way that you don't have to empty out a whole room in your home to be your gallery space, maybe it's possible to find a way to carve out a little space to be with your grief.

What might serve as your own art studio or staging area? A box? A shelf? A notebook?

Remember, whatever you create in this space can be just for you. It doesn't have to be good. It doesn't have to make sense. We are making sense of our losses and experiences in the telling and retelling and exploring. It doesn't matter whether someone else values what we're doing!

In the same way that an artist often creates in solitude, you're not necessarily creating for public consumption at the start. The grieving process, like the creative process, doesn't benefit from harsh criticism or premature feedback. Especially with early grief or tender topics, my hope is that you don't expose your vulnerable self to the critiques or opinions of just anyone. Give yourself space to just be and to be curious, away from judgmental eyes—even your own.

PROTECT YOUR SACRED SPACE

What do we do with sacred space? Think of churches, cultural sites, places of religious significance, or holy ground: We honor it, preserve it, and protect it. I encourage you to do the same with your sacred grief space. Our daily lives rarely give us room to just be with grief, and our everyday responsibilities can easily encroach on this precious time and space.

Be vigilant about who you let in. You might notice throughout these pages that when I tell stories about being in my mother's house after she died, I usually say what it was like for me—not us. After a couple of attempts at having company for sorting through my mom's belongings, I decided I preferred to be in solitude (I am, after all, a prickly, introverted only child). Even my husband was not invited to my personal grief retreats and creative studio! He loved me—then as now—but he didn't love or understand how I grieved. He wanted to help me, but in his way. As a designer himself, his default was to offer constructive criticism—and I didn't need criticism, constructive or otherwise. As hard as it was at the time, I believe now that recognizing our relative strengths and protecting my grief space were crucial for preserving our marriage in the long-term.

———

GOOD QUESTIONS

What is your sacred place?

Where do you feel safe? At peace? Connected to true yourself?

What might you set up as your sacred grief space, and creative studio for curating?

PART FIVE
COLLECT: CURATING FOR AWARENESS

CHAPTER 19
WHEN EVERYTHING BECOMES PRECIOUS

After my mom died, everything in her house became precious. In addition to the soy sauce in her kitchen, there was also the box of Band-Aids in her bathroom. And her toothbrush on the sink. And the calendar in her living room. Everything felt precious. Everything felt important because they belonged to my mom.

Have you experienced this phenomenon yourself? Did things just look different, after you lost someone?

WHAT'S YOUR "SOY SAUCE"?

What's your equivalent of the soy sauce? A seemingly prosaic object that paralyzed you or you feel inexplicably emotional about?

Here are a few poignant examples people have shared with The Grief Gallery that may spark an idea or memory for you.

It's just a simple, functional watch that was steadfast and unwavering in its operation — no surprise that my mother chose it, Kate wrote. *She had a variation of this watch for as long as I can remember, from my childhood to her death, always on her wrist. I think it will be forever charged with her essence.*

I found myself getting tearful over a screwdriver because I remembered it being in the house I grew up in. It was a red screwdriver with the name of a hardware store on the handle. I put it in the donate box and took it out so many times! Eventually I did let it go, a griever shared on Instagram.

Every day my Grandmother Jackie would put her hair up in a banana hair clip. I don't have any of hers, but it will always be an object that reminds me of her, shared Omni.

Sticks, rocks, and bark remind Alica Forneret of her mother Deborah, who was Canadian. "My dad always said, 'Every time we would go to Canada, we would bring an empty suitcase because your mom was just going to bring back a bunch of sticks, rocks, and bark from trees in the woods near the cabins where they grew up,'" remembers Alica, who is the founder and executive director of PAUSE, a nonprofit enhancing the grief and end-of-life experience for people of color. "I don't know if it's illegal, but I guess she's dead now, so it doesn't matter," she adds, with the matter-of-fact, dark humor a lot of us grievers know well.

You may be surprised what you feel attached to after a loved one dies. I expected to get emotional about my mom's jewelry and family photos. I did not expect to feel so strongly about my mom's own collection of random rocks or a bottle of soy sauce!

ANCHOR OBJECTS

Let's take a look at that soy sauce in my mother's kitchen. Why was this half-empty bottle of soy sauce so meaningful to me?

I remember its general shape. I remember the golden maple color of her kitchen cabinets. I don't remember the label or the brand of soy sauce (but it wasn't Kikkoman). I do remember trying multiple times to throw it away and finding it impossible.

Why did I need help throwing it out? Let's get curious. Let's shine the spotlight on the soy sauce, put it on our imaginary display pedestal and see: What stories, memories, and meanings are attached to it?

It's an anchor object. Anchored to that bottle of soy sauce were many memories, connections, and feelings:

Memories of the turkey she would make as part of a traditional American Thanksgiving. It calls to mind a photo of my mom as a teenager with her family at their first Thanksgiving after immigrating from Hong Kong. With a huge turkey on the table.

My mother was a great cook, but the turkey is turkey. It was never my favorite part of the meal. The best part was what she would do with the leftovers: make congee (aka *jook*, aka rice porridge). The turkey carcass with plenty of meat still attached would go into her biggest pot with rice, peanuts, and aromatics. After my parents' divorce, she'd try to make it with a turkey leg, but it wasn't the same.

Chinatown on Christmas Day. We adopted the New York City Jewish tradition of going to Chinatown on Christmas Day. During the last trip home, we went there on Christmas Day for roast duck, one of my favorites.

Soy Sauce is also a connection to my ancestors. The ones that I knew and didn't know. The ones that I've lost since my mother died.

My maternal grandmother *Pau Pau* died of cancer when I was five, my first memory of losing someone. I'm told that *Pau Pau* made really good *zhong*—Chinese tamales made of sticky rice, sausage, pork meat, and duck egg yolk (the best part, in my opinion), all wrapped up tightly in bamboo leaves and steamed.

There's dim sum with my aunt and uncle, a meal best experienced with a group.

My Uncle Stephen lived next door to us, on the 39th floor of our high-rise apartment in the sky. When I was little, he would pick me up after school.

Everyone knew him in Chinatown. There was always a table for him, no matter how busy the dim sum parlor. My uncle always arrived first. My aunt would turn to me and ask, "What do you want?" She would flag down the waiter or manager and expertly order my favorites: Chive dumplings. Steamed pork ribs.

But they're all getting older. Uncle Stephen died in May 2022.

There are fewer people at the dim sum table these days. Often there are only three of us or not even enough for dim sum. Sometimes I'm the one placing the food order (as if I was the adult or something).

And I feel a pang of sadness. *Gosh, there's so much meaning attached to this soy sauce. No wonder I feel so emotionally invested in it.*

The soy sauce anchors fond memories of meals with my family, but for a while it also anchored plenty of regret:

I didn't learn how to cook all that great Chinese food.
It's shameful that I don't know how to cook those traditional dishes.
I missed my chance to learn from my mother.
Does that mean I was a bad daughter?

All these painful thoughts and questions, tethered to the soy sauce!Sometimes, acknowledging these difficult internal ideas and ruminations can allow them to loosen their grip and eventually be released.

Simple objects can have a lot of stories, memories, and meanings attached. The soy sauce represented my mom's love for cooking, our Chinese-American identities, my guilt as a daughter, and so much more.

DO YOU SEE IT DIFFERENTLY NOW?

Now that I've told you the story of the soy sauce, when you go to dim sum . . . are you going to look at the soy sauce a little differently? (By the way, if you're wondering what I ultimately did with the soy sauce in my mom's kitchen? Check out chapter 35.)

Knowing the healing power of these stories is why I disagree when people say dismissively that it's "just stuff." Technically, these everyday objects and belongings *are* "just stuff," but when they are anchor objects, with so many stories, memories, and meanings attached to them, they're so much more to us as grievers.

Later in the book, we'll take a deeper look at the meanings attached, but for now, let's take a look at what might be attached for you.

———

CREATIVE EXERCISE

This is your invitation to get curious about what you feel attached to—without judgment. You can answer the question, "Why am I so attached?!" from a place of curiosity and compassion.

I often do a mapping exercise with clients because it reveals so much. I like to use mind mapping software like MindNode, but you can do this with pen and paper. It's one of the most powerful creative exercises I offer in the Curating Grief process, both with clients and during The Grief Gallery's monthly gatherings.

Step 1: Pick a meaningful object: It can be the mundane object you felt inexplicably emotional about. Or a possession that you can picture so vividly in your mind.

Step 2: Ask yourself:
Why is this so meaningful?
What does it represent to me?
What are the memories and the stories that are anchored to this?

Step 3: Create a visual of what is attached to your meaningful object, with memories, stories, and phrases branching out from it.

GETTING OBJECTIVE

In this exercise, we are putting the meaningful object on the plinth and we practice seeing it in different ways:

Seeing Objectively: There's the object itself and its inherent qualities: shape, dimensions, materials. It's how the object would be described on the label in an art gallery or museum.

Seeing Subjectively: Then there are the subjective qualities: how we see and perceive the object. Our perceptions are going to vary, from person to person and from day to day.

LEARNING FROM THE OBJECTS

What can we learn from the belongings and the meaningful objects? Over time, as I've worked with thousands of grievers through individual coaching and group workshops, I found that the objects can tell us a lot . . .

About our grief
About our relationship with grief and emotions
About our relationship with the loss
About our relationship with the person

That's another role that the objects and the belongings might play. If you find yourself feeling attached to an item like a pair of glasses, a box of matches, try asking yourself:

Why am I so attached to this?

And again, ask from a place of curiosity, compassion, and love. Sometimes we ask ourselves that question in an almost accusatory way, like, *Why am I being so silly? Why am I so attached to this? Grow up!*

Let's try looking with curiosity:

Why am I so attached to this?
What do I see when I look at it?

———

GOOD QUESTIONS

To wrap up this part of our inquiry together, I invite you to look at the meaningful objects you've been considering above, and now looking through the lens of everything being precious, everything being important:

What do you see now?

Is there anything that surprises you?

CHAPTER 20
OPP: OTHER PEOPLE'S PERSPECTIVES, PROCESSES, AND PRIORITIES

Imagine again that we're in an art gallery. White walls with framed paintings. On a display pedestal in the middle is a sculpture. I might come in and love the artwork immediately. Maybe I recognize the artist—it's a Rodin! Or I instantly love the beautiful shape—it's a Barbara Hepworth.

Someone else might come into the gallery space, look at the same piece of artwork, and say, "I don't get it." Maybe they don't like abstract art. Maybe they don't like sculpture in general. That happens often and very naturally in an art space.

But what if it's something more intimate, more personal? What if, instead of a famous sculpture on that display pedestal, there is a meaningful object that belonged to a loved one?

In chapter 6, "Who Else Is in the Room?" we introduced the concept of OPP, which stands for:

Other People's Processes

Other People's Pain

Other People's Perspectives and Perceptions

Other People's Priorities and Preferences

Other People's Problems

DO YOU SEE WHAT I SEE?

All the different expressions, expectations, and experiences that individuals have after major loss can be the source of so much conflict, pain, and suffering.

> **What Hurts?**
> *Why can't they see it my way?*
> *Why don't they understand why I'm so attached?*
> *Why won't they help me with the estate and stuff?*
> *Why do they have such strong opinions about what I'm doing and not doing?*
> *Why is it so hard for me to choose?*
> *Why is it so hard for them to help the way I want them to help?*

OTHER PEOPLE'S PERSPECTIVES

Just as we looked earlier at how you might be surprised by your own grief responses, likewise, you might be surprised by how other people respond after a significant loss. In chapter 2 we talk about how individuals grieve differently. People have different relationships with the deceased. People also have different relationships with: Death, Life, God, The Universe, and themselves.

When it comes to the belongings and objects, this can be a hard truth for grievers:

What is meaningful to you
may be meaningless to someone else.

How is it that an object can be full of meaning for you—so imbued with love or significance—and yet be devoid of meaning to someone else?

Let me give you an example of an object that is meaningful to me—and potentially meaningless to you. One of my favorite objects from my mom's house is a miniature chair, about four inches high. It's plastic, with a white curving back that scoops forward to cradle a black seat cushion. Instead of four legs, it has a single, sleek pedestal base that appears poured from the bottom of the seat, pooling into a perfect circle on the floor.

If you like design, you might immediately recognize the little chair as a model of a Tulip Chair by the Finnish-American architect and industrial designer Eero Saarinen. It's a design classic.

But what if you're not a fan of design or designer chairs? How might you see this miniature chair? You might think, "Oh, a little chair. Is it a toy?" Maybe you think it's cute, but you don't have the additional context.

The way we see and interpret an object is influenced by factors like prior knowledge, our lived experiences, and our expectations.

For me, there's another layer of interpretation, because this chair was a gift from my mother. She knew nothing about designer chairs, but she knew *I* loved them. We did share a love for cute and small things. She bought this toy chair for me. It was part of a collectible series, and she brought the whole set all the way back from Hong Kong to New York to surprise me.

Through my eyes, the miniature chair represents my mom wanting to connect with me. What might it represent for someone else? **Same object. Same plastic chair. Same dimensions: Different meanings and interpretations.**

Let's continue imagining that we are in an art gallery.

I've placed the miniature chair on a plinth to show you and tell you about it. Now imagine that a stranger walks into the room. What will their perception of the little chair be? They haven't heard my story. It likely doesn't have the same meaning for them as it does for me. Even though it's *so* full of meaning to me, it's meaningless to them. (I'm not offended, really.)

Unless they have another association . . .

Maybe they had a similar chair in their childhood home. Maybe learning about Eero Saarinen inspired them to become an architect. Maybe then it evokes a meaning and emotion for them.

In chapter 19 we talked about seeing the belongings and meaningful items as anchor objects. This object, this simple toy, has all these stories, memories, and meanings attached. That's what makes it meaningful for me. For someone else, they might have different stories and meanings attached to it, different interpretations. That's what determines whether it's meaningful to them.

When we talk about our loved ones and we share why certain objects are important to us, it's also an invitation for others to develop their own associations and their own attachments to the item.

Now that I've told you the story of my little chair and the meaning it has for me, do you see it differently? *Feel* differently about it?

To me, that is the beauty and brilliance of meaningful objects as anchor objects, and why I believe so passionately in curating these objects as a potential source of comfort and connection.

But not everyone is going to take you up on that invitation . . .

"I DON'T SEE IT THAT WAY"

A lot of friction happens in families when something meaningful to one griever is meaningless to someone else. Belongings are thrown away without consent or consultation. Siblings can withhold items, reflecting an old relationship dynamic or a new rift after the loss.

What Hurts?
They threw away the thing that was most important to me.
My sibling is withholding our aunt's jewelry from me.
My father threw away all of my mom's clothes after she died.
They swooped in and put everything in garbage bags.
Why was that object meaningless to them?
Didn't they love them?
Don't they care about me?

Again, same object. Very different perceptions of value and emotional attachments. Why is that? Here are a couple of ways to look at it:

- Maybe their stories are attached to something else.
- Maybe their relationship with the person was very different than yours.
- Maybe their relationship with grief and style of grieving clashes with yours.
- Maybe their relationship with stuff is different.
- Maybe they really are a jerk and intend to hurt you. (This is, unfortunately, the case at times.)

OTHER PEOPLE'S PROCESSES AND PAIN

When a close family member or a loved one dies, it brings up a whole range of reactions and emotions. It can be helpful to remember that these differences in emotions, reactions, and expressions can be a big source of conflict after someone dies because people will respond in various ways.

These grief responses and expressions are influenced by several things:

First, the relationship that you have with a person will affect your experience with grief. How you feel personally and how you think about that person is going to affect how you feel about their loss—and their stuff.

Then there is a person's relationship to grief itself. In addition to different ways of grieving, individuals also have varying *capacities* for handling emotions and scenarios. This can manifest in various responses to the physical stuff:

A widower throws away all his deceased wife's clothes because it's too painful to look at them. He might think that having them out of sight will help reduce his grief. (It's similar to how some grievers believe they'll feel much better after the funeral because it's a major grieving task done.)

A parent might insist on keeping their child's bedroom precisely as they'd left it. Maybe they close the door and keep it like a shrine or museum. Maybe they go in every day and say good morning.

A child moves all their parent's belongings into a storage unit and never sorts through it. Or they keep the family home for seven years, untouched, like a family friend did after her parents died.

In the next chapter, we'll take an even deeper look at our relationships to stuff.

Tip: When I'm frustrated by otherwise well-meaning people intruding on how I prefer to grieve, I imagine them in oversized clown shoes. 🤡 👞 I visualize them stumbling around in their own grief, shock, and uncertainty, trying desperately to help—but they're creating a racket in my peaceful gallery space and stomping on my toes accidentally, when I just want quiet and tranquility. It's absurd. It's tragic. It's hilarious (at least the mental picture is for me).

OTHER PEOPLE'S PERCEPTIONS

What's your answer when you put on your curator hat and ask yourself, "If I were to present an exhibition about my loved one, which objects would I put on display?" Your reply is going to be so personal to you and to your relationship with the person based on your interactions and shared history.

Now imagine another person answering that question, say a sibling, colleague, or former spouse. If that person were to present an exhibition about the same person, about your loved one, their exhibition might look radically different. So different that you might not even recognize the exhibition as being about your loved one! Their relationship may be vastly dissimilar, based on factors like their own circumstances, their interactions with your loved one, or their own view of the world.

If my aunt were to curate an exhibition about my mother, it would be unalike from mine in many ways. As her sister, their relationship was very different from the one I had as a daughter. On a practical level, she has access to divergent belongings and objects, but also memories and experiences that I don't have. My aunt's exhibition about my mother would likely include objects from their childhood in Hong Kong before they moved to the United States, and moments and stories from their years growing up together.

Different Curations: Your person is represented by the imaginary exhibition as a whole. Different people will present very different exhibitions about a person, depending on their relationship with them and their interactions. If my mother's coworkers at Hewlett-Packard were to curate an exhibition about her, they would likely not include soy sauce!

The items on the plinths represent various facets and aspects of your person, as well as disparate parts of your relationship with them. Remember, as curator, *you* get to choose what you highlight and what you show.

A reminder: This OPP work of practicing seeing from others' perspectives is for *your* benefit. You make the call as to whether you stay in touch with a person! And it can be a privilege to be able to cut off contact. If you cannot due to circumstance, duty, or desire, this is also for you.

"BUT I WANT THEM TO SEE IT MY WAY"

When I was in high school my parents had a poster of a painting by Mark Rothko in the kitchen, next to the phone on the wall. It was the kind of poster you find in museum gift shops, albeit cheaply framed, and was an everyday presence in our lives and home decor. Even after my mom divorced and moved into her dream house across the country, she took that framed poster with her, and it eventually found a home in her sunroom.

I liked the poster all right, but I didn't think that much about it. I'm not sure why my parents loved that particular painting so much, but if I had to guess, they saw it at a museum and the poster reminded them of that trip.

If you're not familiar with Mark Rothko, he was an American abstract painter. He's famous for his Color Field paintings composed of blocks of color layered one atop the other.

If you and I were to go to a museum with a Rothko painting on view, we can imagine a range of reactions from visitors.

Some people would appreciate the depth and vibrancy of the color in person, the multiple layers of paint. Some visitors would know the history and impact of Rothko's work and be excited to finally see his work in person.

Others might learn from an art docent, curator's note, or a wall label that Rothko described his work as "painting emotions" and thus see the work in a new light.

And other people would look at this iconic painting—this painting valued at hundreds of millions of dollars, the pride of a museum's collection—and they would shrug. "Oh, my kid could make that," they might say.

That's a fascinating aspect of abstract art and art in general! It's subjective. People will see it in different ways. If they hear an explanation from an art docent or learn more about the artist's intentions, inspiration, or technique, they *may* change their mind.

It's a good reminder of how subjective many things are in life. Generally, we aren't surprised or offended if this happens in the setting of an art gallery. That said, it is possible to spend a portion of our lives arguing with strangers and family members about whether a Rothko painting is beautiful or ugly or even art at all. (But that's not how I personally want to spend my time and energy!)

There can be a similar hard truth after a loved one dies. Earlier I mentioned that my amazing mother is the villain in some people's stories. They would choose entirely different objects, moments, and stories when curating their imaginary exhibition about her.

Just like I could try to convince a person who hates abstract art of the brilliance of Rothko's paintings, or to offer a dissertation about the cultural context and significance of Yves Klein's *Blue Monochrome* ("It's just a blue rectangle?!), they may never get it.

I could talk forever about how much my mom contributed to the world and how much she tried to help her community. And some people will *never* see it my way.

I can only shrug and say: OPP. Other People's Perspectives. Other People's Perceptions. Other People's Problems.

OTHER PEOPLE'S PRIORITIES

What hurts?
Why don't they want this heirloom or special object?
Why aren't they making time to help with the house?
Why won't they talk about them?

Here's how I see it: Your relatives may have different life priorities determining how they allocate their resources. For example:

How they use their space: Even if they care about you and loved your person, they may prefer to decorate their living space differently. They may prefer to have new artwork from Etsy or even IKEA instead of an heirloom.

How they use their time: They may choose to prioritize time with their family or career over time spent sorting through the belongings.

How they use their energy: Maybe they know that therapy might be helpful, that talking about your loved one could be cathartic. And maybe they don't have the energy to spare or are choosing to spend it elsewhere.

The mismatch in priorities can be *so* painful. *And,* I suggest letting other people's processes and priorities (OPP) be their own and embracing what feels good to you.

Tip: My grief coaching clients have noted that "of course they did" can be one of the most helpful phrases I offer them. It's a phrase I associate with Radical Acceptance, a concept often referenced in dialectical behavior therapy (DBT) and derived from Buddhist and Eastern philosophy.

It's a stress tolerance skill, of accepting reality (including people and their actions) as they are, not as we want them to be. A handy, maybe even vital, skill for grievers!

My dad doesn't ask how I'm doing. "Of course he didn't. He never does."

My sister is playing the role of martyr. "Of course she did. It's how she's always coped."

We don't have to approve, but it takes away the shock. We can accept the reality of the world and human nature, so we can decide how we want to respond.

I find that practicing Radical Acceptance gives me the space for hope, love, and compassion, even after major loss.

I am sad and angry. "Of course I am."

I still believe in hope and beauty. "Of course I do."

CHAPTER 21
OPP: OUR RELATIONSHIPS TO STUFF

I was, on many levels, the worst equipped person to deal with sorting through, packing, and getting rid of my mother's belongings. I find it very difficult to let go of stuff. I get very attached.

For instance, when I moved from San Francisco to New York with my husband, decades ago, I took so much time to sort through my books, jewelry, and art supplies that we missed our original flight. My husband, a minimalist by nature who owned very few items at the time, was baffled. My mother drove up to the city to lend a hand. She patiently helped pack our dishes and cooking pots, while I cried and my husband fumed. We had to book a whole new flight to make that move.

It was a similar story when we moved from New York to Europe for his studies. I took so long sorting through clothing, cookware, and books that I had to change my flight and delay the move. (Making decisions about what to keep, and then doing the actual packing, were clearly not my strong points.) My husband was furious. My mother was likely shaking her head, but she comforted me and called the movers to change the move date. All the books and furniture we wanted to keep but couldn't move with us found a temporary home in her attic.

No wonder I found myself so overwhelmed as I stood in

my mother's house, trying to decide what to keep and what to let go of after she died!

———

GOOD QUESTIONS

What's your relationship to physical stuff?

Has it changed since your person died or over time?

How does it show up in your experience with grief?

———

In chapter 13, "Curating Grief Is a Form of Interior Design," we explored how a person's relationship to grief may manifest in how they approach the physical objects. What other factors can shape our relationship to stuff? What contributes to OPP: Other People's Processes when it comes to the belongings?

CHILDHOOD EXPERIENCES WITH POSSESSIONS CAN SHAPE YOUR RELATIONSHIP WITH STUFF

Maybe you grew up moving a lot. Maybe you had to let go of things all the time, against your wishes. Maybe things got thrown out without your consent. Maybe you didn't have your own space for your childhood treasures.

My husband and I have contrasting relationships with stuff. We both grew up with big moves. His father worked with the United Nations, and his family moved many times, often internationally. He lived in Italy until he was ten. He's also one of five kids.

I'm an only child. When I was ten, my parents and I moved across the country, far from my mom's family in New York's Chinatown.

I'm fascinated by how differently we've responded to these formative experiences. My approach: We had to move multiple times and things sometimes got lost. *So I better hold on tight to my belongings* was a prominent belief that took root in my psyche. My style is to cling to things. That feels stabilizing to me. I feel safe and secure with my belongings around me.

Does that sound familiar to you?

In contrast, my husband's approach is to not have many physical objects. Because you might have to move again. Because things will likely get lost. Does the "better to not get attached" approach resonate with you?

OUR RELATIONSHIP WITH A LOVED ONE'S BELONGINGS AND OUR PERCEPTIONS OF STUFF—ALL CAN BE SHAPED BY OUR EXPERIENCES WITH OUR OWN POSSESSIONS

It often ties back to what we have owned and how our stuff has been treated. Let me give you an example: the Hello Kitty figures in my mother's house. My mom had a collection of them dotted through her rooms on various shelves. When I see my mom's Hello Kitty toys, they represent our shared love for cute things. They represent connection and love. When I look at them, I also smile because I imagine her permitting herself to have childlike things in her home. This is significant because she didn't really feel like she had a childhood.

"I never had a toy, not a single one," my mom wrote in an essay I found (she went back to school for her master's degree in her fifties). "I guess my family was so poor in the 1950s and '60s in Hong Kong. At the time, we had nine members in the family, with two parents, five children, and two grandmothers. I don't think my parents had extra money to buy us toys, books, or candy, like my daughter's generation."

After my mom moved to New York City when she was fifteen, her spare time before and after school was spent working in the family laundry instead of playing with her friends. I love that in her later years, she treated herself to these adorable toys. When I look at the Hello Kitty figures now, I see evidence of my mother's self-care. This is my perception and interpretation.

"When I Was a Kid"

When I was growing up in Manhattan's Chinatown, my mother would buy me Hello Kitty toys and stickers as rewards if I was good. (She kept them in the top drawer of our bedroom's wooden dresser. Now and then, I would sneak open the drawer and gaze lovingly at these goodies.) It's another reason I have fond associations with Hello Kitty toys: They represent good things and my mother's care for me.

But what if you had a different childhood experience? What else could be represented by an item like a Hello Kitty toy? What if you didn't get treats and rewards as a kid? What if you didn't have toys? Maybe your family couldn't afford them. Or a parent withheld toys as a way of withholding affection or approval?

What if there was a toy that you really loved that got broken, taken away, stolen, or lost?

What if you grew up with parents who didn't care, or with family members who neglected your emotional needs? As I noted, the Hello Kitty figure represents caring to me. If you didn't get that kind of caring or feeling cared for, it might represent a *lack* of caring for you.

Maybe you have a specific negative association with Hello Kitty. A traumatic childhood experience, or maybe you're freaked out by her lack of a mouth? Clearly, that object will represent very different things to you. Maybe instead of looking at Hello Kitty and feeling happy and comforted (the way I do), you might feel a pang of loss. You might feel angry, resentful, betrayed, or sad. Sad for you now, sad for yourself as a child.

If that's the case for you, I hope you might be able to take inspiration from my mom and treat yourself now—as an adult. To delight your inner child with that plush toy, that action figure, or another cute item. Feel free to start with a Hello Kitty figure!

Fun Fact: The labels next to artwork? The big explanatory text on the wall of a museum's exhibition display? These are all called Interpretive Text. After all, even with artwork in a gallery, there's the artist's intent and then there's the viewer's interpretation, as well as the curator's.

"We don't see eye to eye"

It's not uncommon for siblings to have very different reactions to or interpretations of the same object. Losing a loved one, especially a parent, can heighten or bring to the surface a range of family dynamics.

Was one sibling the favored child, and another sibling considered the black sheep and relatively neglected? Is something of that nature being triggered when you're looking at the same item? Is that what's influencing some of the feelings and heightened emotions that are coming up?

"I see security"

I grew up with stories about my grandmother and great-aunt being raised in poverty in China. Stories like my great-aunt not being allowed to go to school because she was a girl and walking barefoot behind the cows to pick up their dung to use as fertilizer. And those were the good years!

When we cleaned out my great aunt's apartment in the senior home, her closets were filled with unused stockings and polyester shirts still in their packaging, plus the few garments she actually wore, patched multiple times. We carefully checked the linings for hidden cash, as she was known to stash extra money away—just in case.

Maybe your relatives lived through the Great Depression or were refugees and migrants. Growing up with scarcity (or with excess!) will influence your relationship with stuff. If stockpiled items represent security, it's no wonder it may be hard to let them go.

"I see a burden"

If your parents or other family members were hoarders, that will surely shape your relationship with physical objects. Maybe you grew up with stacks of junk in your home. Perhaps you didn't have clear surfaces to do your homework or unobstructed pathways from one room to another. It would be no wonder if the belongings represent clutter and limitation to you.

Maybe physical stuff represents oppression or mental illness. And if you had responsibilities for hiding the situation or trying to clean things up, it might represent an obligation or a burden to you. In some families, belongings are, unfortunately, used as a tool for control and manipulation.

No wonder there is a wide range of relationships and responses to the physical stuff, from negative to neutral to positive!

SAME OBJECT, DIFFERENT ANGLES

So, what do we do if we realize our partner, siblings, or other family members have very different interpretations and ways of looking at the stuff, especially after a loved one dies?

Communication is key.

I find it helpful to name some of these different interpretations: to share what you see and feel, and then invite the other person to share what they see and what they feel.

"When I look at this, I see X, Y, Z. What do you see?"

"When I look at this, I feel A, B, C. What do you feel?"

210

The goal is to invite and spark conversation about the different ways that you're seeing and interpreting things. We want to approach this from a place of curiosity and compassion.

Curiosity: "That's so interesting! I see this object in all these different ways. I have these associations. I feel this way when I look at it. When *they* see it, they see a totally different thing. Fascinating."

Compassion: "Can I access some compassion for both how I'm interpreting it and how they're interpreting it? In other words, can I find within myself a softening and feel compassion for both of us?"

And a reminder, your family members, partner, and friends don't need to understand *why* you are feeling a certain way to respect your choices and views.

We can look together at the same object from different angles, as if we are in a gallery space, keeping in mind our various backgrounds, our lived experiences, and our unique relationships with the person.

———

GOOD QUESTIONS

What roles did belongings play in your life?

Did they help you feel safe or protected? Cared for?

Did belongings feel like a burden?

What roles do belongings play in your life now?

CHAPTER 22
WHAT ROLES DO THE OBJECTS PLAY?

Meaningful objects can play different roles in our lives. In this chapter, we will place the belongings and items in the spotlight, to take a closer look at these roles. By seeing and honoring their individual roles, we can see more clearly why we might feel emotionally attached to certain items, and thus confirm or affirm our reasons for keeping them or letting them go.

For our curating purposes, an object can be:

Evidence
A Souvenir
An Artifact
An Heirloom
A Talisman
An Anchor

EVIDENCE

Some objects serve as evidence. Evidence of how the person died. Evidence of how the person lived. Evidence they were here.

As I shared earlier, because my mom died so suddenly, the items in her house initially felt like potential clues or evidence of what might have happened. Over time, her belongings have taken on new meaning. They are now: Evidence of her kindness. Evidence of her love for life. Evidence of her adventurous spirit.

For my client Heather, a metal lunchbox was beautiful evidence of how hardworking her dad was and of the loving relationship she had with him. After his death, she found in his lunch pail a note that she'd written for him. She wrote a stunning piece about it; here—in its exhibition-ready form complete with wall label—is an excerpt:

His Lunch Pail

Aluminum Lunch Box, Repaired Handle
Contributed by Heather Campbell, 2023
In memory of her father

2023.NY.HC.2

"When my father died, I didn't ask for valuables; money and status weren't what my dad stood for. I saved things that helped me feel him around me: a shirt I could snuggle in, to be wrapped in his hugs; Obsession cologne and Chapstick, to smell his essence; the blanket that always lived in his truck, to spread out for picnics and star gazing; methiolate wound care, for mending any hurts; and his lunch pail.

That battered pail is older than I am. Made of aluminum with a Bakelite handle that had long been replaced with rubberized grips as the plastic deteriorated decades ago; the dilapidated exterior was a testament to his hard work. The man never missed a shift and that showed in the tarnished facade.

I remember the racket it made as it clattered against the counter and echoed through the house when he packed it each evening on overnights; the creak of the hinges as I stealthily opened it to hide 'I love you' notes in it for him to find during his shift.

I was compelled to ask for the pail; it had been part of our story. I took the box home with me, and for weeks it sat out of sight until I could bring myself to open it and mull over the contents.

I ran my fingers over its dented carcass. One latch absent completely, the other barely hanging on with a makeshift clasp, I pulled at the pin and the fastener limply gave way, clinking against the side. A nostalgic sound as it rattled open and I laid my eyes upon a familiar scene: a handful of napkins, his spoon and knife, Chapstick, a stained baggie full of crumbs, three pens, one Sudafed, a pouch holding three Band-Aids, Tylenol, an empty plastic tube, a film canister containing three Tums, a toothpick, three sticks of Wrigley's spearmint gum, one blue raspberry candy cane, half a pack of Life Saver's Spear-o-mints, three Werther's Originals, one peppermint melt-away, and an individually wrapped Life Saver's mint. At the bottom, a paper towel for cleanliness scattered with crumbs. All inventoried and accounted for.

I lifted the towel to wipe the sediment into the garbage and beneath found another sandwich bag. I was about to drop it in the trash bin when I realized it was sealed shut with something hidden inside. I could feel that it was paper, but years of stains and wear had made it thick like plastic. I unfolded it. The page was decorated with clipart hearts, and the words 'hug' and 'kiss' spray painted, graffiti-style. I began to read as my eyes welled with tears, 'Thought I would put a note in your pail for old times sake. Love you, Daddy, have a great day at work!!!'

I wept, wept for this blessing, out of gratitude because this silly nothing I wrote half a lifetime ago was meant to make him smile, and instead, brought me closure. I never doubted the love we shared, not for one moment, but the page in my hands, with its bleeding ink and food spatter, was a tangible measure of that bond.

SOUVENIR

Some objects are souvenirs. A memory of a person, a memory of a place or a period in time. Of course, the word souvenir is from the French for memory.

My mom's house had lots of souvenirs because she loved to travel. The souvenir from Brazil made me smile, reminded of her happy vacation snapshots. But it was also bittersweet. She would never travel again. We would never go to Machu Picchu together.

What makes the best souvenirs? Something that's "so them"— so characteristic of a person, unique to a place, calling to mind a specific meal, moment, or meaning. Poppy Chancellor of The Griefcase identified only one thing of her father's she wanted: His Sex Pistols poster. It was "so him."

The following piece is the introduction to a touching tribute that Heather wrote for her mom's memorial—another poignant example of a souvenir.

Her Walkman

1980s Sony Walkman
Contributed by Heather Campbell, 2023
In memory of her mother

2023.NY.HC.1

"In 1979, Sony invented a device that would allow individuals to create a personal stereo experience they could carry on their hip with ease: the Walkman. For my mom, a small-town mountain girl who grew up in a family of musicians, this was a magical advancement. Her dad was one of 13 children, all with impressive musical prowess, virtuosos who could play any instrument with ease, and their family jam sessions planted a seed of music in her heart.

By the mid-'80s, she was the proud owner of her own Walkman, and for the first time, at the push of a button, she could wield music from her bygone years. Her cassette collection ballooned. She would slip her headphones on, along with her short shorts, and bop around, singing off-key while doing the dishes and picking up the house. She had a lovely singing voice, but with the volume cranked up, it was hard to interpret as anything but tone-deaf, much to our mortification when we had friends over. But company never deterred her concerts."

What I see: The Walkman that Heather's mom cherished was "so her," but I also see a souvenir of a bygone time. Her mother's eventual multiple sclerosis diagnosis and multiple falls lead to significant cognitive and physical decline, limiting her mobility. I also see in the beloved Walkman that Heather describes a souvenir of a sweet period when her mom was young, happy, and active.

ARTIFACT

Some objects are artifacts, relics from another time that we uncover as we go through a loved one's home or that surface after someone dies. We examine them with fascination, an item of great archaeological or historical significance. For example, my mom's address book is a microcosm of her life, a time capsule of her priorities.

These artifacts can also be long forgotten but instantly familiar pieces that transport us back to another time. Like my mom's favorite Benetton T-shirt from the 1980s. Or the VHS tape of a movie your family often watched on the weekend.

Sometimes these artifacts are curiosities, sparking more questions. Like an archaeologist on a dig, you might excavate a remnant, a shard of pottery or a piece of fabric that's like a puzzle piece. You might say: *What is this? Why do they have it? What did it mean to them? Is it significant?*

Though you might feel like an archaeologist as you dig through belongings and memories, a curator and archaeologist do different things! See chapter 29 for more about the distinction.

HEIRLOOM

Sometimes objects are heirlooms. Meaningful possessions that your family passes down through generations or relatives.

My grandmother's vase. A blue and white porcelain sugar bowl from a set my mother bought in Beijing, China, when I was a toddler. (I don't know why it was so important to her, or why she carried it back and forth across multiple international and cross-country moves. But she did.)

For author Claire Bidwell Smith, it's a coffee table:

The Coffee Table
Marble
Contributed by Claire Bidwell Smith, 2023
In memory of her parents

2023.CA.CBS.1

"Of all the belongings my parents left, a heavy, marble coffee table is one of my most beloved objects. My parents bought this table in Oaxaca in the '80s, and it was a part of every living room in every house I grew up in. I've been carting it around for over two decades myself.

It's been across the country more than twice. It's almost always surrounded by friends and covered in books, toys, and cheese plates. I have found each of my children sitting on top of it shortly after they learned to pull themselves to standing.

I love that this table will be as much a part of my children's lives as it was mine, and I can't imagine that my parents ever imagined their grandchildren playing on it when they bought it. But wherever they are, I bet they're glad."

TALISMAN

Some objects are Talismans, helping us to feel protected, comforted, and connected to our loved ones. After my mom died, I hoarded her cashmere sweaters, and I still feel so cozy and loved when I wear them.

Even the concept of my mom and her love can be a talisman. When I was little and scared of the dark, I would say to myself, "My mom loves me, so I will be OK." I said it for the comfort and courage it gave me. And I still do, sometimes.

When I met Lindsey Whissel Fenton, creator of Speaking Grief and Learning Grief, hearing about her "Love Talisman" made a big impression on me:

"I've often described my first dog Birch as the love of my life. As someone who did not grow up with pets, I was astounded by the intensity of the bond I shared with that little seven-pounder. Her death was sudden and devastating. I will never forget how my apartment felt when I came home from saying goodbye to her: empty and silent.

I didn't know how I was going to feel about the presence of her belongings. I knew several people who had immediately boxed up their pet's things because seeing them was too painful. It was the opposite for me. I found great comfort in any physical reminder of Birch that I could get my hands on. I dumped all her sweaters and costumes (she had quite an extensive wardrobe) onto the bed and burrowed into them. I wrapped myself in the blankie my now ex-husband and I had given her for Christmas. I wore her collar on my wrist.

When I got her ashes back from the vet, it was initially heart-breaking, but soon that gritty gray dust became my biggest source of comfort. I slept clutching that wooden box to my chest. I carried it around the apartment with me. I touched it constantly. I hated when I had to go out and couldn't take it with me.

Eventually, I had an idea of how I could keep her with me all the time. I went on Etsy and bought an urn necklace. Now, when my grief gets loud and my missing her feels unbearable, I rub my fingers over the smooth gold disc that contains some of the precious pieces of my little Birch and it helps to ground me.

One day, I decided to add some ashes of both of my grandmothers to the vial. When Piko, my friend's smooshy orange kitty who did the impossible and turned me into a "cat person" died, I added some of his fur as well. I've begun to refer to this necklace as my love talisman. While no object can ever replace the physical touch of a special soul, I am grateful that this simple accessory has given me a literal touchstone to so much love."

In my experience, the relationship individuals have with the belongings and objects often reflects their relationship with grief and death in general, as well as their relationship with the deceased. Lindsey has a much higher comfort level with death and grief than many people do.

Fun Fact: Talismans can also serve as transitional objects after a big loss and during times of change. The term *transitional object* was coined by British psychoanalyst Donald Winnicott in the 1950s to refer to soothing objects like blankies and stuffed animals that can help comfort a child when separated from a primary caregiver or making a big transition. As grievers, we are experiencing many big transitions too!

ANCHOR

As we noted in chapter 19, sometimes objects are anchors. Anchoring you to the person, anchoring stories and memories to your mind. Sometimes it's an anchor that helps grievers to feel close or connected, what is often called a "linking object." Sometimes the meaningful object helps an individual to feel grounded and secure, like an anchor for a boat.

A good question to ask: *What kind of anchor is this?* You don't need to decide right now, but at some point, it can be helpful to consider this perspective. Go to chapter 24 for more about when an anchor keeps us stuck.

CREATIVE EXERCISE

As you sort through the belongings and consider the meaningful objects, I encourage you to consider what role the items play in your life. Turn toward them with curiosity—similar to the way you might look at objects on display in a museum—and wonder about the roles they played in your loved one's life.

Choose one to start. Imagine a meaningful object in front of you as if it's been impeccably placed on a pedestal in a gallery:

- What role does this object play? For you or other people?
- What might it be evidence of?
- Is it a souvenir of a person or place?
- Is it a talisman? How does it make you feel?
- Is it an heirloom or an artifact?
- What does it represent to you?

———

TIP: Here is a helpful phrase when people don't understand why the object is important to you and what role it plays in your life: **You don't understand it, and that's OK. Please respect it anyway.**

The fact that an object is important to you makes it worthy of respect. Feel inexplicably attached to a T-shirt, a pair of socks, or a mug? It's almost certainly playing a role in your life or your grief. That role may change over time and as your grief evolves. Let's see, witness, and honor those object roles.

In the next chapter, we'll dive deeper into the role of objects as Evidence because it's such a potent category.

CHAPTER 23
CATEGORY: OBJECTS AS EVIDENCE

What do we leave behind? Bodies and belongings. Memories and mementos. Evidence of who we were. Evidence of What Happened.

Sometimes objects serve as potential evidence of what happened. As I shared earlier, immediately after my mother died, one of the ways I saw the objects in her home was as if they were pieces of forensic evidence from a crime scene.

Because my mother died suddenly and unexpectedly, I never saw her sick. I never saw her body before she was cremated. She was just gone—as if she'd been spirited away or abducted by aliens.

By the time I got to her house after flying in from London, my aunt had already done some cleanup and tidying. Still, I walked through my mother's house, taking photos with my Canon digital camera. (It was 2013.) I took photos of her bedroom and the objects in her home. It felt like I was capturing all the evidence with crime scene photos.

Because it felt like a crime *had* occurred.

I'd gotten the call. They told me she'd been found on the floor of her bedroom. And that's all I knew. I didn't know what happened. None of us knew.

Like an investigator who studied the scene of an accident or crime, dropping little plastic tents with numbers on them next to a skid mark on the road or a bullet on the floor, I studied the details and objects in my mother's home, and I documented them.

Gathering evidence: Her socks on the floor. Notes on scraps of paper. Food in her refrigerator. What was that evidence of?

In those earliest days, I didn't want to discard or even move anything. It was all potential evidence! As far as I was concerned, my mother had vanished, and I moved and snapped photos with urgency, as if the answers to the question of what happened might also disappear.

Over the weeks and months that followed, we gathered more information. More evidence. Through the paper day planner in her purse. The monthly calendar on her kitchen table. Receipts in her wallet. Voice messages on her answering machine. Conversations with friends and family.

I pieced together her final days. Yes, just like a crime investigation. I read the autopsy report. I spoke to her doctor. We learned she died from a stroke and likely had died immediately —for which I was grateful.

OUR RELATIONSHIP WITH OBJECTS CAN CHANGE

Those first photos that I took of my mother's belongings were not pretty. There was no intentional artistry nor beauty to them.

I didn't want to revisit them. But over time, I decided that I wanted to document her belongings in a beautiful way. I commissioned a photographer in Lisbon to take photos of a selection of my mother's belongings, like her lipsticks, favorite jewelry, and hair clips. The photographer I chose specialized in shooting beauty products for Instagram. I wanted my mother's special items to look attractive and gussied up—like the Glamour Shots offered at malls in the 1980s.

That difference in how they were photographed and presented by the product photographer's photos represented the change in what kind of evidence my mom's belongings are now for me. They are no longer evidence of a crime having happened, of the terrible thing that took place. They have become evidence of how she lived.

Her lipsticks and her jewelry are evidence of how she liked to dress up now and then, even though in her day-to-day she didn't wear makeup. She wore a certain shade of lipstick. She had a favorite rhinestone pin she would wear on the lapel of her jacket at company events. Her hair clips and combs were always tortoise shell-patterned. I think she associated the pattern with being classy.

I'm reminded of how she had very fine, slippery Asian hair, so it was hard for her to keep a clip in there. She and I had that in common. She had a whole assortment of clips. I look at them now and remember how she often had wisps of hair around her face and how she would wear her hair when I was growing up, like wings over her ears.

———

GOOD QUESTIONS

What are the meaningful objects potentially evidence of?

What answers are you seeking?

Is it proof you're looking for? Proof of what?

What would be different for you if you found that proof?

———

EVIDENCE OF OUR RELATIONSHIP

Some objects and belongings become evidence of the relationship we had with our person who has died.

One of the last things I threw away was my mother's toothbrush and the ceramic cup it was in. It lived on her bathroom sink. But it wasn't just any ceramic cup—it was a ceramic yogurt cup, earthenware with a matte lavender glaze, that she'd brought back from London when she visited us.

In our home in East London, we had dozens of these ceramic yogurt cups. Holding pens, holding plants, and sometimes just filled with potential. My mom was very charmed by them, and asked if she could take one back with her.

When I saw her toothbrush in the ceramic cup on her bathroom sink in New York, I was so touched. It meant that every night and every morning, when she brushed her teeth, that yogurt cup was there. A reminder of her trip. A reminder of me.

I also felt guilty because I'd been impatient with her on that trip. It was right in the middle of a design festival, and as usual, I had overscheduled myself. *Why hadn't I been more patient? Didn't I know she'd die just a couple of years later?* (Actually, I didn't know.)

The meaningful objects can be evidence of the relationship we had—or wish we'd had. Notice how the yogurt cup with my mom's toothbrush in it brought up fond memories *and* difficult emotions. I felt the guilt of being impatient with her for years. I wrestled with the story that I had been a bad daughter. There were plenty of objects that I could interpret as evidence to support my belief that I had been a bad daughter. As if I was on trial and standing accused, and evidence was being presented against me.

But, ultimately, I let go of that belief and that interpretation.

———

GOOD QUESTIONS

Are some belongings evidence of the relationship you had? The good parts? The bad parts?

Are you using any objects as evidence against yourself? Evidence of what?

———

EVIDENCE OF MY MOTHER

At my first exhibition with my mother's belongings, I had an installation called "Evidence of My Mother.' Each item had its own little display pedestal, and a number. I look back now at my notes in preparation for that exhibition in October 2015, and see that I had jotted down what each item represented. The list of evidence included:

1. Mini perfume bottles — Sophistication, admiration for French things, worldly and Western.
2. Pill box for travel in mini tin — Both a collector of cute containers and a health conscious consumer of daily vitamins.
3. Hewlett-Packard work badges — So proud of her work, working her way up from temp to valued permanent employee at HP Labs, to taking early retirement. Part of her American Dream.
4. Passports and travel tags — She was a traveler, always curious.
5. Paper 9J tickets — From visiting *Yee Pau*. The good niece. Connection to older generation, she spoke their dialect.
6. Lipsticks — Always similar shades. Special occasions marked by application of lipstick. Smelling them when nauseous in parking garage, not sure how effective!
7. Misspelled grief label — Organized. Not a great speller. Studying to be a social worker, had MFT degree. Actually read the grief articles she clipped.
8. Postage stamps for reuse — Frugal, well-intentioned. Holding on to old ways, though could spend.

9. *Kuo Feng* business cards — Exciting time. First real job. Colleagues and friends who kept in touch and pursued their American Dreams. Bank officers, government officials, university professors, authors.
10. Sewing kits from hotels — Practical. Cautious. Potential hoarder.
11. PanAm soap and United fork and glass salt shakers — I come from a long line of purloiners of travel things. A traveling, exploring family. Hold down the fork.
12. Large pin from the laundry — Lee's family laundry. How they spent their afternoons when young, resentment sometimes. Chinese-American experience, many limited to laundries and restaurants. How family achieved American Dream, from parents sleeping in back of laundry to buying a home in Queens with cars and holidays.
13. Small, cute things — Hello Kitty figures, keychain.
14. Illegible labels and writing — Scrawls on paper everywhere. Notes we could barely read. But always conveying something helpful or heartfelt. She wanted to write a book about her life and our family.
15. Blue and white sugar bowl — That pattern, same as photo from Beijing.
16. Name chop — So many names. Chinese names and English names that she couldn't really pronounce. Variations and combinations.
17. Graduation tassel — Education. Once a source of shame, now of pride. Her resolve. Her blossoming in the last decade of her life. Kept it with mine from my UC Berkeley graduation.
18. Eiffel Tower souvenir — She loved Paris. Last email was about Paris.
19. Statue of Liberty souvenir — Mom a proud New Yorker. Photo of her by Manhattan Bridge.
20. HK acrylic block — Birthplace. Spiritual home of Chinese-Americans. Travel agent days.

21. Mütter Pass — Doctor checks in West Germany. Baby photo of me. My German grandmother "Flau Weiss." Only later did I realize she meant *Frau Weiss.*
22. Ankle X-ray — Weak ankle. Blamed on cycling mishap in Beijing. Bones. Hard evidence.
23. Brooch, turquoise rhinestones — Photo of her at HP event with it pinned to her suit
24. File folder labeled "scarves" — With clippings about how to wear scarves in different ways.
25. Receipt from her last day, change in her purse — She didn't know it was coming. She was active and healthy and socializing. She'd had lunch with her brother, tea with a friend, gone shopping for groceries.

With each of these featured objects, I was painting a picture of my mother for the exhibition's visitors. To me, they were all evidence of how she was:

Funny
Sentimental
Smart
Kind-hearted
Curious
Generous
Adventurous

How my mom had been when she was alive and thriving—that's how I wanted to remember her and how I wanted her to be remembered.

PART SIX
CURATE: CURATING FOR CLEARING OUT AND MAKING SPACE

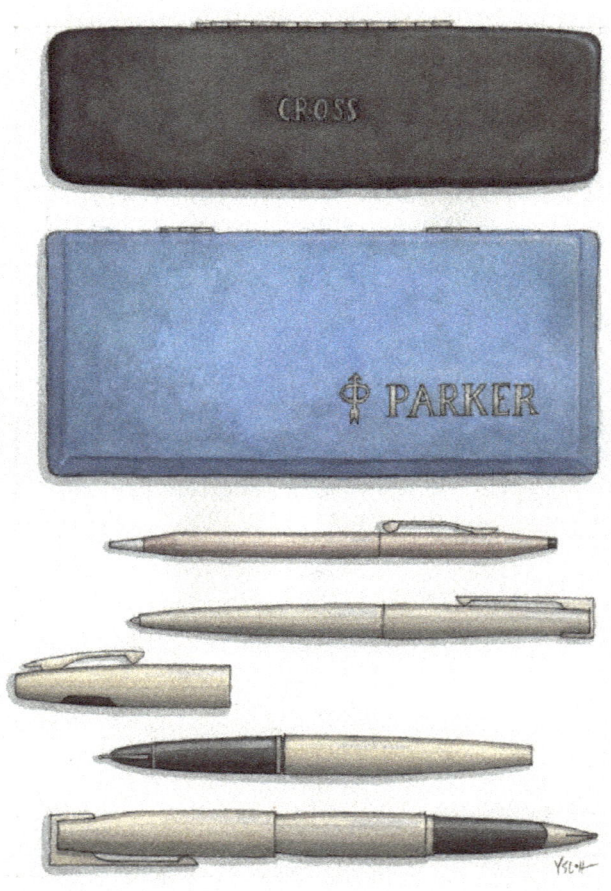

His Collection of Pens

CHAPTER 24

ANCHORING AND UNANCHORING: WHEN IS IT TIME TO LET GO?

I remember the exact moment I *knew* I had to let the house go. I was in my mom's house, and I was cold. It was always cold. Wearing one of my mom's many fleece jackets, a scarf, and fuzzy slippers, I shuffled down the hallway. *Surely, it doesn't make sense to keep a house that's so hard to heat,* my brain reasoned. In the five years my mom lived in the house, it had always been too chilly for comfort. Shoes aren't worn indoors in Asian households but going barefoot or even just with socks was unbearable. She kept a basket of slippers by the door and issued us a pair upon entry. That day I was wearing the fur-lined slippers she'd bought when she visited Russia.

For a year, I'd flown back and forth between London and New York. My husband stayed in the UK, ostensibly for work. But really because he couldn't reach me where grief had taken me. There was much more than an ocean between us.

My husband didn't understand why I needed to look at everything. "Why don't you just turn over all the contents to an estate liquidator?" he suggested, oh so helpfully.

No! This was my mom's house. It was my responsibility.

I had to sift, I had to sort. My mom's things were here. All that I had left of her. Sometimes it felt like *she* was here.

I padded into the sunroom, with its many windows overlooking the lake and the surrounding woods. By day, we had views of the trees, water, and swans. By night, the windows were black rectangles. Impenetrable darkness, though there was a neighbor's house just yards away.

From a table, I picked up a tchotchke from her trip to Brazil and paused, remembering the barbecue my mom had held the summer of 2008. Family had gathered on the patio. My aunt had bought my mom a huge, fancy grill. It was before the massive house extension project. Little did we know my mom would be dead in just a few short years.

With the souvenir from Rio still in my hand, I flopped down on the L-shaped white leather sofa my mom was so proud of, to eat my dinner in front of the TV. Beside me, a pile of paperwork. Another mortgage bill to pay. Another utility bill.

The math had made sense to me, at first. If I rushed to sell her house, I might save money on mortgage payments, but the future therapy bills would cost me even more. It was making less sense as time passed, as I processed the initial shock and as bank balances dwindled.

But this was my mom's dream house . . . a voice inside me said plaintively. *How can I let it go?*

I sighed, and prepared to bring my dishes back to the kitchen. My plan: I would walk quickly down the hall, past my mother's bedroom. Now locked because it was nighttime. During the day, I could go in there. I could stare at her clothes, only partially pared down. I could linger over the photos on her bookshelves. Sunlight would stream in, landing in dappled patterns on the light green paint I'd helped her select.

But once it got dark, I locked the door. Scurried past it. She had died in that room. Her ashes were kept in there. *What if she haunted it?* I couldn't bear the thought. And I certainly couldn't bear seeing anything inexplicable.

I got up from the sofa and headed toward the doorway of the sunroom. And caught sight of a figure. I stopped, startled.

Dark hair
Dark eyes
Light robe

The house *was* haunted . . . by me.

That was me, reflected in the sunroom's darkened windows. In my mom's clothes, rambling around her empty house. Shuffling to and fro in a space I didn't have much reason for being in anymore.

It was her dream house, not mine. Her life, not mine.

My life was waiting for me, back across the ocean.

I nodded at the reflection. She nodded back.

I got the message.

It was time to go.

ADRIFT

During that first year of flying back and forth across the Atlantic, burning through savings, airline miles, and my husband's patience, I traveled with my mother's purse slung across my chest, on top of my purse. In her purse was her wallet and her death certificate.

(Why was I carrying her death certificate? I think, on some level, I thought I would need to prove to someone that she was really dead. Looking back, I think I was the one who didn't fully grasp that she was really gone. That she was not coming back to that dream house. I was like a lost child waiting for Mommy to come back to help me.)

During this terrible time of feeling adrift, I found an anchor in my mom's house. It was my safe place. I could cry or not cry, be sad, be angry, be confused. Just be!

What my mother had imagined as her dream home, where she'd enjoy her last decades, became my safe cocoon. Looking back, it was yet another way she always took care of me.

Surrounded by green leaves in the spring and clean white snow in the winter, I made time to be with grief. As I sorted through her belongings, I sorted through my emotions and memories. I was also figuring out a different way to relate to my mother.

I wasn't making much progress with the physical stuff, but at least I felt cushioned and cared for in her house.

A TURNING POINT: FEELING WEIGHED DOWN

After a while, there was a shift. I began to feel the weight of being anchored to my mother's house. I had been paying the mortgage on the house for over a year. And everything started to feel heavy.

I had a recurring vision of me tethered to the house, and it was pulling me down to the bottom of the ocean. I had a vision of myself stretching, gasping for air, reaching for light, and getting dragged down all the way into the darkness. I felt like I was drowning.

That's the funny thing about anchors. On the one hand, an anchor can keep you safe and stable, keep you from drifting out into the open ocean, keep you from getting dashed to pieces on the rocks.

And an anchor can keep you stuck. Stuck in one place for too long, not moving forward. And that's where I was: I was stuck. Stuck in my dead mother's unoccupied house, far from my home, my husband, my work, my life.

WHAT KIND OF ANCHORS

If you're considering whether you should keep a home or an object, ask yourself: What kind of anchor is this? Is it an anchor that helps you feel secure, safe, and connected, or is it an anchor that makes you feel stuck—dragging you down and holding you back from something else you want to pursue?

Sometimes we hold on to anchors because they help us to stay connected. In chapter 22, we talked about the different roles that meaningful objects can play for us. I've had audience members at my talks say they held onto everything, like all the medication and the hospital bed because they were evidence of what happened. This was a very real part of their grief and loss story, and sometimes we want those objects as anchors that help us to feel connected to our loved one, or as evidence of what we went through, at least for a period of time.

––––––

GOOD QUESTIONS

What are you holding onto?

What do you need now? What did you need then?

What kind of anchor is it for you: Is it keeping you stable or is it keeping you stuck?

Is it a helpful anchor or is it an unhelpful anchor now?

––––––

DO YOU WANT A MUSEUM?

If I had all the money and resources in the world, I might have kept my mom's house forever. I might have turned it into a museum, preserving all her belongings as is, and maybe visited in the summer as my art studio and retreat. But I couldn't afford to do that.

I'm not alone in having that impulse. My client Deborah considered doing the same with her childhood home in Austin after her parents died. Her teenage bedroom, in particular, was a wonderful living portrait of a special time in her life.

When I asked her what it represented, she said, "My bedroom is a literal time capsule, but it also represents an innocence both in my life and in the greater context of society. My bedroom represents the infinite possibilities that the future could bring (for any child), the backdrop for the imaginings of what you envision the future might be like, offering a protected space from the unexpected pain of reality.

If my bedroom walls could talk, they would recall laughter, endless gossip about classmates and teachers, the master-minding of countless plans to get a crush to notice you, and the hysterical melodramatic role-plays if improbably they *did* talk to you. Fashion shows, scrutinizing yearbook photos, makeup tips, getting ready for dances. My mom patiently watching me pack (or unpack) while reclined on my twin bed. My bedroom represents a connection to my childhood and home—and my parents —when they were here, while they were dying, and now after they are gone."

Ultimately, Deborah had a novel solution: She hired a company to shoot a 3D video of the house, paying special attention to her bedroom. She can take a virtual tour of the house whenever she wants, lying in her bed and looking up at all the posters surrounding her. Today, she is carefully preserving the collages and posters on her bedroom walls to potentially recreate them in another space or to use them in another artistic way.

HOUSE MUSEUM

Some houses *do* get preserved as museums. For instance, the Frida Kahlo Museum in Mexico City, the Blue House we discussed in chapter 10, occupies the home where she once lived. When I visited, I marveled at her paints and brushes beautifully arranged in her studio space—not necessarily preserved exactly as she'd left them, but artfully arranged in a recreation of how it might have looked, as there was a clear intention for the home to eventually become a public museum and gallery.

The museum website sets the stage for visitors this way:

"The Casa Azul (Blue House) is Frida Kahlo's private universe. She spent most of her life here, first with her family and, years later, at Diego Rivera's side. They hosted a fascinating array of luminaries from Mexico and abroad, drawn by the charisma of both artists.

Frida and Diego wanted to leave her house as a museum for all Mexicans to enjoy. At her death, the couple's friend, museographer and poet Carlos Pellicer, did the exhibition design. Its administration was assigned to a trust, the Fideicomiso de los Museos Diego Rivera y Frida Kahlo, under the central bank, Banco de México, and constituted by Rivera himself in 1957.

Since its inauguration in July 1958, the Casa Azul and its gardens have displayed personal objects and paintings by both artists, folk art, Pre-Columbian sculpture, photos, documents, books, and furnishings that were part of the ambience where Frida was inspired to create."

Another favorite museum of mine is the Noguchi Museum in Astoria, Queens. This building was originally the studio space of the Japanese-American sculptor Isamu Noguchi. In his lifetime, he decided to turn it into a museum, preserving some of his studio space and showcasing many of his sculptures and processes.

Other examples of house museums and studio museums include American industrial designer Russel Wright's home and studio, Manitoga, in Garrison, New York. Or Spanish artist Joan Miró's Sert Studio on the island of Mallorca, which is on my must-visit list, as I've only experienced a variation of it as a traveling exhibition in London. I can only imagine the level of documentation and care it takes to faithfully preserve and recreate these spaces!

For instance, the Margaret Olley Art Centre (MOAC) features a recreation of the home studio of its namesake, Margaret Olley, "Australia's most celebrated painter of still life and interiors," as the website proclaims. "The recreation features original architectural elements such as windows and doors, relocated from Olley's home studio at 48 Duxford Street, Paddington, Sydney. The interiors are filled with over 20,000 items that Olley collected over many years as subject matter for her paintings."

I asked the museum pros on Reddit how they would have recorded and preserved a space with so many objects, and they explained that methodically and with great attention to detail, the museum's teams would have mapped every square inch of the artist's studio, down to each individual cigarette butt!

That's amazing! was my first thought, with the same wonder I felt when I took my first field trips to the Metropolitan Museum of Art and the Fraunces Tavern Museum in New York as a child. My second thought: *That is* so *much work!*

So, I'll gently turn the questions back to you: Do you actually *want* a museum? Do you want to do that much work? Do you have the resources to maintain or recreate their home, or to preserve *all* the things?

I had the desire to keep my mom's home and all her belongings. I had the impulse to keep it preserved as a museum. But I didn't have the resources, and eventually, I no longer had the desire.

Here's what I did do: At my design residency in Toronto in January 2022, I displayed the blueprints from my mom's dream house. I jotted down my reflections too:

Once a house of dreams
Now a museum
. . . or a mausoleum?

I am glad I unanchored from my mom's house.

BACK TO LIFE

In my bedroom, on what I consider my mom's shelf, there is a beautiful ceramic sculpture by Japanese artist Midori Takaki. The name of the piece, a pale-faced female figure with staring eyes, is *The Last Journey*. Perched on her head is the boat that carries souls across the River Styx. When I visited Midori at her studio in Cambridge, England, and spotted the sculpture, I knew I had to have it.

When I visualize my work with grief, I often imagine individual grievers standing on the banks of the River Styx, peering out into the fog toward where they last saw their loved one. Their person is gone, their soul ferried to the land of the dead, according to Greek Mythology, by Charon. As a grief guide, I now see my role as gently walking alongside grievers to help them return to the land of the living—to their own lives.

When I finally unanchored from my mom's house, it was like I'd been standing on the banks of the River Styx for so long that my own home, health, and livelihood—"livelihood" in the monetary sense of the word—were crumbling away from neglect. My mom was never going to physically occupy her dream house again, and I'd been wasting away tending to it—trapped in one spot, her belongings scattered on the ground all around me. By unanchoring, I chose my own livelihood in a different and now expanded sense: my own fullest, most vibrant life.

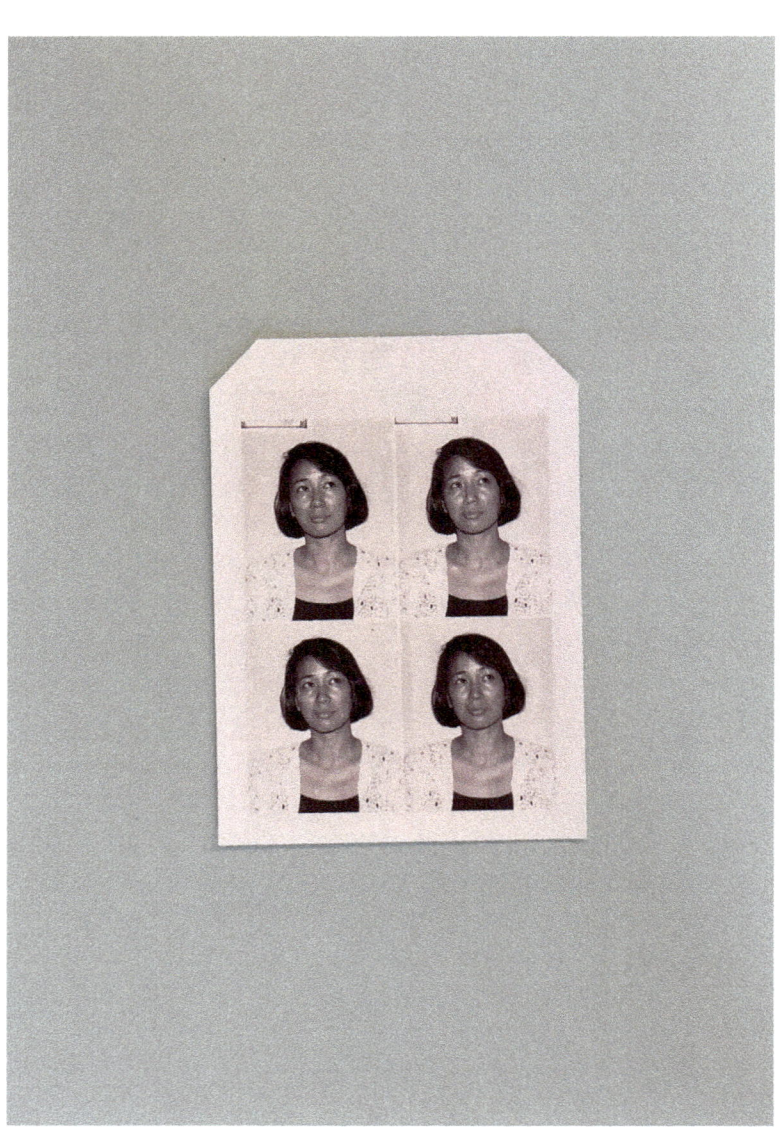

CHAPTER 25
HOW TO CHOOSE: START WITH WHAT'S IMPORTANT

Eight months before my mother died, we posed together in a photo booth. We were at my cousin Conroy's wedding reception (which was, of course, at a Chinese restaurant).

We all had so much fun in that photo booth, playing around in different combinations: Me and my cousin Eva, with my aunt and my mom, making funny faces. My husband and I, sharing a kiss. My mom on her own, trying different poses. My mom and me, our heads tilted toward each other.

I treasure these photos and study them often: The background was red, as fitting for a Chinese wedding. My mom wears a black dress with white dots, with an aqua chiffon wrap around her shoulders. I'm wearing a fuchsia pink dress from J Crew, with a white crocheted cardigan as a cover up. I had borrowed this white crochet top from my mother, not for the first time.

I track the crocheted top through more photos:

A high school photo of me, with a textured gray backdrop. I'm wearing silver earrings—the pair my mom gave me and called "the good-looking earrings." Sometimes she would borrow them back for special occasions. I still remember how disappointed she looked when I later lost one of those earrings in the park by our house. She kept the remaining single earring in a box. I don't remember if she ever told me where the earrings were from. I still have the widowed earring.

I also find photos of my mother in the crochet top. Young, with short hair in a black and white passport photo. (I have no idea where she got the top or why it was her favorite. Yet another thing I should have asked.)

I do remember how every time I would ask to borrow the top, my mom would excitedly, joyfully prepare it for me. "I've cleaned it," she'd say. "I bleached it, so it's ready for you." (Yes, bleach. My mom was a 1980s mom, not a textile conservator!)

PILES OF STUFF

My mother had sacks and stacks of clothing in her closets. She loved to shop! They were a burden to me as the estate executor, but as a daughter, I took comfort in knowing that in her last years, she had achieved a financial comfort level that meant she could afford to shop as a hobby.

Some of her clothes were just plain T-shirts from Gap. Those were easier for me to donate to Goodwill. Other pieces were harder to let go of, like her favorite dresses. Or sweatshirts from the 1980s that I see in photos from our family vacations, reminders of a happier time.

My mom in a baggy sweatshirt in front of Devils Tower National Monument in Wyoming. That favorite yellow Benetton T-shirt. The suit jacket with big shoulder pads that she wore to my high school graduation.

THE PROBLEM WITH CONVENTIONAL WISDOM

A lot of the conventional advice about organizing starts with getting rid of things. Designate big bins for what you can donate, recycle, or trash, they advise.

But I found that to be an impossible task when my Mom died, and I had to clear out her house. Letting anything go felt like letting her go.

CURATING PUTS THE FOCUS ON WHAT'S IMPORTANT

By curating—by asking ourselves, what would we choose if we were to curate an exhibition about our person?—we reverse the approach. We ask ourselves:

What do I want keep?
What do I want to elevate?
What can I identify as truly important?

Answering these questions helped me to elevate some items to VIP status. It made it easier for me to say, *OK, I don't need to keep **all** of my mother's T-shirts.*

Because I had already identified other pieces as important:

- The Italian wool suit she saved up to buy as a teenager.
- That crocheted top she let me borrow for my cousin's wedding.
- The silk and satin cheongsam (traditional Chinese dresses) that belonged to my mom and grandmother.

Because I'd already designated some items as *most* significant, I realized I didn't need to keep *all* of the things that had *any* significance.

THE CROCHET TOP NOW

These days, the white crochet top lives on a shelf in my bedroom. It's one of the few pieces of clothing I still have from my mother's house.

Last year, I wore it in Los Angeles during one of The Grief Gallery's pop-up exhibitions and when I spoke on a panel about grief and creativity. I don't think I even told anyone the significance of the top. But it was meaningful to me. I loved being able to wear my mom's top in those moments, the top she treasured so much that she kept it for decades.

Our relationship wasn't perfect. I still wish I could have been a better daughter. She wasn't my best friend, the way I've heard other people describe their mothers. But the top is a reminder of the bond that we *did* have.

When I asked myself: *Which of my mother's clothing pieces, out of all these sacks of off-season garments, out of all these stacks of clothing, was most important?*, it was the white crochet top that immediately surfaced as an answer, rising in my mind's eye above the piles of dresses and T-shirts. I mentally placed it on a gallery plinth, reflecting its elevated status.

Having chosen it and recognized its importance, it made it easier for me to let go of most everything else.

SHEDDING IN LAYERS — "MAYBE I'LL WEAR IT"

You know how experts say that a good strategy for packing for travel and planning for inclement weather is to wear layers? You may need to shed the possessions in layers, too, if you have the luxury of taking the time. "Maybe I'll wear it," was a category I assigned to my mother's clothes. Never mind that we were very different sizes and body types. (My mom was relatively tall for a Chinese lady, all of five feet, five inches.)

Maybe I'll get pregnant, and I can wear these dresses she bought at Ross Dress for Less as maternity outfits, I thought hopefully. (Never mind that these loudly patterned dresses were not my style at all, and they still had their bright red clearance tags on them, indicating my mom had never actually worn them.) I tucked the garments away in rubber bins before eventually shedding them during the big storage unit clear-out years later. Looking back, I needed to hold on to them and that hope for a while before letting them go.

———

GOOD QUESTIONS

Which items are most important? What would you grab in a fire or rescue after a flood?

What would you choose to include in a gallery about your person?

Which pieces might you feel ready to shed? Which items do you need to hold onto for now?

———

OPP: OTHER PEOPLE'S PROCESSES

After I went through my mom's closet and picked out what was most meaningful to me, I invited my aunt to pick out what she wanted to keep. She brought black trash bags and cleared the entire top shelf into the sacks with a sweep of her arm.

I was startled, and my compulsion at the time was to be upset: *Why couldn't she be more selective? Isn't it disrespectful to dump all the clothes into trash bags?*

Then I accessed compassion: She had lost her big sister. Just like I had known my mom all my life, so had she. They had a close relationship, even with ups and downs over the years.

My aunt wore my mom's fleece tops for years afterward. Maybe she also needed to shed in layers.

CLARITY CAN COME FROM ACTION

What if you can't tell what's important, because *everything* feels important? What if you feel the need to look at each individual item? I'm not going to try to convince you to do otherwise!

You might find it helpful to just start sorting and categorizing. You can even record each item in a spreadsheet, or in a notebook, so you have a catalog. Or place each document in a protective sleeve, like an archivist. This process can itself be clarifying.

My client Caroline's husband kept the boarding passes from every trip he made, from business trips to vacations. At first, she found it difficult to even consider letting any of them go. We explored the idea of making a display of them for her family, which meant looking through them. The first boarding pass she took out of the box elicited an immediate laugh: A trip to Indonesia for their anniversary during which a monkey stole his prescription glasses. But as she continued looking, she quickly realized not every piece of paper elicited such potent emotions. "This doesn't have any meaning to me," she said, squinting at a faded handwritten ticket. Yes, the boarding passes were meaningful for her husband. They helped to tell a story about his life and their lives together. *And* not every boarding pass is needed to tell that story.

A hierarchy gradually emerges.

I'm reminded of when I helped my friend Maren to catalog a private collection of art prints. As an art registrar, her role is to document and track all the pieces in a collection. At first, it was fun, but by the time we documented the fiftieth individual, identical print from an edition of 100, it grew tedious. Her eyes were bleary from squinting at penciled artist signatures, and my spreadsheet was monotone with repetitive rows of information. (I still remember her lamenting, "My eyes!")

Not everything is actually, equally important. You can certainly start by picking up each individual object if you want! Thinking in categories can be helpful too. Sure, I fixated on the bottle of soy sauce in my mom's kitchen at first, but I eventually placed it in the category of "my mom's cooking sauces and oils" —which I finally discarded. I didn't need to weep over the sesame seed oil as well in order to honor the role these objects played in my mom's life and in my memories of her.

CHAPTER 26
STORAGE UNIT CONFESSIONS: THE COST OF KEEPING AND LETTING GO

Confession: I spent over $20,000 on storage units in the ten years after my mom died. She died in January 2013. I sold her house in September 2014 and got the first storage unit at that time. I didn't plan on having a storage unit, but it soon became clear that I didn't have resources, namely time and emotional capacity, to sort through and make decisions about everything in her house.

In January 2022, I downsized from the original storage unit to the smallest size they had. Again, I didn't plan on keeping a storage unit, but it became clear that I still didn't have the time or emotional resources to discard everything that remained.

If you still have stuff in storage, whether it's a rental unit or boxes in your attic, you are not alone.

And you don't have to be ashamed.

Validating our experiences as grievers is such an important element of caring for ourselves. You're not crazy. It's totally normal to feel like you can't take this step that *seems* logical. When I shared my storage unit confession with my grief colleagues, I was so relieved to hear echoes of my own story in their responses. A grief therapist I admired a lot shared that she still had a storage unit as well, with belongings from her mother and grandmother.

A hospice worker said, "Oh yeah, my equivalent is the attic.

There are boxes there that are haunting me." A fellow grief coach affirmed, "Yup, my mom's things are in the basement, and every time I walk by them, I shudder."

Hearing their experiences, I felt less ashamed. If grief experts, therapists, and colleagues I respect so much had their own "stuff" in storage, maybe I wasn't deficient or weak either! I was not alone. You are not alone.

We first met grief therapist Litsa Williams, co-founder of What's Your Grief, in chapter 16, where I shared our candid conversation about our storage units. Like me, she didn't have enough emotional and mental capacity to sort through all the belongings after selling her mother's house. Like me, she got a storage unit and then eventually downsized to the smallest size, shedding stuff in layers and iterations.

We both employed various filters:

- What are the things I'm not ready to part with now?
- What might I want to have in my home, or what might someone in my family want?
- What had meaning for them—my loved one?
- What has meaning for me?
- What might I feel ready to look at now?

Litsa advises checking in with ourselves regularly, to see if our capacity has changed. It's an approach she's taken with her own storage unit: "I tend to do a little look around and see what I can part with that I couldn't part with before. It's helpful for me because it reminds me that I'm in a different place now."

It's a phenomenon I've seen at The Grief Gallery's in-person exhibitions and online gatherings as well. The ongoing invitation to share a meaningful object gives grievers an opportunity to check in with themselves and their grief. A Zoom attendee who could only stay off camera and listen might find that, just a couple of months later, they feel up to sharing in the chat or even coming on camera to share an object and story about their loved one. A visitor may find that contemplating the belongings I've curated for an exhibition sparks for them the hope that they may also be able to see their person's possessions in a different way someday.

PAST VERSIONS AND VISIONS OF OURSELVES

Not surprisingly, I shed the contents of my storage unit through the lens of curating and exhibitions. By the start of 2022, I finally felt ready to look through some of those boxes that had been too painful to deal with—I was actually burning to let them go!

In chapter 27, I share more about the January 2022 exhibition I presented as part of a design residency in Toronto, Canada—including what I did with my mother's urn. I used the that exhibition as a creative brief for tackling the storage unit. That made it an artistic, poetic process—much gentler than telling myself: *Suck it up, Charlene, you've spent too much on this storage unit already. Now go tackle this grim task!*

Instead, I asked myself:

- Nine years after my mother died, what would I choose for an exhibition about her to present to the public in Toronto?
- What might I want to convey about my relationship with her now, and about my experience of grief (especially while we're still in the midst of a pandemic)?
- What do I feel ready to let go of now? What is from a past version or past vision of myself?

For example, the storage unit included boxes of my possessions, like dishes from our apartment in Chinatown, squirreled away for our move back to New York someday. But by then, my tastes and life had changed. I had plenty of beautiful plates in London, made by talented British ceramicists. I no longer needed my chunky white bowls from Crate and Barrel.

In the process of sorting through the storage unit's contents, I made an effort to acknowledge, honor, and say goodbye to past versions and visions of myself: The past version of me that couldn't look at the paperwork. A past vision of moving back to New York and using the same dishes.

I felt compassion for September 2014 Me, who couldn't face the most painful pieces: The divorce paperwork. The paperwork from the sale of my parents' house in California after their separation. In theory, all of it could have been either shredded or burnt. They technically no longer served a purpose. But back then, I just couldn't let them go. *What if I needed to refer back to them for some reason? It was legal paperwork, wasn't it? That's serious stuff.*

Beyond my anxiety about getting rid of legal documents, there were also more emotional meanings to the boxes of papers. The divorce and house sale paperwork represented what should have been—the perfect family life my mom had imagined. Had *deserved.*

I booked a room at a motel in the town that my mother had lived in. The motel's décor was outdated, complete with a pastel-tiled bathroom, but there was a view of trees and my room was spacious, with two queen beds. A family friend brought me boxes of Chinese noodles for breakfast, lunch, and dinner that his wife had made. My aunt brought me dim sum. My room had a microwave, and I treated myself to popcorn and snacks from my mom's favorite grocery store.

During the day, I made quick decisions about the many boxes of household items. I spent all my evening hours looking through the papers, making choices about whether I could let them go or not. *Mom, why did you keep so many bank records, boarding passes and documents?* I despaired. But I also accessed compassion and understood: As an immigrant, you never know when you might need to prove that you have the money, the right or the moral character to enter or stay in a country!

It was *so* hard. But I got through it.

Even in the fog of reactivated grief and the overwhelm of being surrounded by stacks of potential emotional landmines, it was interesting for 2022 Me to marvel at how far I'd come from 2014 Me. Back then, when I sold my mother's house, I couldn't even *look* at those boxes. It was all just too painful. My grief was too raw. I was already exhausted from the millions of decisions that went into selling her house and getting it ready.

You, too, may have the category labeled "too painful to deal with right now". *And* you may find your relationship with these items will change at some point. I hold the hope for you that you *will* be able to face them. I encourage you to keep checking in with yourself, to see what you feel more ready to handle.

Keeping the peace with partners and others . . . My husband did not come with me on these trips to the storage unit. He wasn't invited! For the sake of our marriage and our sanities, we decided to respect each other's very different relationships with *stuff*. What I needed for my mental wellness—spreading everything out in a hotel room, looking carefully—is exactly what would have sent him over the edge. Instead, we identified our respective strengths and weaknesses and planned accordingly.

See chapter 4 for more about our grief guides and getting the type and flavor of support we need.

THE COST OF AVOIDANCE

"I could teach funeral directors about grief," said the manager of the storage facility. It made sense. A storage unit typically only comes into someone's life during a time of transition. A move (voluntary or otherwise), the sale of a house, downsizing, a death. He has met people at the worst times in their lives.

On one of my visits, he told me the story of a longtime customer. The customer rented a large unit, one of the biggest sizes they had. And he wouldn't pay the monthly fee for the unit until it was at risk for seizure and auction. Then he would pay the whole amount due at once to hold on to the unit.

This continued for *fifteen* years. When the payments finally stopped, and the time came to open up the unit and assess it for auction, they found all the belongings from his parents. And a thick layer of dust. In 300 square feet of storage space, enough space to store furnishings from a two- or three-bedroom apartment or house, he had preserved the contents of his parents' home. Like a museum collection no one visited or saw. Or a full-scale doll house with no occupants.

How many times over the fifteen years had the customer thought, *Maybe this month, I'll clear it out. Make a decision. Make some choices. Start to let things go . . . start to let* them *go.*

What is the cost when we don't eventually make some hard choices? When we don't let go? There can be a monetary cost. In this customer's case, fifteen years of fees totaling over $60,000. And potentially fifteen years of monthly agony when the bill came due and then overdue.

When I told Litsa the story from the storage unit manager, she had a great insight about avoidance:

"It's a good example of how avoidance works in our brains. When we avoid something for so long, it builds up because we don't think we can cope with it. As time passes, it becomes harder and harder because our brains lack evidence to disprove the belief that we can't handle it."

The emotional cost can be debilitating. Ask yourself: Is there something you've been resisting letting go of? What are you avoiding? What is it costing you?

GIVING OURSELVES EVIDENCE

Litsa recommends giving ourselves opportunities to keep checking in with ourselves, whether we're dealing with a storage unit, a house, or a room, even without the intention of doing anything. "Just being there, opening the door, looking around, and regulating your emotions can be beneficial. It serves as a reminder that you can be there and, as time passes, you might find yourself able to open a few things or look around and realize, *Oh, I don't need that.*

You might see that you're a different person now than you were nine months ago or two years ago, which allows you to approach the space differently. It's important to push ourselves a little if we have the opportunity to do so."

COST-BENEFIT ANALYSIS

The question of what it costs us to keep something—not just monetarily but also emotionally—is important to keep revisiting. The cost of keeping became apparent to me when I realized how much mental space was being occupied by that storage unit, which started to outweigh the benefit of having it.

We also have to consider the cost of letting go, actual or implied. For instance, if I think letting go of my mother's house means betraying her, I'm not going to want to let go of it or the things in it.

Keep checking in with yourself and doing that cost-benefit comparison!

EXHIBITIONS AS ITERATIONS

The subsequent exhibitions I've curated in the years since my mom died reflect the evolution of my grief and my relationship with the stuff. Though some featured objects may recur, each exhibition is different, iterations on the theme of Curating Grief.

By January 2022, the way I carried the loss of my mom and how I related to her through her belongings had changed. The hard work of grieving had brought me to a very different place than I was immediately after she died, when selling her house was one of the worst things I had ever experienced. Even though I couldn't throw away my grandmother's vase, even though I couldn't completely let go of the storage unit, recognizing the progress I had made felt amazing. It really did feel like I had more emotional space.

In April 2024, I emptied the last of the storage unit. I marked the occasion with a mini exhibition called, unsurprisingly, "The

Last of the Storage Unit." It included photos of little me, my mom, my grandparents, and other caregivers. A tribute to all that had played a role in caring for me, including the sometimes-maligned storage unit.

Each exhibition is an opportunity for me to mark a transition, to acknowledge the grieving and processing I've done. I am not static, I am not stuck. My relationship with my mother isn't static —it's a living, growing, and evolving relationship.

I invite you to keep yours growing and evolving too.

Fun Fact: The January 2022 exhibition in Toronto was the first time a bottle of soy sauce made an appearance as a featured object! It represented the soy sauce in my mother's kitchen that paralyzed me, but it also represented my longing to feel connected with my heritage. In clearing out the storage unit, I also uncovered grief about not having many memories of my grandparents and ancestors.

CHAPTER 27
HOW TO CHOOSE: HAS THE OBJECT PLAYED ITS ROLE?

My mom's urn broke on the way to Toronto.

But I'd planned it that way. Or at least I'd planned to bring it to Canada to break it. (American Airlines just gave me a head start.)

The custom urn, as I mentioned in chapter 4, was created in East London shortly after my mother died, and it was accustomed to traveling. Handmade in the UK, the urn crossed the ocean to my mother's house in New York, where it held a tin of her cremains in her bedroom for over a year.

When I finally sold my mom's dream house, the white porcelain vessel moved from its sunny window spot to the gloom of a storage unit. It sat empty and lonely in a brown cardboard box for many years. During that time, I scattered my mom's ashes in lakes, rivers, and oceans on different continents. My mom loved to travel, so covering this expanse felt meaningful and fitting.

On a cold January day, eight years after my mom died, I contemplated the urn again. I was trying to clear out the storage unit I'd had since selling her house while making some hard choices about what to keep and what to discard—again.

MY CREATIVE BRIEF

Once again, I had a creative project: an exhibition in Toronto, Canada, as part of a design residency during the city's annual design festival. As with all the exhibitions I curate for The Grief Gallery, the show invited visitors to acknowledge personal and collective losses through the contemplation and celebration of objects: the belongings of loved ones lost.

The event description read, "This edition of The Grief Gallery explores the bridging of distance: between personal and collective grief, between loss and recovery, between physical locations and disparate cultures, between then and now, and between the dead and the living."

Remember, a creative brief is a statement of the purpose and parameters for a project. I *needed* a creative brief. I had dreaded dealing with the storage unit and its contents. I'd kept it for years after I sold my mom's house, with the COVID-19 pandemic adding more layers of difficulty, logistically and emotionally.

My brilliant idea: Use the design residency's exhibition as the impetus for clearing out the storage unit! I knew enough about how my brain and creative processes work to know I needed a deadline—ideally a fun, meaningful one. This is why exhibitions work so well for me, both as an artist and designer, and as a griever. If I have a date, time, and space, I can work toward it—I have a *reason* to curate. A reason to choose.

FRIGID WEATHER, WARM RECEPTION

That's how I wound up putting my mom's porcelain urn in a suitcase and traveling with it north to Toronto, Canada. I wasn't sure how exactly, but my plan was to smash the urn at the end of the show . . . you know, in an artsy way.

Can we talk about the cold again? It's *cold* in Ontario in January. A record storm dumped many inches of snow that year, and in preparation for the trip, I bought waterproof boots lined in fake fur. But during those ten frigid days, when I slowly trudged through snow and ice to get to my gallery space, I couldn't have imagined a more heart-warming experience.

My gallery space was in the back of the MADE custom furniture showroom, whose owner, Shaun, welcomed me kindly. I put my mom's urn on display on a plinth in the exhibition space, one last hurrah and chance for it to be admired before I let it go. You might recall that I designed the urn to also function as a vase, because my mom loved flowers—and at this show, she got her flowers in grand style.

Next door to the MADE showroom was a gorgeous floral design studio, owned by Shaun's partner Todd. What beautiful synchronicity! (Through my experiences as a griever and in doing this work, I've learned to leave plenty of room for uncanny coincidences. I encourage you to be open to synchronicity too, in your own process.)

I was so touched when Todd offered to make a custom floral arrangement to display in my mother's urn. The fragile flaring rim of the urn had broken on the flight from New York to Toronto, but the body remained intact and could hold flowers without problem.

Walking carefully across the icy driveway, we carried the urn next door to the floral studio. I picked out the flowers I wanted for my mother's bouquet: ranunculus and roses in vibrant pinks, oranges, and reds. As lovely and lively as my mother had been.

With care and consideration, Todd made a stunning arrangement. It was such a fitting tribute. My mother would have adored it: a high-end florist who counted major brands, weddings, and celebrities as clients, making *her* bouquet. She would have emailed photos to all her friends. It was such a meaningful way to celebrate the urn, to acknowledge the role that it had played, and to say goodbye.

A JOB WELL DONE

You might be thinking, "But if the urn was so beautiful, why did you decide to destroy it?" Simply put, it had done its job. The urn was created to contain my mother's ashes, and her ashes had been scattered.

Could I have just kept it as a vase? Yes, but it didn't meet my curatorial and collection criteria. In chapter 15, we looked at how curators work with a set of collection criteria to decide what to keep and how to allocate limited resources. Here were my considerations:

Space: After clearing out most of the storage unit, and after the Toronto exhibition, I was going to fly back to Europe with several heavy suitcases. They were already packed full of my mother's vintage clothing, family photo albums, and my grand-mother's costume jewelry. There wasn't room for the porcelain urn, which was both delicate and heavy. And I didn't want to put it in storage again, unused and taking up space. I didn't have room in my small apartment at home either.

Purpose, Mission, and Role: The urn had been a home for the ashes. Without the ashes, what was it now? An empty vessel. (There's a connection there with my mom's house being just an empty shell without her, and even our human bodies becoming just empty vessels after we die, but I'll leave that for another book!)

The urn had once been a blessing and a beautiful tribute to my mother. But at this point in my grief and in my life, to keep it would have allowed it to become a burden.
It had completed its role.

CRITERIA FOR KEEPING

I have mixed feelings about the way author Marie Kondo approaches clearing out possessions. But I do like her suggestion of thanking items and then letting them go. I thanked the urn and let it go.

Nineteenth-century British designer William Morris famously said, "Have nothing in your house that you do not know to be useful, or believe to be beautiful."

My variation is:

"Have nothing in your house, head or heart that you do not know to be useful, or believe to be beautiful."

During that Toronto exhibition, a visitor shared that she had kept her deceased friend's distinctive Doc Martin boots and turned them into flower pots! What could have been clutter, she made both beautiful *and* useful.

A REDUNDANT ROLE

Another example of a possession that I kept and eventually let go was an aqua blue T-shirt. My mother had many T-shirts, but this one was an anomaly: a bit frilly, with a deep scoop neck, a very different style than her norm. But I knew why my mom had bought it: it was *my* shade of aqua blue. What she called "Charlene blue." My favorite colors have long been teal, turquoise, aqua, mint, and robin's egg blue. My logos are typically in these shades, and my exhibitions feature design elements in these hues. (My friends already know to wear these colors to my memorial.)

When I found the T-shirt, it was stark evidence of my mom buying it purely for the color. I kept it for the same reason. Even though it was too big and unflattering on me, and I never wore it. But eventually, I decided it was time to let it go. Because if its role was to serve as an aqua blue item that represented my mom's love, I already had plenty of other pieces that served the same role. The treasured photos of my mom and me in the photo booth at my cousin's wedding? She's wearing a shawl in that aqua blue. The melamine bowls she had in her kitchen? My blue.

I also honored the role of aqua blue in our relationship in a poem:

Aqua Blue

Because of me
My mother wore aqua blue
To my cousin's wedding

"Charlene's blue"
She called it
My favorite hue

Most everyone knew

And we smiled in the photos
Against a background red
My mother in aqua blue

And none of us had a clue

In 8 months time
My mother would be dead
Gone too soon
Everybody said

If only we knew

Because of me
My mother wore aqua blue

Because of my mother
I wear aqua blue

Fun Fact: The process of removing an item from a museum's collection or an archive is called *deaccessioning*. A museum may re-evaluate whether an object still fits the organization's mission, or whether they still have space and resources to preserve it.

As grievers, we can do the same.

We may choose to deaccession an item from our collection. I evaluated the items in my collection of objects from my mom's house, and decided I had enough to play *that* role—to serve the purpose of representing aqua blue.

It was official: I could deaccession the aqua T-shirt.

LET YOUR ANCHORS HAVE THEIR SEASONS

Everything has a season. Even life's anchors. As I've shared, after my mom died, her dream house by the lake became my refuge. As the months passed, I spent weeks at a time in her otherwise unoccupied house, figuring out what to do with her estate and processing her loss.

Eventually, with the bills piling up and my savings dwindling down, the house became less a safe space and more a burden. Its season as a reassuring refuge was over. It was time to let it go. In chapter 24 I share the exact moment I knew I had to let the house go, and the concept of different kinds of anchors.

A similar shift happened with the storage unit. At first, the storage unit was a gift to myself, a granting of grace to set aside what I couldn't deal with at the time that I sold my mother's house. It was a parking space, an opportunity to keep the unmade decisions flying around my brain in a holding pattern. An archive for multiple generations of women in my family: My grandmother's coffee table. My great aunt's sewing supplies. My mother's papers and jewelry. Family photo albums. My books and artwork.

The storage unit kept it all safe. An island of climate-controlled calm. An anchoring address for my life in flux. But eight years after my mom died, I found the anchor of the storage unit was weighing me down. It was time to let it go.

That's what happened with the urn and the T-shirt. Their seasons had ended.

There may be similar kinds of anchors in your life. Situations, relationships, or objects that are helpful until they aren't.

This is the case with any anchor: It can stabilize you and keep you tethered for your own safety, or it can keep you from moving on, to your detriment. When it's time, acknowledge the change of seasons. Accept the transition to come. Unanchor and let go.

———

GOOD QUESTIONS

Is it beautiful?

Is it useful? (Not could it be useful, but is it useful?)

What role has this object played for you?

What role does this object play now?

Has it completed its role?

Is there another object or piece that already fulfills this role?

CHAPTER 28
HOW TO CHOOSE: IS IT THEIR COLLECTION OR YOURS?

Growing up in New York, I lived next door to my Uncle Stephen, my mother's younger brother. He was in 39K, and we lived in 39L, on the thirty-ninth floor of a forty-four-story building in Chinatown. My Uncle Stephen loved penguins. I remember throughout my childhood admiring the various black and white figurines in his apartment. (I guess liking cute things runs in my family.)

I cherish the one item I have from him: a big magnet from his fridge of a skiing penguin wearing a light blue hat and scarf.

For me, this sporty sea bird represents Uncle Stephen's playful and affectionate nature beneath an often stoic exterior. His big heart and large stature. Every time I see the magnet on our fridge, it evokes memories of him picking me up after school to walk the one block home. It sparks a vision of that time we got off the subway in Queens on the Fourth of July, so a twenty-something Me could ooh and aah as I watched the fireworks from the outdoor platform.

Did your person have a collection? Susanna's father had a collection of wooden ducks. Rebecca's father had an impressive collection of rocks—not like my mother's random rocks, but a world-class collection that she and her brother donated to Harvard. Yeesan's dad had a collection of pens (which she beautifully captured in the watercolor illustration at the start of Part 6).

His Collection of Pens
Classic metal pens from Cross and Parker
Contributed by Yeesan Loh, 2021
In memory of her father

2021.NY.YL.1

"I chose to keep my dad's pens because that was something he used on a daily basis," she says. "I have always had a love for writing myself, so they feel like appropriate objects to remember him by . . . like an extension of him."

I find the items that immigrants collect and carry with them especially poignant. If you're moving with suitcases or in a rush, an item must be incredibly significant to make the cut! A favorite photo I share from The Grief Gallery's exhibitions is of the model of a boat that Vanessa's father made. That wooden boat, large enough to need both hands to hold securely, traveled with him from Africa to the United Kingdom and eventually to Ontario, Canada. I can only imagine how much meaning it must have had for her father to have warranted crossing those many miles and years with him. The boat now lives in a prominent spot on her bookshelf in Ontario.

In previous chapters, we've been looking at the belongings through the lens of an exhibition about your person. In chapter 22, we looked at the role of a particular object. In this chapter, let's explore the concept of collections—those that belonged to your loved one, and your own permanent collection.

To guide your decision-making process, here are a couple of ways to look at your person's collections:

REVISITING COLLECTION CRITERIA

In chapter 15, we talked about the concept of Collection Criteria —how a museum or archive decides what to add or keep in their permanent collection. It's a helpful concept when we're trying to answer essential questions for ourselves: *How do I choose what to keep? How do I determine what is important after someone I love dies?*

To recap: This concept involves thinking of the curator not just as someone who selects items for exhibitions but also as someone who may choose what goes into a museum's collection. Many museums have collections of significant objects, artifacts, papers, and other items that they own and/or have responsibility to care for. They often draw from their own collections to create exhibitions. They can also borrow items from other places, assuming temporary custodianship of them. (Fun Fact: Did you know the contents of the Louvre in Paris actually belong to the people of France?)

DETERMINING WHAT GOES INTO A MUSEUM COLLECTION

Museums have different purposes and missions. Whether it's a natural history museum, a museum centered around a particular culture or group of people, a specific art form or period, or the work of a particular artist, their stated mission influences their collection. Practical constraints also affect what gets included. One constraint is whether it serves the museum's mission. Physical space is another constraint. Museums don't have endless storage, and caring for objects requires money and other resources, such as electricity for climate control and funds for restoration and cleaning.

For example, the Museum of Modern Art in New York focuses on modern art, a specific time period. MoMA has its own collection and borrows from other collections for exhibitions, but even a well-funded museum like MoMA faces space constraints and must make choices.

Applying this to the belongings of our loved ones, consider:

- What would be the purpose of a museum about your person?
- Do you *want* to have a museum about your person?
- If so, do you want it to have a permanent collection, or would you want to bring in items temporarily?

ART INSPIRATION: SONG DONG

In 2012, the year before my mom died, the artist Song Dong presented a stunning installation at the Barbican Centre in London called "Waste Not."

In the curving gallery space, over 10,000 objects from his mother's house in China were displayed. Not just the significant ones; everything from used tubes of toothpaste, empty glass jars, and old shoes were arranged on the floor.

Each individual item was laid out on the ground of the gallery space, interspersed with the wooden walls of his mother's house. The installation originally started as a way to help his mother after the death of his father, when the trauma of the loss exacerbated her hoarding tendencies.

I remember being touched by the artist's filial effort to comfort his mother. I recall being disturbed by how reminiscent parts of the exhibition were of the homes of hoarders in my own family.

I also marveled that all of these items that the mother had squirreled away were now part of an art installation. Each pair of shoes, now cataloged, preserved, contained, labeled, documented. Each bottle cap, placed one-by-one by exhibition installers in a soaring gallery space in London. The prosaic items had gone from being belongings to art objects. Simple possessions to parts of an artist's collection or body of work.

Looking back now, there's no doubt that Song Dong's work influenced the creation of The Grief Gallery and my decision to curate my mom's belongings when she died. I think of the "Waste Not" installation often, wondering what we, as everyday people who are not world-class artists, do when we don't have warehouses to store the items that we've inherited, nor institutions willing to pay to transport, store, and install all of these pieces. What do we do? You likely know what I'm going to say:

We choose, we curate.

MY MUSEUM COLLECTION

I do have a mini museum of my mom's stuff, but I think it serves a purpose. Having a selection of her belongings was—and still is—important for me as a daughter, and it's a privilege. But in very real ways, some of my mom's and other family members' belongings are now part of The Grief Gallery's collection. My mother's Hello Kitty figures appear regularly at my exhibitions and in my talk presentations. My grandmother's tomato pin cushion gets recognized at shows because I share it often on social media.

I did have to consider physical constraints when choosing what made it into my collection, such as:

Transportation: How do I get things from New York to London? And then to Portugal? Am I shipping them or putting things into my suitcase? How much will it cost?

Storage: I live in a small apartment, so where does it get stored? What kind of care does the collection need when it's in storage? For instance, most of my mom's belongings are in boxes to avoid constant dusting and to protect them from sunlight.

Display Space: I have limited display space in my home, just a shelf here or there. Exhibitions are primarily where I present my mom's belongings, other than the clothing and kitchen items that have been easier to integrate into my life.

Over the years, I've let go of more belongings of my mom's, deaccessioning them—removing them from my collection when they no longer fit my mini museum's purpose, or my physical space.

When you're considering what's in your museum collection, keep in mind the limited resources mentioned in chapter 15: **space, money, energy, time!**

IS IT THEIR COLLECTION OR YOURS?

Another way to apply this collection analogy is the creative thought exercise of imagining that your museum preserves their lives and their things exactly as they were. In chapter 24, we explored the concepts of house museums and studio museums, like Frida Kahlo's Casa Azul. However, most of us do not have the resources to keep a whole house or room dedicated to an accurate recreation of a person's home, like a full-scale dollhouse.

What's more, we are not obligated to, even though sometimes, as grievers, we feel like we should or need to keep everything.

One way I like to think of it is this:

When the person was alive, what they accumulated in their living space, what they kept in their closets and in their kitchen, was *their* collection. It was the collection of what they chose to have in their lives, whether deliberately or not.

When you inherit those items—that house and those belongings—you don't necessarily have to take on the whole collection. That accumulation of items was *their* collection for *their* lives.

When we take on the role of executors or decision-makers for choosing what to keep and maintain, we then get to decide what is now ours—in *our* collection.

Questions to ask yourself:

- Do I want a museum collection of my person's things?
- Or do I just want a selection for myself as a grieving person who loved them?
- Do I want to keep everything they had in my collection?
- Do I want to take on the role of caring for this collection?

THE STUFF OF LIVING

Imagine you were to die today . . . Too morbid? It's a favorite pastime of mine, so we can also use me as an example. If I were to die today, there would be so many items in my home, drawers, and purse that are not actually significant. Tissues, cough drops, and a million pens. Sweat pants that I've forgotten I own. Sure, I excavated my mom's purse like a forensic archaeologist, but that was just the purse she was using when she died—I didn't mine and catalog the contents of all of her purses. And I did, eventually, discard the tissues and cough drops she had in it.

It's what Litsa Williams calls "the stuff of living." "When someone dies or we're clearing out a family home, it can feel like everything they touched has meaning," she says. "But I had to remind myself, 'This probably wasn't important to my grandma; it's just a random item.'"

ARCHAEOLOGIST OR CURATOR

Have you ever considered what the difference is between an archaeologist and a curator? I have! Here are some big differences:

An archaeologist is required to keep everything that they find. The most important pieces from the dig may wind up in a museum. Remember that we're defining curating as choosing with intention. A curator *chooses* (sometimes with the help of a collections team) what goes into a collection or archive, what goes into a gallery space, what is kept, and what gets displayed.

In this way, curating is as much about what gets left out as what gets kept in. What gets elevated? What is worthy of making the cut?

An archaeologist is past-focused, excavating historical sites. They study their finds to glean new knowledge. A curator manages and interprets collections to educate the public now and in the future. For exhibitions, curators explore how the artifacts in a collection relate to the present, taking past context and culture into account.

I want to highlight here a key difference between us as grievers and the roles of both archaeologists and museum curators: *They have a responsibility to the public and the world's greater knowledge base. We do not.* As important as my mom's belongings are to me, and how passionate I am about The Grief Gallery, I am OK with her items only lasting as long as my lifetime. They do not need to be preserved into perpetuity. They will have done their job. I am capturing their significance—in images, as experiences, and with this book—while I am alive.

And here's a similarity between us as grievers and professional curators and archaeologists: *Interpretation is still required.* In order to figure out the significance of an artifact, archaeologists and their colleagues consider the context of the civilization and what they know about the culture—and there are still many unknowns.

It can be the same for us grieving people doing our own excavations. I found a religious statue in my mother's bedroom: Jesus resting in the Virgin Mary's arms. I was puzzled and a bit alarmed: Had my mom found religion in her later years? Maybe it originally belonged to my grandmother? I dutifully gave it to my mom's churchgoing friend, who would know what to do with it.

Only later did I realize it wasn't just any religious statue—it was a reproduction of the *Pietà* by the master sculptor Michaelangelo. Internet sleuthing revealed that the *Pietà*— carved from solid Carrara marble—had been transported from the Vatican to the 1964-65 New York World's Fair. The same World's Fair that was such a formative experience for my mom and her family as new immigrants. The figure was likely a souvenir! I now imagine my mother rediscovering the *Pietà* statue when she moved back to New York and reconnecting with that wondrous experience in her youth. I trace her love for European art back to seeing the *Pietà* at the New York World's Fair as a teenager, the same love of art that she would pass on to me. More archaeology!

Are you finding yourself in the position of archaeologist?

When we're opening boxes, closet doors, and drawers, we may well feel like an archaeologist. Maybe your loved one was the family historian or archivist, their home the repository for the collective belongings. My mother's home contained items from my grandmother and great aunt as well. (Fun Fact: In the *Manual of Curatorship*, the book notes that for the purposes of conservation, archaeological objects are considered things that were "interred or entombed!")

You might find yourself digging through layers of family history—and, potentially, drama! You may be sorting through generations and a whole family narrative as well as an individual's life story.

But I want to remind you: You are not an archaeologist, even if you may feel like one.

What's more, we are just *playing* the role of curator here, as a creative exercise. We can wear our archaeologist and curator hats with great earnestness and focus, the way children who role play do, *and* it's not too deadly serious. (No pun intended.) We have to laugh: when we unearth twenty packs of unopened nylon stockings, or we find a decade-old slice of cake in the freezer.

———

GOOD QUESTIONS

What have you been uncovering?

Can you think of an example of an artifact that you immediately recognized and could identify the significance of?

Is there an example of an artifact that left you puzzled?

Do you want to play the role of archaeologist? For how long?

What are you hoping to find? Is there a Holy Grail item you're desperately seeking, like Indiana Jones?

PART SEVEN
CURATE: FEELING STUCK? CURATING FOR HEALING AND GETTING UNSTUCK

CHAPTER 29
PROVENANCE: SEEKING ANSWERS AND DETAILS

My maternal grandmother, *Pau Pau*, had a favorite green and white vase. It had a classic shape, with a long neck and floral pattern on its body, and was as tall as a toddler.

The vase is ever present in photos from my childhood in New York: On the side table next to me as I sit on the sofa eating cherries, grinning at the camera. In the foreground of a snapshot of my mom playing with me and my cousin Eva.

When we moved out of that Chinatown apartment, I put the vase in the Donate box. It wasn't my style. But my mother said wistfully, "Oh, your *Pau Pau* loved that vase." She told me how my grandmother had carried that vase on her lap on the plane. After hearing that, I moved it to the Keep box.

The vase then lived in my mother's house. When she died, of course I kept the vase, because it had been so important to my grandmother that she had carried it on her lap! But when I, hungry for more stories, asked my aunt to tell me more about the vase, her answer surprised me. My aunt corroborated that my grandmother had indeed cherished the vase, but she said my grandmother had bought the vase in New York.

So, what was the truth? Had my grandmother bought the vase in Hong Kong and then flown with it in her lap, or had my grandmother bought the vase in New York and brought it back by car? I don't know. And ultimately, I don't think I need to know.

WHAT HURTS? "I'M MISSING DETAILS"

Provenance is an important term in the art and museum world. Records need to be kept about who made the piece, where it's from, when it was made, who owned it, and who owns it now.

However, I suggest that for my purposes as a griever, and likely for yours, knowing the exact provenance is not actually that important when you're assessing what's meaningful to you. Do you really need to know who bought it first? Where they bought it? How much they paid? Unless you are on *Antiques Roadshow*, you likely don't need to know in exact detail.

It can be painful to realize that we don't know the full backstory. But is the pain from not knowing, or is the pain from realizing yet again that we can no longer ask our loved one? We can acknowledge that we feel sad or angry that our loved one is no longer here. We can acknowledge the regret we may feel for not asking more questions and getting more stories when they were alive. *And*, I suggest that if it's meaningful for you, that's all that matters.

You don't need to know all the minutiae. You are not the Metropolitan Museum of Art. You are not the British Museum. You do not need to know all the details in order for it to be OK to keep an item, in order for that item to be meaningful and special to you. I know my grandmother loved the vase, and that's enough detail for me.

Here's when we DO want to consider provenance: When we're dealing with painful, unwanted, or unhelpful stories about ourselves. Inside your unique situation, consider the provenance and decide if it fits your life's collection criteria. See chapter 31 for more about guilt and regret.

WHAT HURTS? "I DON'T HAVE ANSWERS"

Often as grievers, we're grappling with unanswered questions. Sometimes we hold on to objects because we think they may contain or reveal the answers we're seeking.

Jamie hoped his father's notebooks would hold the key. A native of Bristol, England, Jamie lost his father to cancer a couple of years ago. He brought a curation of his dad's few remaining possessions to Lisbon and told me about them, flipping through the slim red notebooks filled with his dad's handwriting.

Here's what he said in our short film *Curating Grief: Loss and Objects*:

"When he died, he just had so many books just full of stuff and, and he would just fill them up with crap. Mostly, probably, when he couldn't sleep, which was very often.

When he died, I just went poring through them, trying to find some kind of answers. Thinking that there would be some kind of, you know, some kind of reason in there. Something that might pertain to me or how I was feeling. And there wasn't.

I think a lot of this was him kind of working out how humans interact, which he was always fascinated by. He loved people, and he loved trying to understand people, and he loved talking about people. I would always have really long conversations with my dad about my friends. He loved hearing about all of my friends, and kind of understanding them. And then he loved telling me stories about his friends and people he's met in the past or somebody he's met down the pub last week.

That's all kind of summarized in his writing. Some of them have been thrown away. And then some of them, before he died—because luckily he had the knowledge that that was going to happen—he redacted a load of stuff from it. He drew these big black lines like a CIA dossier or something. Because he was like, well, this is personal stuff for me.

But the stuff that he left, he obviously wanted us to read because otherwise he would have thrown the whole thing away. And so that's why I felt that, you know, I should read it because he's left that for us to read. He's curating and censoring, which is something I think I definitely do."

Do you see how Jamie was seeking answers through the belongings? It sounds like he didn't find the exact answers he was looking for. That can be a hard experience for many grievers: Not finding the answers we want.

Sometimes we will never get the exact answers we're seeking. Sometimes questions will remain open.

Here's what I also see with Jamie: A son finding evidence of the kind of relationship he had with his father. A relationship where they were close enough to talk often, where they felt comfortable enough to share about their respective friends. Evidence of a father who was curious about people and valued connecting with his son. Evidence of similarities between father and son, as thoughtful individuals driven by curiosity and a desire to engage with the external world, even while having a rich internal world.

Sometimes we're trying to make sense of situations that will never make sense.

How can your beloved daughter be murdered?

How could your brilliant brother die by overdose?

How does a healthy young person get cancer and die?

How is it fair for a parent to die just before their hard-earned retirement?

Not having answers or resolution can be painful. We may never be able to make sense of it all. And we can choose our interpretations and meanings. And we can live a fulfilling life, with the option of bringing our loved one forward with us.

GOOD QUESTIONS

What do you want to know?

Why are these details important to you?

Do you have painful unanswered questions?

What do you think would be different for you if you had answers?

What if you never get the answers?

WHAT HURTS? I'M FORGETTING DETAILS

I'm starting to forget the details.
I can't exactly remember his voice.
I worry my memories are fading.

Grievers often find it upsetting when they find themselves forgetting details about their loved one, or when they can't recall what exactly happened when recounting a story.

My understanding of how memory works is that our brains are always recreating what we "remember," so even our most precious memories that we think are most clear to us may very well have have changed over time—but I'm not a neuroscientist.

I think of it in this artistic way:

There is the exact thing and there is the essence.

For instance, what if I asked you to tell me about an amazing vacation that you had with your family? You might tell me about the meals that you had. A beautiful beach. The amazing sunset.

That time you went on a whale watching trip and saw a baby whale.

Now, can you tell me what shirt your sister was wearing during lunch on your third day? Do you remember? Is it a problem that you don't remember that little detail?

Likely not, because it's not important to your overall memory.

That's how I think of remembering our loved ones: It's more important to remember the essence of them rather than the exact details.

I remember how she made me feel.

I remember the way he'd look at me.

I remember the way I felt when I was around them.

That's what is vital, that's what keeps their memory alive. That's what keeps us connected.

WHAT ARE WE REALLY TRYING TO HOLD ONTO?

The soy sauce on the cover of this book is not my mother's bottle of soy sauce. It is a watercolor illustration of a bottle of soy sauce. It is a *representation* of my mom's soy sauce, but it is not even an accurate depiction of my mother's bottle!

As I noted earlier, I don't remember what brand of soy sauce my mother favored. But it certainly wasn't Kikkoman.

What's important about the soy sauce, about the ingredient, about the flavor, is that what I'm **actually** trying to hold onto.

I could become obsessed with tracking down the exact brand. I could hire a hypnotist to put me under to try to visualize the label on the bottle of soy sauce that was in her kitchen cabinet.

(I did ask my aunt what brand my mother used, because the brand of soy sauce is very particular for many Asian families. Every household has their own preference. Chinese families often have multiple kinds: light soy sauce, dark soy sauce. There's the oyster sauce. The fish sauce. So I asked my aunt and she named a brand, but I looked it up and it was not the brand in my mother's cabinet. It was a totally different bottle shape and label! I don't know if my aunt is remembering incorrectly or if my mother had different favored brands at different times in her life.)

I could also obsess about not being able to get the brand of soy sauce here in Portugal and making that a problem. But it's not about the brand. And it's not even about that specific bottle of soy sauce. Even though it was my mom's. Even though it likely still had her fingerprints on them.

I could have tried to smuggle that specific bottle of soy sauce into my luggage, and then dealt with explaining it to airport security—but that's not what I was trying to hold onto.

I was trying to hold onto those memories, the stories, the meaning. That bond and that connection. That's what was most important.

In my kitchen in Lisbon, I now have multiple bottles of soy sauce. Every time I use them, every time I have dumplings, I feel connected to my mother, to my grandmother, to my ancestors.

Through the flavor.

Through the ritual.

Through the ingredient.

That's what I was trying to hold onto.

GOOD QUESTION: What are you *really* trying to hold onto?

CHAPTER 30
HOLDING ON: WHEN IS IT UNHEALTHY?

When we moved from New York to California, my mom thought she'd lost the box containing her childhood photos. I was ten years old, and I can still remember the note of despair and what I now recognize as grief in her voice. *Losing things hurts,* was the lesson I absorbed. *Best to hold on tight.*

The box of photo albums must have eventually been found, because I have her childhood photos with me now. Black and white images of my mom and her siblings, small and shy on their balcony in Hong Kong; my grandmother, young and smiling. All carefully arranged in old-fashioned albums by my mom —her own curation.

When a family member suggested that I send the photo albums to her instead of keeping them in a storage unit, I was startled by how fiercely I rejected the suggestion. *No! It's all I have left of her*, my mind and heart roared. I felt almost feral in my defense of the precious photos.

I was surprised again by the pain of loss when my mother's burgundy belt disappeared in Marseille, a couple of years after she died. In that moment—and luckily, for just a moment—it felt like I'd lost her again.

Have you experienced a similar pain? Maybe a flood or other natural disaster meant you lost photos and clothing that can't be replaced. Maybe it was an unnatural disaster—a theft or other injustice that took away what you weren't ready to let go of yet.

When do we know it's time to let go?

One of the questions that often comes up when we're talking about keeping belongings after the death of a loved one is, "When is it unhealthy?" It might be in the context of a widow who can't bring herself to throw out her husband's clothes. Or a parent who keeps a child's bedroom untouched. Or the way I found my mom's everyday belongings so incredibly precious after she died: her glasses, the soy sauce in her kitchen. (Did I mention the five expired tubes of Neosporin I still have?)

Here are a couple of ways I look at it:

IS IT HELPFUL?

As a coach, I prefer to phrase the questions as, "What is helpful?" and "What is unhelpful?" as opposed to healthy and unhealthy. (A medical professional might look at it as "functional vs. dysfunctional.") And the answers will vary from person to person, and will likely change over time.

If a child's bedroom is helping a grieving parent to cope, who am I to say they should empty it out? If wearing a wedding ring helps a widower get through his day and brings him the comfort of feeling connected, who are we to try to convince him to do otherwise?

Megan Devine, the psychotherapist you met in chapter 4, is a fierce defender of grievers taking things in our own time. "You don't get to rush people through their grief," she says.

Remember how we talked about anchors earlier? An anchor can be stabilizing, or an anchor can keep you stagnant and feeling stuck. In my view, you get to decide, in your own time.

IS IT MOVING AND EVOLVING? IS IT EXTERNAL OR INTERNAL? IS IT STATIC OR DYNAMIC?

What else do the experts say? In chapter 11, we talked about the Continuing Bonds model, the major shift in our understanding of grief and loss that suggested we can stay connected to our loved one even if the physical bond is severed.

"The research shows that continued bonds with objects are helpful when they are dynamic and internalized (so meaningful for what they represent)," explains our friend Litsa Williams. "Those bonds can be more difficult and complicated when they are stagnant and externalized (when people are attached to the objects in and of themselves)."

As we've been exploring here, we can honor the belongings and meaningful objects for what they represent to us, while recognizing that it's the stories and memories, and the ongoing relationship, that are most precious, not the object itself. Hopefully, the external objects can help us to access internalized bonds.

An example from a What's Your Grief training session that sticks with me is how a child who hasn't been able to develop a picture of a person's personality and values via their own memories, or from stories others might share, may attach fiercely to a specific memory or object. What helped was when adults and others helped them to create new connections and a more dynamic relationship across their lifespan. This is why stories are so important! If all we have of our person is an object, no wonder we're going to hold onto it tightly!

PAST, PRESENT, AND FUTURE

The belongings and meaningful objects can also help us to move our bonds with our person from past to present to future. For instance, when you take belongings out of a box, when you integrate a meaningful object into your daily life or incorporate an item into a ritual, you are creating new memories and renewing bonds.

The object is no longer locked away in a dark archive, unseen and forgotten. It is brought into the light—and into your life.

A yellow melamine spoon from my mom's kitchen is now my husband's favorite spoon, and he uses it every day for his yogurt bowl.

Julie used her late sister's stethoscope to listen to her daughter's lungs, extending her legacy of care. Her wife Erica cherishes the game of Yahtzee that originally belonged to her grandma's and the accompanying score-cards in her distinctive handwriting, with the names of various family members. "We are a big board game fami-ly," she declares.

Yeesan unearthed her father's pen collection for the illus-trations featured in this book and started using them, giving them new life.

Eric dedicates a beer to his brother every time he visits a new pub or new country.

In the process of writing this book, I created a makeshift writing altar, as a way to bring people and memories from the past into this exciting and challenging process with me. On it, I have:

- Photos of my mom in her younger and bohemian artsy days
- Photos of ancestors I knew and those I didn't get to know, including grandparents and various aunties
- Souvenirs from a trip my mom and I took to China together that I rediscovered in the storage unit
- A photo of my child self, doodling at a museum

- Artifacts from my mother's desk, including vintage metal pens and a notepad from HP Labs, where she worked for decades
- A box of decorative Portuguese soaps labeled Poppy Lover, in memory of my colleague Poppy Chancellor of The Griefcase, who didn't get to finish her second book

I feel so connected, cared for, and aligned when I look at this writing altar. I'm reminded of my purpose, that I'm writing for them, writing for me (then and now), writing for you and all grievers who might benefit from these ideas. Past integrated with present and future.

When I asked on Instagram what others have on their altars, my friend Mila described how she incorporates her mother's belongings into her life in a range of ways like a makeshift or living altar: "Photos as bookmarks, mom's ring and recipes, her scribbles where she noted baking temperature conversions from Fahrenheit to Celsius—I keep them in the recipe book. Her shawl I cover my head with when I'm in church."

She also integrates her mother into her actions, to make new memories:

"My oldest kid asked me to make Mom's pancakes—he calls them 'baba Nadia's pancakes.' I first said no because they take time and require extra care because she made them so thin (I always burn my fingers on the pan), but then I thought about the altar . . . and got to work.

I suppose seeing Mom's recipes through is also part of my makeshift altar. I thought how it would make her happy that her grandson asks for her pancakes—had she still been around. I hope that makes her happy still, somewhere."

When we move the objects and our relationship with them into our present and our future, we are also moving our relationship to our loved one from past to present to future.

THE IMPORTANCE OF INTEGRATION

Notice the verbs that are used here: Incorporation. Integration. My friend and colleague Gina Moffa, the grief therapist you met early in the book, has a whole chapter about integration in her book *Moving On Doesn't Mean Letting Go.* I asked her to tell us more about why integration is so vital:

"In my work, I speak about the idea of integration as the long path forward after loss. Slowly, but surely, allowing in the grief experience without the accompanying feeling of being blindsided by it. Grief would make us believe that we must only ever feel devastated by our loss, but integration shows us that over time there can be a softening and opening towards being able to see our loss with more clarity, compassion, and patience as we make our way in this new world.

This means we are more able to experience sadness, or despair, alongside hope for the future and moments of joy. They can exist altogether as we gently move forward.

With the goal of 'integration' over 'moving on' from loss, we can accept that our life going on means moving forward without our loved one being physically present, but also being able to carry them forward and staying emotionally connected to them in our own ways that hold deeply personal meaning."

IS THIS RELATIONSHIP CODEPENDENT?

Have you heard of the term *codependency* when it comes to relationships? In a codependent relationship, a person loses all or most of their sense of independent self to another person or external factor.

My shorthand for codependency is: "I need you to _____ for me to be OK."

For instance, "I need you to behave this way for me to be OK." "I need you to say this for me to be OK." And by OK, I mean on a fundamental, almost survival level. That mindset can leave us feeling overly vulnerable and dependent on a person or thing.

But the goal isn't total independence either—"I don't need you! I don't need anybody or anything!"

I learned the helpful phrase *emotional outsourcing* as a way to describe codependent thinking and behavior from fellow coach Victoria Albina. She has an inviting, loving, and self-described witchy way of talking about our nervous systems based on Stephen Porges's development of Polyvagal Theory and Deb Dana's important subsequent work.

"I define emotional outsourcing as: when we chronically source or look to find our sense of worth, value, significance, and emotional wellness, from everyone and everything outside of ourselves," Victoria says on her podcast *Feminist Wellness*.

"Instead of believing, in our own beings, that we are inherently worthy of love and care, exactly as we are."

But the solution to codependent behavior isn't complete independence either, she says. It's interdependence:

"We all need each other. We're human mammals, mammaling along, and our nervous systems need each other, to feel safe, to survive, and to thrive. So, independence is not the answer. Because you're not getting what you need there. And, you're not giving to anyone else."

Victoria defines interdependence as "a way of relating based in mutuality, and reciprocity, on a loving and balanced exchange of energy."

As human beings, we *do* need each other. We benefit from and may crave connection. That can extend to our relationships with objects. After a person dies, sometimes it might feel like we need to keep an object—that we might *not* be OK emotionally if we don't have it. A grieving person might find themselves emotionally outsourcing to an object—and we might very well need to! Research shows that these "linking objects" can be a source of solace and stability in the midst of massive change.

"Linking objects are items that belonged to the person who died that you now like to have around you. Objects such as clothing, books, knick-knacks, furniture, artwork, and other prized possessions can help you feel physically close to the person you miss so much."

DR. ALAN WOLFELT, *THE WILDERNESS OF GRIEF: FINDING YOUR WAY*

Am I codependent on this object?

Here's how I look at the belongings and meaningful objects through the lens of codependency and interdependency:

Holding on to an object can be helpful as a coping mechanism, until it isn't. Just as the goal with relationships is interdependency vs. codependency, I suggest it's similar with the belongings and meaningful objects. These items can be so helpful, as external objects that give us a way to more easily access what is inside us. However, ultimately, it's what's internal that's important: the love, the memories, and feelings of being cared for and worthy of love.

I love physical stuff. I love having a selection of my mom's things. It hurts when I lose them. So I hold on, but I try to hold lightly.

Am I codependent on my person?

The codependency question can also extend to the relationship with the person who died. I think of this when grievers say things like "I don't know how to go on without them" or "I can't live without them." On some level, they're saying "I need you to be alive for me to be fundamentally OK."

When my mother died, I had to learn to trust that I would

ultimately be OK without her. Just to clarify, I am *not* OK with my mother dying and being dead. I will never be OK with that! Being OK is not approbation. Acceptance of the reality that she is gone is not approval. But I now know that *I* will be OK. I might be sad, but I will survive. I will always miss her, and I can thrive. I can still live a beautiful life, even though I wish she was here.

We can be devastated by loss *and* be OK. We can feel destroyed by grief, *and* we can rebuild and live full lives of our own. That's my hope and vision for all grievers, including you.

HOLD LIGHTLY

To be sure, you can hold on to things. I hope I've been clear throughout this book that I'm not saying that you *have* to throw things away! You can hold onto things if you want, but I encourage holding *lightly*. The object might be meaningful to you. It might help you to stay connected to the person, to anchor some of the stories that are important to you.

And I suggest that you will be fundamentally OK even without the object.

The stories and the memories, the meanings and the feelings —they are all actually separate from the object. The object is here to help you see the meanings, to help you access a feeling of connection to your person—and yet it is not your person. It is not the relationship and bond itself.

So, again, hold on to the object if you wish, but hold it lightly as opposed to clinging, clutching, holding fast—as if your life depended on it.

What if your life—living your own fullest life—is about holding all things lightly: holding people lightly, holding their belongings lightly?

———

GOOD QUESTIONS

What are you holding onto tightly?

Is this object or meaning helpful for you or not?

Is it helping you to live in the way that you want or not?

Does it enhance your life?

Does it help you to feel connected to your person?

What might you feel ready to hold more lightly?

CHAPTER 31
GUILT, REGRET, AND OREOS

After my mother died, I found a pack of OREO cookies on top of her fridge. Every time I looked at this pack of OREOs, I felt so much pain, shame, and regret. Because it was a special birthday edition of OREOs. She died suddenly of a stroke shortly after her sixty-sixth birthday, and I had forgotten to wish her a happy birthday.

To me, the pack of OREOs was evidence that I was a bad daughter. I imagined her sadly putting the colorful box of cookies in her shopping cart, feeling forgotten because her only child hadn't called or emailed to celebrate with her. The guilt was crushing.

I kept the cookies on top of her fridge for over a year, a silent indictment and reminder of my transgression.

HOW DID IT LOOK FOR YOU?

Did you feel guilt and regret after the death of a loved one?

Do you *still* feel guilt and regret? What stories do you have about something you did or didn't do? Are these stories weighing on you? Is there anything you'd like to bring out into the light? What do these stories mean about you?

So often, grievers can feel shame about these stories. Maybe, like me, you've wondered to yourself:

What kind of daughter does that?
What kind of son would say that?
What kind of sibling, parent, friend, partner . . . would do that?

You are not alone. You are *so* not alone. Guilt and regret are some of the most common emotions that grievers report feeling —and some of the most painful.

Here's what I felt guilty about after my mother died:

- I forgot her last birthday.
- I wasn't there when she died.
- I couldn't make it back in time.
- I couldn't keep her house.

Here's what I regretted:

- I should have replied to her last email sooner.
- I didn't tell her more often that I was proud of her.
- I should have called more.
- I didn't consider that she might have a serious health condition.
- I could have helped out around the house more.
- I should have watched *The Voice* and *American Idol* on TV with her instead of rolling my eyes.

But it was the fact I forgot her last birthday that haunted me the most.

THE GUILT-REGRET CONNECTION

Though we may use the terms guilt and regret interchangeably, there actually are differences. Guilt implies that there was an action that you actually took—or didn't take—that caused harm. In a legal sense, an *intent* to cause harm also comes into play.

When I speak with grievers about guilt and regret, a lot of

them ask, "What do I do about it? How can I stop guilt and regret from taking over my life? How can I stop feeling so bad?"

I like to take a step back to see what's happening. We do and feel things for a reason, whether we're aware of it or not, even if the reason might not be entirely accurate or helpful.

What role is guilt or regret playing for you?

There's a reason our brains, hearts, or bodies want to keep what may be a negative feeling. For instance, we might feel anxious because part of us is looking out for danger and trying to protect us. Or we feel guilt because we want to have a sense of control in a situation where we don't have much control. *Maybe if I focus on what I could have done differently, I don't have to face how helpless we were,* we might be thinking subconsciously. Or we hold on to regret as a way to stay connected to the person.

So ask yourself: What role is this guilt, regret, or other emotion playing for you?

What do you think it might be helping you do? For example, is it helping you to feel like there was something you could have done? Because if we had to face that there wasn't anything we could have done, that would mean feeling helpless. And feeling helpless is really hard.

Or part of you wants to hold on to the regret, to keep beating yourself up over what you did and didn't do, because you want to be a better person. You think it will help you to make a better choice next time.

What would be the cost of letting go of that guilt or regret?

Maybe you believe letting go of guilt means giving up a relationship with the person. Maybe it helps you feel connected to them even though it feels bad.

GETTING OBJECTIVE

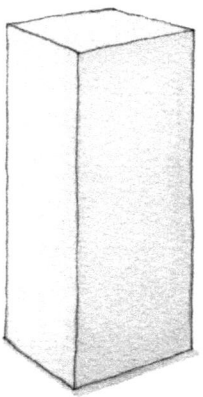

Remember our Getting Objective exercise from chapter 10? If we imagine ourselves in a gallery space, we can put the guilt or regret itself on the display plinth and get curious about it. Take a look at your story about what you did or didn't do, or should have done instead, and ask yourself:

What role is this emotion playing for me?

Do I want to keep this guilt or regret?

If you do want to keep it, I'm not going to argue with you about it. You get to choose! But choose with intention:

- What do you want to *do* with it? Do you want to wield your regret or guilt like a stick, beating yourself up with it mentally and emotionally? Do you want to carry its weight for the rest of your life?
- Is it helping you to create the ongoing relationship you want with your loved one?
- Is it helping you to create the life you want to live?
- If not, see what holding on to this grief or regret is creating for you. Does that insight help you loosen your grip on it, or to consider letting it go?

WHAT HURTS? OTHERS ARE BLAMING ME

They're telling me it's my fault.
They say I should feel guilty.
They say I could have done more.

In chapter 29, I assert that the provenance of an object—the detailed history of it—is actually not that vital for most grievers. Where I think provenance *is* important is when it comes to guilt, shame, and blame.

THE PROVENANCE OF GUILT

Sometimes guilt and regret arise in us as grievers because we're trying to make sense of a situation or, as described above, trying to gain a sense of control. But sometimes, the guilt is assigned to us, stated out loud in someone else's voice or words. Many of my clients come from immigrant families, and I find that in certain cultures, it's more common for people to straight up say, "It is your fault. You are to blame." That can be so painful.

And sometimes the guilt and blame are implied. I suspect that there were a good number of family members and people in my mother's community who thought: "What kind of Chinese daughter isn't present when her mother dies? What kind of child lives so far away from her parents?" (No one actually said this to me. I feel very fortunate that no one said it aloud. I think my mother would have haunted them, because she was very protective of my mental health, and they knew it.)

When it comes to guilt and regret, I find it helpful to look at the provenance:

- Where does this guilt come from?
- Who is the original owner of this guilt?
- Is this guilt or regret that has been assigned to me?

- Is it something that's been projected by others because they're actually feeling guilty themselves?
- Is someone coping with grief by blaming me?
- Am I being told I didn't do enough? How much did *they* actually do?
- Is the guilt something that I've inherited? A result of previous or generational trauma? Passed down like an ugly heirloom?

Just as we can choose with intention which physical items we keep after a loved one dies, we can also choose with intention— we can curate!—the stories and meanings we wish to keep.

MAKING AMENDS

If we feel that our guilt and regret are warranted, what do we do to release them? Grief therapist Claire Bidwell Smith, one of my mentors, recommends writing letters of apology to the person we feel we have wronged, as a form of making amends. I have apologized to my mother aloud and in podcast interviews. On a very real level, my grief work and The Grief Gallery's exhibitions are a form of making amends.

Every year, on my mother's birthday, I sing her praises. I might have forgotten it that fateful year, but I never forget it now.

WHAT I DID WITH THE OREOS

Not only did the pack of OREOS remain on top of my mom's fridge for over a year, but it *haunted* me for over a year. It was the heaviest pack of cookies ever. Attached to it were all those painful thoughts about forgetting my mother's birthday and the belief I was a bad daughter. No wonder I felt weighed down by them.

At one point, my aunt took them when she did a sweep of my

mom's kitchen. I saw the box of cookies in her car, and I took them back, without saying a word. I placed them back on top of the fridge as if I needed them there to remind me of what I had done. I wasn't ready to let them go or to let go of my guilt and regret.

But when I finally sold my mom's house, I did throw away the pack of OREOs. And I didn't want to keep those heavy stories either, so I tossed them too.

Imagine if I had kept those guilt cookies and the accompanying belief that I had been a bad daughter. What would have been the cost of keeping that guilt and its companion belief? Maybe I'd be triggered every time I saw OREOs! Maybe I'd get incredibly depressed on her birthday.

I would likely avoid thinking about my mother and talking about her. I wouldn't be telling you and the world about her and how amazing she was. And I didn't want that. These sad memories weren't wholly representative of my relationship with my mother, which had been a good relationship, especially as we both got older.

This year, my mother would have celebrated her seventy-seventh birthday. I'm not depressed. I celebrate her memory, on her birthday and every day. I dedicate pieces of cake, Portuguese pastries, and Belgian waffles to her. I'm excited to be telling you about her.

Some years, I do a red ribbon dance for her birthday. Regardless, everyone knows it's my mom's birthday because I talk about her. I invite them to remember and celebrate her too. It's part of my process of making amends, of apologizing for forgetting her last birthday.

I've forgiven myself because I think she would have forgiven me too. But more importantly, because forgiving myself allows me to create the ongoing relationship I want to have with my mother.

This is the healing and blossoming that's possible when we make intentional choices about what to keep and what to discard after a loved one dies.

WHY WE RUMINATE

Rumination is often brought up alongside guilt and regret. If guilt and regret feel like a gnawing sensation, an unbearable pressure, or a dark cloud over your head, then rumination might feel like a storm. Rumination might feel like brooding, being in a dark space, going over and over what could have been, what should have been, and all the what ifs.

Why do we ruminate? In *The Grieving Brain: The Surprising Science of How We Learn from Love and Loss*, Mary-Frances O'Connor cites the "rumination as avoidance" hypothesis by researcher Margaret Stroebe and her colleagues: ". . . letting our thoughts run through our mind again and again may be a way to distract ourselves from the painful feelings of grief."

One of my grief colleagues also shared an interesting insight into rumination: The word *rumination* comes from the Latin verb *ruminari*, which means to "to chew the cud" or "chew over again."

Cows ruminate—they chew their cud, which is regurgitated food that they re-chew, trying to extract all possible nutrients from it. It wasn't until the 14th century that the word began to be used as a metaphor for mental reflection. So when we ruminate, we may be continuing to chew on a story, an occurrence, or a meaning. I personally resonate with this explanation.

When we ruminate, is there a part of us trying to extract a lesson?

When we replay a story over and over, are we trying to extract some kind of meaning?

Do we *need* there to be a lesson from this terrible thing that happened in order for it to make sense to us?

CHAPTER 32
REGRET, PERSPECTIVE, AND INTERPRETATIONS

My mom's last email to me was about Paris.

"I am jealous that you are in Paris," she wrote. "Enjoy while you are there. One of the most beautiful cities in the world." She signed it, "Love, Mom."

I remember being puzzled and amused by her "I am jealous"—a phrase she didn't normally use. Most likely she'd picked up the phrase from TV or YouTube, as she was always learning more slang and trying to improve her English.

In my reply two days later, I gently chided her, but said we could go together: "You're jealous? That's funny phrasing—what TV programs are you watching? :) Well, you're welcome to come to Paris anytime! I can meet you there, or next time you come to London we can take the Eurostar over together."

She never opened my reply. She had her stroke and died suddenly the day between her email and my reply. That haunted me for a while.

Why didn't I reply right away? Why did I wait? My mother could have enjoyed her last day with visions of going to Paris with her daughter.

But instead, I left her hanging, again.
What kind of daughter was I?

THAT ONE MOMENT

Do you have a similar regret? A moment you replay and rue? Maybe you declined a lunch invitation, or skipped visiting over the holidays, thinking there would be another chance. Maybe you weren't there when your person died, by chance or by choice, and you find yourself questioning and repeating "what if" scenarios.

Here's how I look at it now: Back then, it was just another email. (Taking only a day to reply to an email is actually pretty good for me!) For you, it might have been just another text and another ordinary day. It's only with hindsight and the knowledge of what happened that it becomes a significant text or significant day. I try to find compassion for our past selves.

We tend to focus on the one phone call we missed, the email we didn't send. The one lunch we skipped. But in the entire arc of our relationship with the person, that is just one moment—it doesn't tell the whole story. I like to try zooming out to see all the other moments that are also there: The conversations we did have, the times we did make up, the meals we did have together. All the hours we *were* at the hospital.

Instead of leaning in and scrutinizing each moment, like looking at a Monet painting from an inch away, can we step back and see these painful stories with more perspective? Can we give ourselves the grace to see the fuller picture? A human being who erred. A caregiver who was tired and doing their best. A daughter who loved her mom *and* was distracted by her travels.

SEEING OUR CHOICES

What hurts? "I couldn't make it back in time."

This is a refrain that haunts many grievers. I couldn't make it back in time when my mom died—in my case, it was actually impossible, as I was an ocean away and my mom died suddenly and instantly (at least that's what her doctor assured me). Maybe you had more notice and tried, but there were too many miles and not enough minutes. Maybe you stepped away for one hour or one evening, and that's when your person died.

The words "I couldn't make it back in time" have another layer: We cannot go **back in time**. We cannot change what happened. We cannot rewrite the facts, no matter how hard our brains try. We *can*, however, choose how we interpret the facts now and in the future.

Here are some ways to see it:

How are we interpreting the facts?

Remember our Getting Objective exercise in chapter 10? In that exercise, we imagine an object on a plinth in a gallery space and separate the objective facts about the item—its dimensions and materials, for instance—from the subjective interpretations, like the stories and meanings we assign to it. We can do a similar exercise with the facts of our stories, including the actions and inactions that we regret.

This is one way to tell the story of my mother:

My beloved mother, Marilyn, died suddenly from a stroke in 2013. She was only sixty-six. Tragically, she died alone in her dream house, which she only got to enjoy for a couple of years after getting divorced. I'm an only child, I had to put my life on hold. There was a big mortgage on the house, and I couldn't afford to keep it. Clearly, I let her down by selling her house.

But what are the facts of the story? What are the objective facts, and what is interpretation? If I were to highlight just the objective facts, they would be the following:

My mother was named Marilyn.
She died from a stroke in 2013.
She was sixty-six.
She was divorced.
She was by herself when she died.
There was a mortgage.
I am an only child.

I sold the house.

Those are the facts. A lot of what I told you previously was interpretation: *I let her down by selling her house. It's a tragedy that she died alone.* (A lot of people will interpret the fact that she died alone as a tragedy, I've noticed. They interpret that fact to mean that she wasn't loved or that she didn't have people who cared about her.)

What are alternative ways to interpret these facts?

For instance, I think a true tragedy would have been if my mother had a stroke while she was arguing with my father in the midst of their divorce. She wouldn't have died alone, but that would have been far more tragic to me!

A lot of people might interpret my mother dying alone as proof that she wasn't loved, or evidence that something had gone wrong. But I know and I *choose* this interpretation: She was by herself because she had bought her dream house and *wanted* to live alone. Everyone was trying to convince her to live in Chinatown, and she insisted she wanted her own space with the view of the lake. The day she died, she had taken the train down to the city and visited with friends and her brother.

So, here's the story retold:

My beloved mother died suddenly from a stroke in 2013. She was sixty-six. She had a lot of plans, including her newfound independence after getting divorced. She had plans to travel, she had a new career, and she planned to enjoy her dream house.

Yes, there was a big mortgage on the house. To me, that's evidence that she thought she'd live a long time. (Why else would you have such a big mortgage?) She hadn't planned on dying so quickly, so young. She thought she'd have many more years. And not everyone has that privilege, right?

I'm glad she got to decorate the house her way. I wish I could have kept it, but it was her dream house, not mine.

Same set of facts, totally different interpretations—and a very different feeling for me!

That's what I encourage you to do, too. Get objective: Look at your story. What are the facts? What are the interpretations here? What are your other possible interpretations?

What were we actually choosing at that moment?

If you left the hospital to try to get some sleep, because you were so exhausted at that moment, you chose yourself. "You chose your father's daughter," I tell Jen, who was racked with guilt for not being there that one night, the night her dad died. "You chose to take care of your father's darling daughter."

If you couldn't be there when your person died, because you had another important responsibility or allegiance—your marriage, your children, another person you were caring for— you were choosing what you *also* valued.

Maybe you were making impossible choices. Like my client Tracy who was at university when her mom died from cancer— because her mom had insisted she go back to school. Like Jamie, who was in Beijing and geographically a world away when his father died, and who questioned his decision even though he had been home just before and had his dad's support to travel.

If you chose to lie to your person because their dementia or delirium meant they would not have understood, if you lied to protect them physically or emotionally: You were choosing to care for them in the best way you knew how.

If you went No Contact or Low Contact with a family member because they were abusive or toxic, you were choosing yourself. You are worth choosing.

I see these all as *beautiful* choices.

TRYING TO AVOID REGRET

What if your regret is an anticipated regret? What if you're worrying you will choose incorrectly? "What if I choose the wrong thing?" is a question that comes up often with clients and in grief gatherings. Sometimes it's in the context of choosing what to keep when we're going through a loved one's belongings. Other times, it's in the context of making difficult decisions about a loved one's care.

I'm going to share with you a couple of different approaches to this question, in the form of more questions.

1. Can you take more time to choose?

If you have the ability, try to give yourself time to choose. That's the advice that a lot of grief experts give: Take your time, if you can. If you have money to throw at the problem and you need to hold on to the house for a little bit, if you need to put stuff in storage, to look at stuff when you are not in the initial state of shock, or when your mind is in a fog or when you're emotionally upset, do it!

In chapter 17, I share my timeline with my mother's house and belongings. I kept my mother's house for over a year after she died, and then I had a storage unit for almost a decade! I was lucky, and I had the privilege of being able to throw money at the problem. Not everyone is going to have that resource and that privilege though.

2. What if there's no such thing as choosing the wrong thing?

What you're really trying to hold on to is not necessarily the object itself—most often, it's what the object represents. For instance, I have a slim, navy blue leather belt that belonged to my mom. I had never seen her wear it because it's likely from her younger years. The belt represents how stylish she was, and a period of her life when she cared deeply about being ladylike. There can be something very powerful about knowing that the belt belonged to my mother and that at some point she wore it —*and* the belt is not actually what I'm trying to hold on to. On some level, you can't choose the wrong thing.

That's not to say that it doesn't hurt when you lose a meaningful object. I had a similar belt of my mother's that was burgundy, with a clasp adorned with a swan. As I shared in chapter 30, I wore it on a trip to Marseilles in the south of France, and I lost it. I remember running around the museum that we were in and going out onto the dock, retracing our steps, seeing if maybe I'd left it somewhere. I checked lost and found to see if anyone turned it in, and I never found it. It hurt like hell to lose it.

Even though I know intellectually that it's not the thing that matters, it can still hurt to not have the thing. It can still hurt to not have belongings from our loved one, either because we did not have access, or we couldn't afford to keep them, or they were taken away from us. It can hurt, *and* we'll be OK.

3. What if you *do* choose the wrong thing?

What's the answer to that question? This "what if" question in our brain is an open loop. It's going to keep asking that question because it's really satisfying when our brains can close the loop and have an answer.

If you find in your grief that you have a lot of these open loop questions— what if, what if, what if—try to answer the "what ifs" to help close that loop. This is something that I learned for better managing my anxiety—because anxiety can look like constant "what if" open loops.

For example, my anxiety might say: *What if I forgot to pack that outfit for my trip?*

What if? Let me answer that question with further questions. Will my trip be ruined? What is the alternative? What would I do to salvage my trip? Answering those "what ifs" closes that loop.

I find this approach to be helpful in grief as well.

What if you choose the wrong thing? Close the loop by answering the question. What are you afraid might happen? The answer will be different for everyone:

- Well, if I choose the wrong thing, maybe I will experience so much pain that I don't think I can handle it.
- I'm going to feel so much regret and that's so uncomfortable. I don't want to experience that.
- If I don't have the right thing, maybe it means I will forget my loved one.

Answering the question offers us more insight into what we're really afraid of in that situation: What is my *actual* concern? Am I afraid that I will forget my person? Am I afraid that it will mean I'm a bad daughter because I've betrayed them? Am I afraid that I can't handle the pain of loss again? Am I afraid that I will beat myself up so much for making a mistake? What is at the end of that "what if" question?

———

I confess: I *have* felt pangs about not keeping some items. In the immediate days after my mom died, the random rocks around her home were puzzling to me, because these rocks—*rocks!*— became so precious in my eyes. Eleven years later, when I finally emptied out the storage unit, I was tickled when I found a couple of rocks that my mother had kept with the words "Cape Cod" written on the bottom with a date. I realized she likely collected rocks because *I* had always collected rocks, from the time I was a toddler.

But at the time, I was trying to get the last of the storage unit cleared out. I had limited space in my suitcases, not to mention weight limits for the flight. *I'm not going to keep actual rocks*, I reasoned. I threw them into the East River by South Street Seaport, a favorite spot for me and my mom. I felt that was a fitting way to release the rocks back to water.

And I still felt a little pang of "what if"—maybe I should have kept those rocks so they could hang out with my rock collection. When I shared the rocks I found on Instagram, well-meaning people suggested, "You could put it in an installation or in your garden" and other lovely ideas.

I felt that twinge of *Oh no, what if? Should I have kept the rocks?*

And I know I will survive. I know I will be OK. I can feel the momentary pain of regret and longing, *and* I don't have to keep revisiting it.

———

GOOD QUESTIONS

Is there anything you regret?

What role is the regret playing for you?

Is your moment of regret representative of the whole arc of your relationship with your person? (If it is, it's OK to grieve that too.)

Are you worrying that you *will* feel regret? Why?

What is your "what if"? What's your answer to the "what if"?

PART EIGHT
CREATE: YOUR GRIEF GALLERY - CURATING FOR CELEBRATING AND MEMORIALIZING

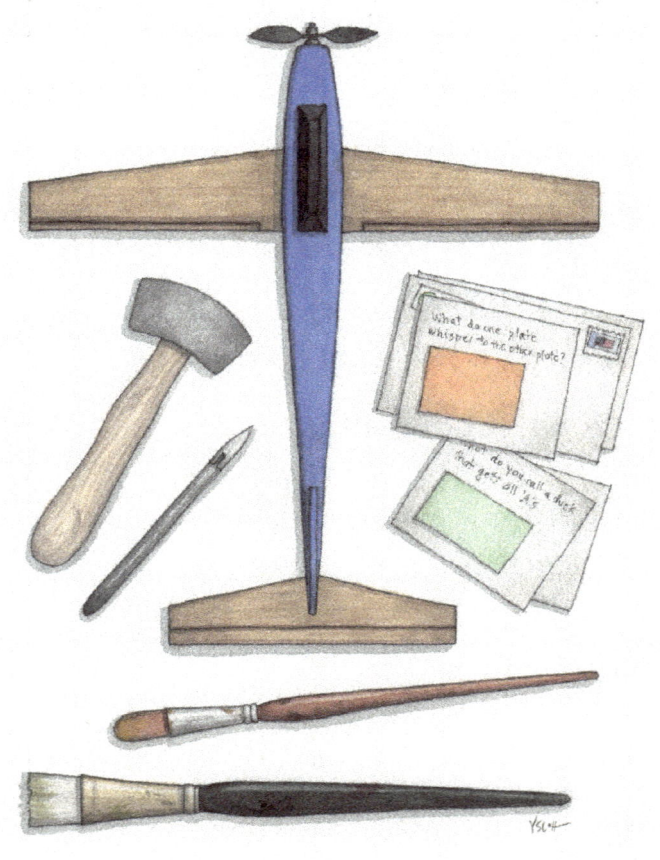

Their Projects in Progress

CHAPTER 33
HOW TO START CURATING YOUR GRIEF GALLERY AND EXHIBITION

Do you feel ready to create your Grief Gallery and exhibition about your loved one? This is where we pull all the elements together! In this chapter, I'll offer you questions to get you thinking about what you want in your exhibition, as well as some examples of different curations.

10 PROMPTS TO GET STARTED

Audience — Who is this for? Who are you inviting? Is this for the public or for private viewing only? One of the key differences between your Grief Gallery and an actual museum is that it doesn't have to be for the public. What's more, your exhibition can be tailored for different audiences. An exhibition can be public or private. You can have a version that's just for friends and family, or a particular interest group, or even just yourself! You can also tailor different versions to be age appropriate, in the same way that we have children's museums, as well as general audience museums.

Purpose — What's the purpose of this particular exhibition? Is it to celebrate a life? To acknowledge a milestone? To process an experience? What do you want to express or convey? What do you want witnessed or acknowledged?

Space — What type of space do you want? As we looked at in chapter 9, you don't need a gallery space or a whole room to curate—but if you want, you can hire one! You can also pick a shelf for an arrangement or altar. Or a wall for a gallery of images and objects. Look at what space you have in your home or in your office and designate that as your gallery space.
If a whole shelf or a wall feels too daunting, start small. Pick one item to elevate: Lift it up, move it out of a box or that jumble of stuff, and make it visible. A clear box, a wooden cube—they can become mini plinths.

Duration — Is this a permanent or temporary display? Museums and galleries may have both. You can switch up the display too, just as museums and galleries do. With The Grief Gallery, I curate pop-up exhibitions that typically range from one day to a couple of weeks, usually during art, design, and grief events. I also have a permanent shelf in my home with a rotating display, and I hope to have a permanent gallery space someday.

Dates and Opening Hours — Is there a certain time of year that's special to you? Is there a date or milestone you want to mark? If there will be visitors, what time can they come by?

Medium and Format — Do you want to have an arrangement of objects? Would you prefer photography, whether you take the photos or you hire a pro? Alexandra Rowley, award-winning artist and photographer/director, created a "conceptual portrait" of her father, documenting his belongings, his life, and his city for her project "PORTRAIT." As mentioned, I've hired photographers repeatedly to take beautiful images of my mom's belongings, in different styles. You can also use collage, paint, or whatever medium you'd like!

Organizing Plan — How would you like to organize your exhibition? You can go in purely chronological order, like a timeline of a life. Or you can group objects by theme or type. For instance, an exhibition about the artist Georgia O'Keefe could span her whole life in chronological order. Or it could focus on just one period of work: when she moved to New Mexico. Or a particular theme: rooms dedicated to her famous flower paintings and skull paintings. Or interesting juxtapositions: a flower alongside a skull painting, contrasted with work from her New York period. There are so many ways to tell a story of a life or a person.

Cultural Elements — Are there ways to weave in elements, rituals, and aspects of your cultural heritage or family traditions? In my case, I did not grow up very traditionally Chinese, so I didn't understand the ceremonial altars. I did not understand the funeral rites. But I adapted elements to my own versions: I do a red ribbon dance, which is a traditional Chinese dance, in memory of my mother on her birthday. I dedicate dim sum to her and my grandmother. I create my own traditions and arrangements with oranges and tangerines, which are considered lucky.

Narrative and Stories — What stories do you want to tell? Which objects help to illustrate these stories? What do you want written on the object descriptions and wall labels? What overall narrative do you want to convey? Examples of narratives include: "She lived a full life and was very loved." "Creativity fueled him, for better or for worse." "They navigated the ups and downs of life together, and triumphed in the end."

Feeling — What feelings and emotions do you want to evoke for visitors? Is it a celebration of life, with a focus on the positive? Do you want there to be space for shadow and darkness as well, acknowledging some of the challenges in your person's life? Do you want your visitors to feel optimistic and uplifted?

CREATIVE EXERCISE: TAPPING INTO THE FIVE SENSES

Are you having trouble deciding what should go into your exhibition? Try this visualization exercise with me! Grab some pen and paper, and jot down what comes up for you.

First, let's imagine an exhibition—it can be about your person, or we can start with something less emotionally charged, like a period of time in your life or a place that you love. Pick the topic of your exhibition.

Then we're going to walk into the exhibition venue, and you're going to imagine looking around the gallery space . . .

FEATURE COLOR: The walls are mostly white, but there is a feature wall that is a single color. What color is this wall? What color comes to mind for you when you think of this person, place, or period of your life?

ITEMS: In this space, there is a display pedestal. There are tables and shelves. What objects are on these plinths and surfaces? Is it a vase? A pair of glasses? A pipe or another item they always had with them? Is it a family heirloom? Is it an everyday object that you just associate with them? Red lipstick, a bottle of perfume. A pen, a distinctive hat. Look around some more: Maybe there are textiles hanging from the walls. Maybe it's the 1970s fabric that was on your grandmother's sofa. Maybe it's something that they wore, like a favorite dress or a leather jacket. A cheongsam or hanbock. A yarmulke or headwrap.

TOUCH: What textures come to you? The smoothness of leather? The plush softness of a beloved pet's blanket? The nubbiness of knit sweaters, or the caress of cashmere, like my mom's favorite sweaters?

AUDIO: There can also be sounds in an exhibition. Is there a certain song playing? Music from a certain period: Is it classical music? Is it the BeeGees? Or the Platters (my mom had that cassette in her car)? What music might be playing that they loved or that you associate with them? Maybe there are other sounds. Maybe it's the shaking out of the New York Times from Sunday mornings. Maybe it is the clinking of a metal watch band. Maybe it's their singing from the kitchen or whistling from the yard as they worked.

SMELL: Maybe there's a smell. Is it the smell of the sea, or the smell of tobacco smoke? For Kelli, it's the aroma of molasses cookies her mom, Walterine, would bake at any random hour of the day.

TASTE: Is there a taste or flavor you associate with this person, place, or time? Maybe the sweetness of Walterine's molasses cookies. Or the tang of tomato sauce made from ingredients from Nonna's garden. Or the cardamom and cloves in Roshni's family chai recipe. (Maybe there wouldn't be tasting happening in the exhibition space, but it could be an experience in the cafe we invite visitors to partake in after learning about our person!)

Now we're going to look at that colorful feature wall again. There is a name at the top in big letters, it's the name (or title) of the exhibition. It can be the name of your person or place, or the way you describe the period in your life. And maybe there is a subtitle as well, a phrase that evokes a theme in their life or a particular facet of your person. Maybe it's a phrase that they would say all the time. For example:

Nonna: A Life Well-Lived

My Mom: The Thread That Held Us Together

Walterine: Love, Peace, and Blessings

. . .

What did you come up with? This visualization exercise can be a way to access the elements you want to include and emotions you'd like to evoke in your exhibition. You can also register your book at curatinggrief.com/book-register for book bonuses like more prompts and an audio version of this exercise if you'd like to close your eyes to visualize!

In the chapter ahead, you'll meet Garret's family and Kayla and get a glimpse of their galleries and exhibitions—more ideas and inspiration to stir your creative heart and mind.

Nonna's Tomato Sauce

Glass jar with metal seal containing tomato sauce
Contributed by Patricia Ritacca, 2022
In memory of her grandmother

2022.TO.PR.1

"Every year my immediate and extended family would wake up at 5am and get together in my grandparents' garage to make tomato sauce for the year. It was a serious affair with my nonna, the matriarch, as our fearless leader, dividing up tasks and keeping us all in check so that our labour would be complete in time for pasta lunch.

My nonna was a force: self-assured, loving, commanding, beautiful. I have four jars left of the tomato sauce we made together just before her passing, 9 years ago.

Knowing that you will never be able to taste the food of a beloved one that has passed away is almost unbearable. The jars will likely sit on my shelf for many more years, unopened. The only remaining possibility of having access to those tastes, our collective labour, and her uncomplicated love."

CHAPTER 34
GALLERY AND EXHIBITION EXAMPLES: GARRET AND KAYLA

As we've explored, there are as many possible ways to tell the story of a life as there are people in the world. Here are some examples of ways real people have applied the Curating Grief approach, illustrating a range of relationships and formats.

GARRET'S GALLERY

Loren created a gallery of her brother's belongings shortly after he died. Most of my clients do not feel ready to curate a public-facing exhibition until months or even years later, but Loren's own comfort level and professional expertise with death, dying, and grief and her family's loving and artistic nature made this incredibly touching endeavor possible. She and her family kindly share with us the story of Garret's Gallery:

"Creating a Grief Gallery with the support and involvement of my parents for my brother, Garret Talbot, allowed me to continue to journey with him even after his death. We had decided that we would display the items that represented who he was at his celebration of life, so I tasked us with making some decisions on what we would bring to honor him. During the last weeks of his life, he had brought some items to his childhood home, so we first spent some time in his room there. The backpacks he hiked with, the books he was reading, the boots he wore to work, the altar he had made of ancestors and close friends who had died were all in this space. Sitting in his room so soon after his death was difficult, but also very affirming to see all the beautiful things that made him who he was.

Later we went to his home and selected more items for the space. Having a reason to collect and go through things gave me a sense of purpose. It was a time to sit with these items and continue to contemplate who he was through objects. There was also an ease to this because it was so obvious what belonged in the gallery we were creating. His chess set, his meditation pillow, his knife collection, his company shirt, his hair product, a photo of the boat he worked on for years, and so on. They all deeply represented who he was and even allowed us some moments of laughter to lift our sunken hearts.

We were fortunate enough to hold his memorial at a former camp which had a ballet studio. I chose this room due to the size, but also because of the large mirror that ran across the back wall. This allowed people to witness themselves while standing with Garret's possessions. To be reflected in the glass surrounded by the things he carried, wore, played—to see themselves with him one last time.

As a lover of music, his friends and I co-created a multi-hour playlist of musicians he listened to throughout his life. This was playing in the room. A recent art show my brother had of his photographs while working was rehung on large wooden panels at the end of the room. Another table held the zine *Bread and Butter*, which he had made in his teens, with copies for people to take home.

The walls held a Magritte-style Halloween mask he created and a jacket he wore frequently.

The room held three rows of three eight-foot tables. We had sections of his journals and writings, the games that he played, the family history, his tools he brought to work each day, and the shirt he was wearing the day he died. A close friend and coworker had prepped some of the tools he had used by polishing them and showing us how an iron worker leaves their signature on their wrenches—another symbol of his life we were able to discover.

Two friends added two very special elements. One was a writing desk that held postcards that she and Garret had sent to each other over the years. She reprinted two of them but left the backs blank so people could write to each other, along with two other postcards (one bearing a beautiful photo of my brother). She added a hand-created mailbox where people could add a stamp and mail the postcard via the box. The other element was a film by a friend who had been capturing my brother for over twenty years. Prior to the memorial, he created a film over weeks that we shared in the gallery space and then later in another room where a deep discussion was held about Garret, his life, and his death.

Over two hundred people passed through this space. Most processing who he was and sitting with Garret for one last time. A few were unable to stay due to the pain the room held for them. For me it was another chance to be with Garret and his community, celebrating a life well lived, surrounded by art, love, dedication, and adventure."

—Loren Talbot

The family and community's love for Garret shines through so clearly in the way they all came together to create his gallery, even though his mother poignantly expresses how painful it was for her:

> "It was so hard to see my son's life laid out on a series of tables. The notice from the day of his birth to the last shirt he was wearing. It was so final. No return. He had done so many things in his forty-seven years. What does a mother remember and what gets lost in the years?
>
> Reviewing the room, the articles, his special things—it provided solace, an overview, and something I still struggle with to accept. It was so meaningful to so many who knew him well and others who got to know him better."

—Marsha Talbot

And from yet another voice, one attendee told Loren, "I only met your brother once, but I am leaving today knowing who he was."

———

KAYLA'S EXHIBITION

My client Kayla curated an exhibition about her grandmother that was just for herself. Her grandmother played a pivotal role in Kayla's upbringing—and she was racist and antisemitic. We explored ways for Kayla to honor the positive aspects of her grandmother in her life, while also protecting her multicultural and biracial partner and child from the bigotry of her family of origin. Ultimately, she arranged a select few objects from her grandmother on a shelf in her office space—a private gallery, just for her, to help her sit with the complexities of feeling love and grief for someone who also caused harm. As her son gets older, she will share age-appropriate details about her grandmother with him.

———

As you can see, these were two very different exhibitions with a spectrum of spaces, from a shelf to a whole room. Different audiences: a private display and an invitation for all to witness. Very different relationships with the deceased. And in both cases, an opportunity was created for grievers to be with the loss and the emotions that came up, and to witness the person who died via meaningful objects.

In the next chapter, I'll offer some more creative ideas for your Grief Gallery and exhibition, whether you have the belongings or not.

CHAPTER 35
CREATING YOUR EXHIBITION: CHOOSING WITH THE 3CS

A jade bangle. Graduation tassels. Scissors she used for cutting my hair. Her work badge. These are all items from my mom that I featured in my most recent exhibition of The Grief Gallery. How did I choose? The same way I've always chosen! Let's refer back to the 3Cs: Collect. Curate. Create.

To recap: When I put together an exhibition, I essentially have three main steps:

Collect: I collect all the things, all the possible things that I can put on display.

Curate: I curate, or I choose intentionally, based on what I want to create.

Create: I bring it into reality in a way that feels most meaningful to me.

Let's revisit the 3Cs as a way for you to consider what you'd like to create. For this exercise, you can use a sheet of paper and pencil, pens, or markers. Or you can download a worksheet and watch an accompanying video at **curatinggrief.com/worksheet**

. . .

Let's go through this together:

Step 1: Collecting Memories and Stories
The first step of the process is to collect. And by this, I mean to collect all of our thoughts and memories about our person. The guiding question to ask yourself is:

How do I remember my person?

In your worksheet or in your journal, put it all down. We're just collecting memories and stories, thoughts, moments—positive and negative, big and small. No need to edit at this point. How do you remember your person? For example, with my mother, I remember delicious meals at her house, how much she loved to cook and feed people, how she loved flowers, getting ice cream together, getting the news from my uncle that she was gone, going to museums and art shows together.

Step 2: Curating Intentional Memories
The next step is to curate. This is where we start to choose. The question I invite you to ask yourself is:

How do I want to remember my person?

Look at what you've written down so far, at all of the memories and moments that came to mind. Now circle the memories that represent how you *want* to remember your person. In my case, I might especially want to remember my mother by the meals we had together, by her love of flowers, by our museum visits. So I would circle those memories. Think of the circle like a spotlight, putting special attention on those particular memories, moments, and stories!

As you're doing this, more memories might come up. Go ahead and add them.

Step 3: Creating Lasting Tributes

The last step is to create. And in order to create, we want to think about what we *want* to create. The last question I invite you to answer is:

How do I want my person to be remembered?

Looking at your worksheet or paper, see what you've circled and then draw a box around the memory, the story, the quality of the person that you really want to showcase. Think of that box like a picture frame around a selected moment or memory that you want to put in a prominent place to remind yourself and others of your person.

With my mother, I can choose to commemorate her love of flowers and the delicious meals we had together. I would draw a box around those items, like I'm framing those memories. I want to remember her in those ways, and I want people to remember her for those qualities as well.

Now that we've identified how we want to remember our person, and how we want them to be remembered, this is when we get creative.

———

CREATIVE WAYS TO REMEMBER LOVED ONES

We can brainstorm about all the different artistic representations and rituals we can create in order to capture this memory, or this essence, or facet of the person. I'll share with you a range of options:

Commissioning Artwork
Every year I commission artwork in memory of my mother.

Back in chapter 4, I shared how, shortly after my mom's death, I commissioned her porcelain urn from a UK ceramicist. Being able to work collaboratively with the right artist or designer on these kinds of projects can be incredibly rewarding and healing.

Tip: You can find many talented artists and makers on Etsy, at local craft and art shows, and open studio events. Allison Gilbert's book *Passed and Present* has many more inspirations for what you can create or have created for you, from memory quilts to commemorative trips.

Illustrations

For the first exhibition I presented with my mom's belongings in October 2015, I commissioned a series of drawings from Spanish illustrator Mercedes Leon. Just like I've shared with you, I asked myself: *How do I want to remember her? How do I want her to be remembered?*

I wanted to create an exhibition that told an inspiring and loving narrative about who my mom was and how she lived. *What do I want people to know about her?* I asked myself. I wanted people to know how smart she was, even though she didn't get her bachelor's degree until she was in her fifties. I wanted them to know how much she loved traveling, how much she loved food, how much she loved feeding people, how much she wanted to help people. (She was studying to be a social worker when she died.)

These are the illustrations we displayed for that first exhibition called "Proof of Life":

Flowers from Her Garden: bright roses, hydrangeas and irises, my mom's favorites

Her Collection of Scarves: faithful renderings of my mom's silk scarves, based on photos I sent

Her University Degrees: a diploma, graduation cap with tassel, and study materials

Notes in Her Illegible Handwriting: sticky notes and scraps of paper with my mom's scrawl

Her Jewellery (spelled the British way): her everyday watch and rings, her special occasion rhinestone brooch

Her Beloved iPad: the device my mom was so thrilled to get and to teach her friends how to use

Delicious Meals Together: including seafood and avocados, with chopsticks alongside forks and other cutlery

Her Love of Belgian Waffles: a bistro table with a plate of waffles with strawberries and whipped cream, alongside the Statue of Liberty and the Unisphere from the 1964-65 New York World's Fair

Her Love of Travel: passport, boarding passes, and luggage tags

Her Dream House by the Lake: a view through big windows of a tranquil lakeside scene

The beauty of illustrations is that they can capture something that's intangible or something that we no longer have. That final one, of my mom's house, is especially meaningful for me. It was so hard to let the house go, but I loved commissioning Mercedes to make a drawing of it. I told her about the view of the lake, trees and swans, and she was able to capture it in a whimsical and beautiful illustration that I cherish and share often during presentations.

Several years later, I added the illustration "Her Love of Music and Dance" for an online exhibition called "Red Ribbon Dance for the Lunar New Year." Because I'm so visually inclined,

I'd forgotten to include music and auditory details in the original exhibition—and my mom loved music! We have the option of continuing to create and to add to our collections over time, if we want—it's not too late.

You can see these illustrations at www.thegriefgallery.com/remembering-marilyn

————

WHAT HURTS? "I COULDN'T KEEP IT"

I also love the process of commissioning artwork because, as we've discussed throughout the book, there can be many reasons we can't keep something. Maybe it belongs to someone else or another family member actually has possession of it. Maybe there's conflict because multiple people really want the item. Maybe we can't keep it because it's too big or we don't actually have physical space for it. Maybe we never had it.

A woman at The Grief Gallery's gatherings told the story of a cookie jar that all the cousins wanted after their grandmother died. She managed to track down that cookie jar via eBay so everyone could have their own. But if she hadn't been able to find it, commissioning an illustration of the cookie jar and giving everyone a print could be a good compromise.

As someone who worries about losing things as part of my grief response, I especially love digital illustrations and scans of original artwork because they can be backed up and reprinted.

Photographs

As I've mentioned, one of the first things I did with my mother's belongings was to photograph them. In the decade since she died, I've taken hundreds more photos and have hired professionals for photo shoots with her belongings as well. Styles have ranged from Instagram-style product shots and flatlays to more artsy images with objects in my hands.

On my wishlist is working with The Heirloomist, a photographer in New York City. You can send objects to her photo studio, and she will shoot them. You can get them in really big wall-sized prints, like you would see in a museum or gallery!

You can also go smaller scale: A photo album is always an option! Or using an online service like Blurb or Shutterfly to create a photo book with the objects and their descriptions as your gallery, or as an exhibition catalog for a physical display.

You can make an Instagram account! Because an Instagram grid can be a gallery too. You're choosing with intention what goes there.

Creating Ritual

You can also create a ritual. On significant dates like my mom's birthday or Mother's Day, or even just when I travel to a place she would have liked, I have a ritual of throwing flowers in bodies of water. I've done this in rivers, lakes, and oceans in Paris, Portugal, and Peru, among others. I usually talk to her when I do this. It's a fun ritual and way to stay connected with her, to bring her forward with me wherever I go, to remember her in the way that I want.

I've also started dedicating flowers for the loved ones of my clients too. Additionally, I now have an art project where I dance with red ribbons and fans, which are often used in Chinese dance.

In these creative ways, I'm choosing my favorite memories, capturing them in a range of mediums, and creating new moments. This is how I curate. This is how I create. Do what feels right for you. And remember: You don't have to do an entire exhibition in a gallery about your person to curate!

GETTING CREATIVE WITH THE OBJECTS:

There are so many reasons you may not be able to keep an object. I offer you some ways to think outside the proverbial box when it comes to honoring and sharing these significant items.

Transform: Valerie couldn't keep her grandmother's piano, so she kept just a couple of the keys and turned them into art pieces.

Redistribute: Susanna hosted a celebration of life for her father's friends and family, with each person leaving with one of the wooden ducks from his collection.

Reconstitute: Alica melted down rings that belonged to her mom, and had the metal integrated into the wedding bands for her and her husband—so they both have a part of her mom in their bands.

Recreate: Carly and her sisters recreated a dress in a distinctive style that their mom loved, so they each have one to wear.

Recontextualize: A therapist friend displays her aunt's textile purse as a decorative piece in her office, a nod to continuing her legacy of helping others.

Transfer the Meaning: As attached as I felt to the soy sauce in my mom's kitchen, it didn't make sense to keep the soy sauce. It didn't make sense to put it in my suitcase and take it back to London with me. (I still needed help to throw it away though— my cousin Eva drove hours to my mom's house to lend a hand. "Is that all you needed?" she asked, bemused, after tossing the soy sauce in the trash. Yes, it was, and it was everything.)

I didn't need to keep the soy sauce, but I *did* want to keep the memories and the stories. The beautiful thing is that I could detach the stories from the soy sauce and attach them to something else. In this case, it was a cooking spoon from my mother's kitchen. I attached those stories of what she cooked and the memories of meals shared, and I took that spoon with me.

And the *most* beautiful thing is, it fit in my suitcase and it fit in my life. It fit in the life that I *wanted* to live. It fit in the life that I wanted to create moving forward.

"In the telling of the stories, mourners befriend their grief and slowly, with no rewards for speed, transform their suffering."

DR. ALAN WOLFELT

CHAPTER 36
CATEGORY: THEIR PROJECTS IN PROGRESS

Notes for a book never written. A woodworking project half-completed. Ingredients for a meal never cooked. "Projects in progress" is a category that can evoke a lot of emotion. These are hobbies or passion projects that reflect the person's interests and how they enjoyed spending their time when they were alive. We may find these projects and their accompanying tools and supplies in studios, offices and garages. The poignancy comes when we think:

"He never got to complete that project."

"They'll never use those tools again."

"She had plans, she wasn't ready to go."

We might also think:

"He got so much joy out of those projects."

"We have good memories."

"No wonder I like making things with my hands as well, we have that in common."

Their creative pursuits and ways of expressing aspects of themselves were probably sources of so much pleasure and satisfaction in their lives. So of course it's understandable that thinking of them can give us both comfort and pangs of missing them dearly.

HELEN'S STORY

Helen's father, Paul, was an engineer and a glider pilot in his spare time. When he died, he was in the middle of restoring a model glider—that is, a scale model of a glider plane. The illustration at the start of Part 8 is based on his model glider.

Model Airplane
Wooden Model Airplane
Contributed by Helen Packham, 2021
In memory of her father

2021.UK.HP.1

"I spent many weekends at the gliding club, going up in the air and reveling in the silence that engineless flight brings," she recalls. "This model glider was given to him to restore by a friend just before he was diagnosed with pancreatic cancer. He started the process but sadly wasn't able to finish it."

WHAT DO WE DO WITH THESE ITEMS?

When we find their incomplete projects, we have some choices to make about what we'd like to do with them. Here are some options:

Complete the Project
After Helen's father died, his friend took back the wooden model glider and finished the restoration. With clear pride and love, she shares a photo of the sizable model glider, its proud golden wings shining, the sleek body in a bold blue with a pert propeller at the nose. She shares, "It now has pride of place on the wall of his house and serves as a reminder of the joy he experienced from gliding."

Keep the Tools and the Memories Close
René keeps his father's tools close. An illustrator himself, René keeps a carving knife his father used to make little wooden animals on his own desk. He considers himself more of a custodian of these objects than the new owner. "I don't think any of his tools will ever feel like 'mine,'" he says. "I'm just borrowing them."

Do What They Couldn't Do
My mother had plans to write a book about our family, but she didn't get far. I found some scant notes and a couple of section names scrawled in a lined, spiral-bound notebook, the kind that school kids use. But that was it.

As an immigrant who learned English as a second language, my mother always lamented that she didn't feel fully confident communicating in either English or Chinese, at least in written form. Maybe that lack of confidence kept her from fully starting her book.

This book that you're now reading is my way of continuing her plans. I'm doing what she couldn't do, what she didn't get to do. Thank you for helping me to complete her project!

GOOD QUESTIONS

Are there projects in progress that you found after a loved one died?

How do you feel when you look at these projects and tools?

What is the significance of them?

What do these objects say about your person?

What stories and memories are attached to these objects?

How would it feel to let them go? Why?

What do you want to do with the projects?

WHAT HURTS? "THEY HAD PLANS"

"What hurts the most is that she wasn't done living."

"He had plans, he wasn't ready to go."

"My sister wasn't done living. She had soup in the refrigerator. A vacation planned."

"My father and I had tickets to see his favorite band together. We had plans."

Sometimes what hurts is the evidence that our person wasn't ready to die. Of a life cut short and plans curtailed:

A calendar with future events circled.

Clothing laid out for the next day.

A to-do list never finished.

A novel never written.

Projects they had in progress.

HOW I SEE IT — THE REFRAME:

My mom wasn't done living either. When she died, she had trips planned to Asia and Alaska. The fridge was full of food, including a fresh fish she'd bought from Chinatown. She was training to be a social worker.

I also realized, if I died tomorrow, it would be the same. I have plans. A fridge full of food (OK, not as full as hers). Plane tickets. Appointments scheduled. After all, how many of us are actually done living when we die, even if it's expected?

My mom didn't know she was going to die that day from a sudden stroke. Over time, I've come to be glad that my mom had plans, that she was just living her life. She shared meals with old friends and her brother the day she died. I'd much rather that she was enjoying her life and looking forward to things than the alternative.

I don't share these musings to discount what you might say or dismiss your pain. Of course it feels unfair and hurts that our loved ones didn't get to continue their lives or fulfill their plans. That's normal, and those feelings are OK. I still feel that pain sometimes. At the same time, I offer the following alternative way of looking at it that's been helpful for me, in case it may be helpful for you.

GETTING OBJECTIVE

Same set of facts, same elements, but I can frame the story in a different way and change the angle of my view. As we did in chapter 32, "Regret, Perspective, and Interpretations," I imagine putting the facts on the plinth.

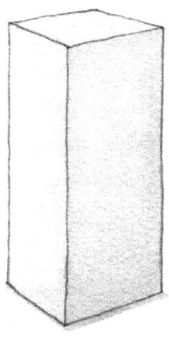

I could focus on how unfair it is that she didn't get to go to Alaska or to complete her plans. I prefer to focus on how I *want* to remember my mother.

I could look at the fact that my mother had plans in a negative light. I *choose* to look at the fact that she had plans in a positive light:

She had plans because she was feeling healthy overall and feeling good. She was vibrant. She had good friends. She was looking forward to the future.

That's how I want to remember my mother.

Your situation might have been very different. Your person might have been sick for a long time, and even been ready to go. You can *still* choose how you want to think about how they died, and how they lived.

————

GOOD QUESTIONS

What plans did your loved one have?

How do you want to frame the fact that they had plans?

Can we acknowledge their unfulfilled plans and grieve the end of their lives, AND choose to reframe their plans in a way that is helpful for us?

————

WE GET TO CONTINUE THEIR STORY

As I finish writing this book, I'm presenting The Grief Gallery's first exhibition in Portugal, at Hospital de Santa Maria, Lisbon's largest public hospital. I've partnered with their palliative care team for an exhibition for the hospital's workers, with objects contributed by nurses, doctors, and other healthcare workers, as well as the occasional patient.

Of course, there are also items from my mother on display:

- Her glasses
- A file folder label that reads GREIF (grief, misspelled)
- My mother's work badge from St. Vincent's Hospital Manhattan, where she had her last job

I tell the gathered audience of supportive healthcare professionals at the opening ceremony, "My mom would have been so thrilled to have her belongings as part of this exhibition in a hospital. *Obrigada.*"

My mother had such an evolution when it came to mental health and talking about grief, death, and dying. Like many Chinese-American immigrants, we didn't talk openly about death when I was growing up—it was considered unlucky in my family.

Her view of mental health shifted when I experienced my first major depressive episode in high school. To my parents' credit, they got me help, including a therapist and medication.

In her fifties, my mom went back to school and got her master's degree to be a Marriage and Family Therapist. She co-founded Chinese American Counseling Services (CACS), a mental health non-profit in the San Francisco Bay Area.

When she died, she was training to become a social worker in New York State and doing outreach to Asian immigrant populations about the importance of healthcare advance directives and mental wellness topics, including grief. After she died, some of the first articles I read about grief were found in her study materials and newspaper clippings, in that file with the misspelled label. I still refer to these resources.

My mother's plans to be a social worker and to help more people might have been thwarted by her untimely death, but I get to continue her work and her story now.

I keep choosing. I continue talking about her and sharing her legacy. I create new memories—another chapter in her life story.

KEEP CHOOSING, KEEP CREATING

You get to continue their stories, too. I invite you to keep choosing, to keep creating—if you feel the desire, and if you have the capacity. Now, in a year, or in a decade or two.

Remember, you do not need a formal gallery space. You don't need to do anything for the public or an audience. But you can, if you'd like! A memorial to mark the ten-year anniversary of their death. A celebration for their birthday. A mourning ritual to help you acknowledge a milestone or transition, and an invitation for you to be witnessed and supported as a griever.

REMEMBER:

- You do not need to keep every item you find because you're not on an archaeological dig. You can also decide to stop digging.
- You are not actually a museum or a historian. Your home is not the Smithsonian or the Louvre. It's OK if you don't know the provenance of every item.
- You get to choose the interpretation and significance of the objects you find and that you keep. Not your family members. Not an institution, nor a board of directors.
- It's OK to keep things.
- It's OK to let things go.

Throughout these chapters, I've painted a picture of my mom. Hopefully an affectionate and truthful one, one that shares many facets of a dynamic woman: smart, loving, and very loved.

This is how I remember her.
This is how I want to remember her.
This is how I want her to be remembered.

Thank you for seeing her and witnessing me. And most of all, thank you for making space for your own grief as we've traveled through these pages together.

EPILOGUE

In the process of painting a picture of my mom for you, I may have also sketched a picture of myself, as a sometimes regretful but hopefully, above all, loving daughter. (After all, *I* am the best memorial for her.)

The picture of my life currently includes:

Hammock time on our balcony with a view of the River Tejo.

A husband who still can't go as deep into the depths of grief and darkness as I can, but says, unprompted, that he misses my mom. He still doesn't love collecting stuff the way I do, but he meets me at the airport to help carry my luggage and helps me unload after my shows. He even made the logo for The Grief Gallery!

Walks by the waterside and hikes along the beach, carrying my mom's colorful LeSportsac backpack.

Plans for retreats and more beautiful exhibitions with The Grief Gallery in Portugal, Mexico, and beyond.

Helping thousands more grievers through the sharing of my story and these *Curating Grief* concepts.

––––––

The picture of me currently includes who I know myself to be:

I am forever changed by the loss of my mom, but I am not diminished.

I am an artist and a curator. A designer of spaces for grief, and the designer of my life.

I'm the keeper of my mother's stories—and *some* of her things.

I am a daughter who could have done better but cared deeply for her mother.

I am a griever who has cultivated unconditional love for herself in the process of grieving and mourning.

My hope is similar for you. What picture do you have of yourself as a griever? In crafting our narratives about our loved ones, in selecting the stories we want to share, in curating about them, we are at the same time, painting a picture of ourselves and creating a narrative of our own lives. May they be beautiful in their own wildly unique ways.

Keep creating. Keep choosing. Keep curating.

INDEX: WHAT HURTS?

Here are some common scenarios that grieving people may find particularly painful. Jump to the corresponding chapter to get the Curating Grief take on it:

ACKNOWLEDGMENTS

This book is for my mom Marilyn and all my fellow grievers. For all my clients.

For Silas and Jordana for teaching me to how to grieve. For Wendy Marx for teaching me how to lead and to treasure every day. For Pau Pau and Yee Pau, and all my ancestors. For Bara, Poppy, and all the people I miss.

Thank you to all my school teachers who saw and believed in me, and saved me with words and writing: Ms Osborn, Ms Sammet, Mrs Taketa, Mr Keplinger, just to name a few.

Thank you to all the people who took such good care of me: Aunt Terry, Uncle Stephen, my cousins and friends, Ah Fei and family, my mom's old friends, my grief guides, my fellow grief professionals, everyone who helped with your heads, hearts, and hands.

Thank you to all the people who saw value in my ideas and championed my work: My editor Debra, Alica Forneret and PAUSE, Regina Anaejionu and my TL coworking crew, the GLC, Claire Bidwell Smith, Meghan Riordan Jarvis, amongst others.

And thank you, Roberto, for finding me in the crowd and always holding my hand, and for putting up with all my stuff.

RESOURCES AND END NOTES

There are so many great grief resources available to us now, with a range of approaches and vibes. This book takes an agnostic approach to grief support —whatever is helpful for you is most important to me. I've collected some of my favorites at curatinggrief.com/grief-resources

Here are some of the grief books I've mentioned:
Anxiety: The Missing Stage of Grief by Claire Bidwell Smith
Moving On Doesn't Mean Letting Go by Gina Moffa
Can Anyone Tell Me? Essential Questions About Grief and Loss by Meghan Riordan Jarvis
It's OK That You're Not OK by Megan Devine
Your Grief, Your Way by Shelby Forsythia
The Grieving Brain: The Surprising Science of How We Learn from Love and Loss by Mary Frances O'Connor
Grief is a Sneaky Bitch by Lisa Keefauver, MSW
The Wilderness of Grief: Finding Your Way by Dr. Alan Wolfelt
Companioning the Bereaved: A Soulful Guide for Caregivers by Dr. Alan Wolfelt

Special shoutout to What's Your Grief and co-founders Litsa Williams and Eleanor Haley for providing such a valuable resource for evidence-based information for grievers—and your patience with all my questions!

Reader, if you're the kind of griever who wants to better understand your grief—or who wants to help others who are grieving—I highly recommend the trainings, resources, and communities offered at www.whatsyour-grief.com as well as their book *What's Your Grief? Lists to Help You Through Any Loss.*

In addition to Continuing Bonds, I also find these grief theories helpful: two-track and dual process models, post-traumatic growth, narrative and attachment approaches, meaning-making and meaning reconstruction.

Visit curatinggrief.com/grief-resources for more, including grief support for BIPOC grievers and community resources, and links to the many references in this book.

 BOOK BONUSES:
Register your book at curatinggrief.com/book-register to get bonus content and resources.

ABOUT THE AUTHOR

Charlene Lam is a certified grief coach, speaker, and the founder of The Grief Gallery. She is passionate about using the lens of curating to help grieving people navigate the aftermath of loss and when they feel ready, to transform their pain into something beautiful.

After her mother died suddenly in 2013, Charlene found herself drowning in grief . . . and her mom's belongings. It's a common problem: Feeling overwhelmed and unable to make choices after the death of a loved one. Charlene's uncommon solution: Curating an exhibition about her mother.

She developed the Curating Grief® framework to help others process grief in a creative, accessible way. (And no, you don't need to be an artist or creative to curate!)

As a triple-certified grief coach, she helps grieving individuals to feel lighter and better equipped to move forward with their own fullest lives. As curator of The Grief Gallery®, Charlene presents international exhibitions featuring the belongings of loved ones lost. As a speaker, she's shared her Curating Grief approach with thousands of grievers and wellness professionals.

She stars in the short film *Curating Grief: Loss and Objects*, directed by UK filmmaker Jamie Max Lee. A proud Chinese-American New Yorker, Charlene is based in Lisbon, Portugal. She works with clients worldwide (and really wants you to ask her about the soy sauce in her mother's kitchen.)

Learn more at www.curatinggrief.com and follow her on Instagram @Curating_Grief

www.ingramcontent.com/pod-product-compliance
Lightning Source LLC
Chambersburg PA
CBHW051607120626
46551CB00014B/1703